The Atlas of Languages

A Buddhist monk at the Labrang Monastery in Xiahe, China writes with the Tibetan script. This writing system, like the monk's religion, has its roots in the subcontinent of India.

The Atlas of Languages

The Origin and Development
of Languages Throughout the World

Consultant Editors
Bernard Comrie, Stephen Matthews,
and Maria Polinsky

Foreword by Jean Aitchison

Facts On File, Inc.

A QUARTO BOOK

For information contact:

Facts On File, Inc.
11 Penn Plaza
New York, NY 10001

A United States of America CIP catalog record for this book is
available from Facts On File, Inc.

Facts On File books are available at special discounts when
purchased in bulk quantities for businesses, associations, institutions
or sales promotions. Please contact the Special Sales Department of
our New York office at 212/967-8800 or 800/322-8755.

This book was designed and produced by
Quarto Publishing plc
The Old Brewery
6 Blundell Street
London N7 9BH

Designer Graham Davis
Senior art editor Elizabeth Healey
Project editor Liz Wyse
Senior editor Sally MacEachern
Editorial assistant Judith Evans
Indexer Dawn Butcher
Cartography Map Creation Ltd
Illustrators Jamie Coath, Kevin Maddison, Mary Noble (calligraphy)
Picture researcher Susannah Jayes
Picture research manager Giulia Hetherington
Editorial director Mark Dartford
Art directors Moira Clinch, Penny Cobb
Manufactured in Singapore by Bright Arts (Singapore) Pte Ltd
Printed in Singapore by Star Standard Industries (Pte) Ltd

10 9 8 7 6 5 4 3 2

Contents

Foreword

Humans, like cows, grasshoppers, woodpeckers, and many other animals, communicate primarily via sounds. Yet language, the human communication system, is the most versatile of all: it can be transferred to writing, or signs, and it can discuss anything, whether it is present, out of sight, or imaginary. Any normal human can produce and comprehend an indefinite number of sentences that have never been said before, even quite bizarre ones, such as "My dodo needs a new toothbrush." And new words are coined daily. Open-endedness is therefore a key characteristic of human language. Consequently, it always has changed, and always will. Yet changes do not cause language to spiral out of control, and become irremediably strange.

Any human can potentially learn any language. An English baby adopted by Quechuan or Turkish speaking parents would grow up speaking fluent Quechuan or Turkish with no difficulty. Language, we now realise, is an intrinsic part of being human, and is biologically programed into the species.

This powerful communication system emerged around 100,000 years ago, probably in the east of Africa, according to current majority opinion. Humans moved northward into Asia Minor maybe 50,000 years ago, then spread around the world. As humans travelled, languages split and proliferated. There are now around 5,000 languages, according to most counts. They can be grouped into around a dozen major clusters, and a number of minor ones.

No languageless community has ever been found. Yet in spite of the importance of language to humans, most people know very little about languages other than their own. Even the names of languages are unfamiliar, and faced with a set of them, say, Abaza, Dyirbal, Hmong, Hopi, Shona, many English speakers would have a hard time specifying even the continent in which they are spoken.

Nor would they know any quick way to find out about them. Even if they found the language listed in an encyclopedia, they would then have to move to a second book, a geographical atlas, to find out the location of the speakers.

One major problem is that languages are spoken by people, and people move around, sometimes in huge groups. The distribution of languages inevitably changes faster than the course of rivers. Views alter on which languages were spoken where in the past: currently, huge controversy surrounds exactly when humans reached America, for example, and how their languages spread. And massive population shifts have occurred

throughout history. So publishers have mostly shied away from the task of producing linguistic atlases.

But not now. This *Atlas of Languages* is an important and worthwhile project. It maps in a useful, clear and easily consultable way what is spoken where at the end of the 20th century. This information may be especially important, because only around one-tenth of today's languages will still be spoken in a hundred years time, according to some current estimates. Hopefully, readers will be inspired to learn more about the splendiferous bouquet of linguistic flowers which exist in the world, and maybe even help to slow down the rate at which languages are dying.

Jean Aitchison
Oxford 1996

Languages are forever changing. Some disappear as traditional ways of life are threatened, others survive but in changed forms. Many of the minority languages in China, for example, are being replaced by Chinese while in Japan it is fashionable for young people to borrow words from English.

Introduction

Long the subject of myth rather than science, the origins of language are becoming less obscure as clues to the pedigree of humankind are assembled from linguistic and archeological evidence. There remains a huge gulf between the rudimentary linguistic capabilities of apes and the complexity of human communication, which serves to emphasize the uniqueness of human language. Investigation of languages from around the world has revealed deep-seated similarities, as well as surprising differences. However, increasingly, this very diversity is threatened as local languages disappear along with traditional ways of life.

A woman in the traditional dress of one of the ethnic minorities of southern China, the Miao. Miao is one of the main minority languages of China, but speakers are dwindling as a result of the gradual Sinicization of ethnic groups.

anguage is perhaps the most important single characteristic that distinguishes human beings from other animal species. Certainly, no other animal species has a communication system with the complexity, flexibility, and range of expression of human language. How and when did this remarkable communication system develop? No complete answer can be given to this question, indeed perhaps no complete answer will ever be forthcoming – no linguists were around to observe human origins. But part of the answer can be given by investigating the linguistic abilities of non-human primates and by studying the archeological record of different hominid (human-like) species.

The most successful attempts to teach a human-like language to non-human primates have been with chimpanzees. Because of the different structure of the vocal apparatus in humans and chimpanzees (*see opposite*), it is not possible for chimpanzees to imitate the sounds of human language, so they have been taught to use gestures or tokens in place of sounds. The successes that have been achieved over the last few decades by dedicated researchers on chimpanzees' linguistic abilities have certainly gone beyond what most linguists would have predicted, but chimpanzees never attain a level of linguistic complexity beyond the approximate level of a two-year-old child. The further development of language in human children, in particular the development of grammar, appears to be beyond the grasp of chimpanzees. In this sense language can be seen as a species-specific characteristic of humans. It should also be noted that, in the wild, non-human primates do not spontaneously develop even the linguistic abilities of a two-year-old human child.

Turning to the archeological record, it is possible to trace the development of the vocal apparatus of different hominid species from skeletal remains. The comparison of these

Several attempts have been made to teach human-like languages to primates, most successfully with bonobo chimpanzees. The male bonobo Kanzi, trained to use signs by Susan Savage-Rumbaugh at the University of Georgia, acquired the linguistic ability of a two-year-old child.

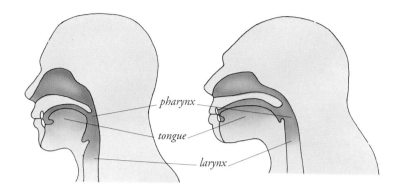

Sounds, produced in the larynx, are modified to form consonants and vowels by the shape of the mouth and pharynx. In Neanderthals, the pharynx was limited by the high position of the larynx, while the size and position of the tongue restricted movement, allowing only a limited range of sounds.

findings with non-human primates throws light on the range of different articulate sounds that these different species could make; this is important because one of the characteristics of the human vocal apparatus is that the flexibility of the tongue makes a wide range of readily distinguishable sounds possible. There appears to be a significant difference between the vocal apparatus of modern humans (who appear in the archeological record from about 100,000 years ago) and of Neanderthals, who lived from about 230,000 years ago until about 30,000 years ago. In Neanderthals (*see diagram*), the larynx may have been higher than in modern humans, which means that the tongue is much less mobile. If so, the Neanderthals would have been able to produce less differentiated speech than modern humans. The position of the larynx in modern humans represents a marked departure from the larynx position in other hominids and in non-human primates. Interestingly, the human larynx at birth occupies a high position, as with other primates, and only subsequently descends to the position it will occupy in the adult. The lowering of the larynx, though clearly facilitating articulate speech, is in other respects a decided disadvantage; humans, unlike other primates, can not eat or drink and breathe at the same time without choking.

The archeological record, unfortunately, tells us nothing significant about brain development. The size of the brain can be deduced from the dimensions of the skull, but brain size tends to be proportional to overall body size, and since the Neanderthals may have been stockier than modern humans it is not surprising that they had, on average, the larger brains, but this tells us nothing about the development of their brains. On the other hand, the archeological record does provide clear evidence of complex social behavior among Neanderthals, including perhaps care of the old and infirm and burial of the dead. This may indicate the existence of at least a rudimentary form of language as a prerequisite for organizing social behavior.

The evidence thus tends to indicate that, while non-human primates lack linguistic abilities characteristic of modern humans, Neanderthals possessed such abilities in a rudimentary form. Language in its modern form must have appeared no later than about 40,000 years ago, when there was an explosion of complex behavior in areas such as art and technology (tool-making, construction of huts and storage pits), and the colonization of harsh environments on a long-term basis became possible. Language may indeed have been present from the appearance of modern humans over 100,000 years ago.

LANGUAGE DIVERSITY

It would seem likely that further light could be thrown on the evolution of human language by studying more and less complex human languages spoken today. However, while it is possible to find parts of one language that are simpler than the corresponding parts of another language, no evidence has ever been produced that would suggest that one particular language as spoken by modern humans is more or less complex than any other. If a language is less complex than another language in one respect, then in some other respect it will be more complex.

A simple example comparing English and Latin illustrates the difficulty in comparing linguistic complexity. In English, regular verbs have only four forms (for example, "walk," "walks," "walked," "walking"), and even the most varied irregular verb has only eight forms ("be," "am," "is," "are," "was," "were," "been," "being"); some verbs have even fewer forms (for example, "cut," "cuts," "cutting"). A Latin verb by contrast has well over a hundred forms, so that whereas English uses the same form in "(I) walk," "(you) walk," "(we) walk," and "(they) walk," Latin distinguishes these as *(ego) ambulo*, *(tu) ambulas*, *(nos) ambulamus*, *(ei) ambulant*. In terms of the number of forms that a verb can take, Latin is clearly more complex than English. However, by combining forms of different verbs, English can make a much richer range of distinctions than Latin. To refer to an event in the past, Latin has basically two forms, as with *ambulabam* versus *ambulavi*, both of which can, under appropriate circumstances, be translated as "(I) walked." However, under other circumstances the appropriate English translation of *ambulavi* will be "(I) have walked," while that of *ambulabam* will be "(I) was walking" or "(I) used to walk," not

Language in its modern form had probably appeared by about 40,000 years ago when Paleolithic society was transformed by unprecedented developments in both technology and culture. New tools and technology allowed Stone Age hunters to colonize and settle remote and inhospitable regions. At the same time, the extraordinary florescence of cave art, illustrated here by a 14,000-year-old bison drawing from Altamira cave in southern Spain, demonstrates a significant development in both perception and communication.

to mention rarer forms like "(I) have been walking" or "(I) used to be walking." These examples show an area where English has six distinct constructions while Latin has only two.

The comparison between different languages is interesting because it reveals how different languages can be from one another while retaining more or less the same degree of complexity. Much of the material in this book will serve to illustrate this proposition. For now, we will look at just one example, comparing English with the Australian Aboriginal language Dyirbal, spoken near the town of Cairns in Queensland. In an English sentence such as "the man saw the woman and came here," the second clause "came here" lacks overt specification of *who* came here, but we have no difficulty in supplying the missing information, and concluding that *the man* came here. Even though the other interpretation, namely that *the woman* came here, would make perfect sense, English grammar does not allow this sentence to have that meaning. If we translate the English sentence literally into Dyirbal, the result is *balan jugumbil banggul yaranggu buran, baninyu*, although Dyirbal has relatively free word order, so that *banggul yaranggu balan jugumbil buran, baninyu*, would also be

possible. Interestingly, however, this Dyirbal sentence translates as "the man saw the woman and the woman came here." The grammar of Dyirbal is just as strict in requiring this interpretation as the grammar of English is in requiring the opposite interpretation. Both languages have rules of equal complexity; but the particular rule cited above is different in the two languages. We might note in passing that yet other languages, such as Chukchi – spoken on the Chukotka peninsula, the easternmost tip of Asiatic Russia – would allow both interpretations for the literal translation of this sentence.

It is a mistake to assume that a language will have a simpler structure because it is spoken in a culture that has simpler political structures or a less advanced technology. Linguists are continually surprised by the distinctions that are made in languages outside the mainstream of more familiar languages. In English, for instance, a sentence like "John saw Bill as he was leaving" is ambiguous, depending on whether we take the one who was leaving to be John or Bill. There is no ambiguity in Plains Cree, an Algonquian language of central Canada and adjacent parts of the USA, where different verb forms for "see" mark the difference in meaning: *John Bill-wa waapameew, eesipwehteet* means that John is leaving; *John Bill-wa waapameew, eesipwehteeyit* means that Bill is leaving. To take a different kind of example, most speakers of English have only the one term "salmon," with perhaps a couple of additional terms for varieties of salmon; by contrast in Nuuchahlnuth (a Wakashan language spoken on western Vancouver Island, Canada), there is a rich vocabulary identifying different varieties of salmon (*see Part 2, Chapter 6*).

LANGUAGES UNDER THREAT

As shown by the few examples given above, and even more so by the many examples scattered throughout this book, human language is extraordinarily diverse, and it is necessary to examine phenomena from a large number of different languages in order to appreciate this diversity. In the last decade of the twentieth century, it is estimated that over 6,000 languages are spoken in the world; when lay people are asked to guess how many languages are spoken in the world today, they typically underestimate the total by several degrees of magnitude, with answers ranging from a few score to a few hundred. The distribution of languages across the globe is very uneven; this can be seen clearly by comparing the vast area over which Mandarin Chinese is spoken in China with the area of greatest linguistic diversity in the world, the island of New Guinea and surrounding smaller islands, where some 1,000 distinct languages are spoken by a total population of approximately 5 million.

Like the more publicized areas of diversity in the world today such as animals and plants, this diversity of languages is threatened, and it is almost certain that in the not-too-distant future neither professional linguists nor

A wood engraving of the Margarita Philosophica Nova, published by J. Gruninger in 1512, depicts the Institution of Languages, with God distributing the various languages of the world.

interested lay people will have access to speakers of the range of different languages that are available today. It is useful to make a three-way distinction among languages with respect to endangerment: a dead language is one that no longer has native speakers (such as Latin or Sumerian); a moribund language is one that still has native speakers but is no longer being acquired by children (such as Dyirbal or many native languages of North America); a living language is one that is still being acquired by children. A moribund language

will normally die out within one or two generations, except in truly extraordinary circumstances – for example, children whose parents did not acquire the language learning it from their grandparents. In an article that appeared in the leading American linguistic journal *Language* in 1992, Michael Krauss of the Alaska Native Language Center estimates that of the languages spoken in the world today, 90 percent will be either dead or moribund a hundred years from now. This represents a far higher rate of endangerment than for animal or plant species. Language death is taking place across the world, ranging from moribund Dyirbal in the Cairns rainforest to Manx, the indigenous Celtic language of the Isle of Man in the Irish Sea, whose last native speaker died in 1974. On the other hand, the successful revival of a dead language though rare, is not impossible: the clearest example is Hebrew, revived as a spoken language from the late nineteenth century and now a native language for over 3 million people.

Of course, languages have died out throughout recorded history: Sumerian, the language of the first of the great civilizations of Mesopotamia (modern Iraq), died out around 2,000 BC, while its successor, Akkadian (the language of the Babylonian and Assyrian empires) had in turn died out by around the middle of the first millennium BC. But the extent of language death is undergoing rapid acceleration in the modern world. Until recently, it was perfectly feasible for a small speech community to survive in reasonable isolation, preserving its own language, and perhaps also using a language of wider currency for communication with the outside world where necessary. However, the growing centralization of life in the late twentieth century makes this kind of situation increasingly rare. Whether governments are providing health care and education or collecting taxes and recruiting armies, they bring small, isolated communities into the mainstream of their country's life, and this invariably leads to the increased importance of languages of wider currency. It is simply not economically feasible for governments to provide services in every language, including languages spoken by only a few hundred or a few score individuals, even if the will to preserve these languages is present. The growing popularity of the mass media, now spread to the most remote regions by means of satellite communication, also serves to increase the importance of a relatively small number of languages of mass communication, again in part because of the difficulty of justifying the cost of programmes in the languages of small speech communities.

The issues involved in this situation are not purely linguistic, but of a more general social and political nature. Certainly, preventing people from gaining access to a language of wider currency, at least as a second language for wider communication alongside the native language used within the community, cannot be justified. If an individual or community has decided to abandon its ancestral language, there is little anyone can (or, perhaps, should) do to stop them: in Tanzania, for instance, younger people are increasingly abandoning their ancestral languages in favour of Swahili, the dominant and official language of the country. In some cases, however, communities have a strong desire to preserve their language, alongside other aspects of their culture, even while acknowledging that they must also be fluent in a language of wider currency. In such cases linguists can provide an invaluable service to the community by assisting in the preservation of the

language, for instance by devising a writing system for the language so that it can be used in a wider range of functions.

But even with the best will in the world on the part of speakers and those with whom they interact, we must accept that a good proportion of the languages currently spoken will no longer be spoken one to four generations from now. Given this situation, it is imperative to salvage as much knowledge of these languages as possible, so that posterity will not lose completely the richness of this aspect of human diversity, of so many solutions to the problem of coming to terms with our environment through language. For linguists, the urgent task is to document endangered languages by providing a grammar of the language, a dictionary of the language, and a collection of texts illustrating various functional uses of the language (ranging from traditional stories to everyday conversation). If you enjoy this book, even more so if you are encouraged to read further about the various languages of the world, please be aware of the fragile ecology on which this description of the world's languages is based.

The development of satellite technology, which enables television broadcasters to reach remote and hitherto inaccessible regions, such as rural India, means that languages of mass communication, in particular English, are becoming increasingly dominant.

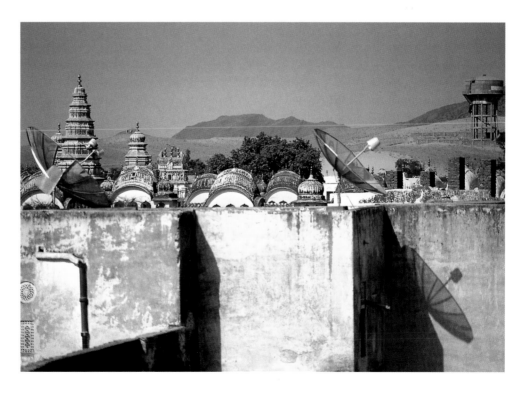

Development and Spread of Languages

Human languages are far more diverse and numerous than most speakers of major world languages think. There are presently over 6,000 tongues spoken around the world, with distinctions ranging from regional dialects of English and Chinese to great language families like the Indo-European and Sino-Tibetan. Linguistic histories can be reconstructed by comparison of vocabularies and of grammatical structures, and today the search continues for ever more distant relationships, which may perhaps indicate a single origin of all language.

Dating the origin of a language can only be speculative. The chronology opposite is intended as an approximate guide to the emergence of human language.

CHRONOLOGY OF HUMAN LANGUAGE

2000	
	SPREAD OF STANDARD LANGUAGES; ACCELERATION OF LANGUAGE LOSS
	COLONIAL PERIOD: RISE OF PIDGINS AND CREOLES
1500	
1000	
	EMERGENCE OF ROMANCE, GERMANIC LANGUAGES
	OLD ENGLISH
500	
0	CLASSICAL LANGUAGES: ANCIENT GREEK, LATIN
	OLDEST RECORDS OF INDO-EUROPEAN LANGUAGES: HITTITE, SANSKRIT
	? PROTO-INDO-EUROPEAN
5000	? EXPANSION OF AUSTRONESIAN: COLONIZATION OF TAIWAN
	SECOND SETTLEMENT OF NEW WORLD: ?NA-DENE
10,000	
	FIRST ESTABLISHED SETTLEMENT OF NEW WORLD: ?AMERIND
	END OF LAST ICE AGE; ? EXPANSION OF EURASIATIC LANGUAGES
15,000	ESTIMATED PEAK OF LINGUISTIC DIVERSITY: 10-15,000 LANGUAGES
20,000	
25,000	
30,000	
35,000	EXTINCTION OF NEANDERTHALS: AT MOST PRIMITIVE LANGUAGE
40,000	HOMO SAPIENS: EVIDENCE OF COMPLEX BEHAVIOUR IMPLIES MODERN LANGUAGE
	COLONIZATION OF AUSTRALIA
45,000	
50,000	?Emergence from Africa

This book aims to give an up-to-date, accessible overview of the languages spoken in each part of the world, of the relationships between them, and what we know of their origins. A subsidiary goal is to show something of the range of diversity of the world's languages, at a time when concern is mounting over the loss of both cultural and linguistic heritage. Languages are dying out at an accelerating rate which has begun to alarm linguists, anthropologists, and others concerned with the diversity of languages and cultures. Unique languages, such as Ainu and Ubykh, have become extinct in the last few

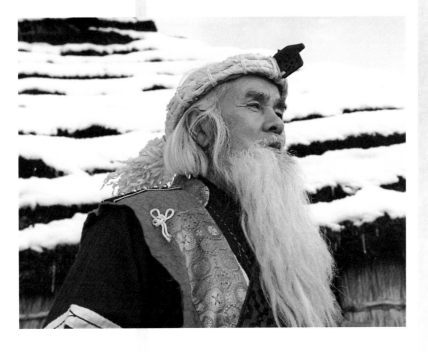

Ainu, formerly spoken in parts of Hokkaido and Honshu, is the now extinct language of the Ainu, an aboriginal people of Japan.

decades of the twentieth century, and it has been estimated that half the world's remaining languages will become extinct over the next hundred years.

Our picture of the world's languages is changing in other ways too. Since the 1960s, substantial advances have been made both in our understanding of language in general, and of particular language groups. Many of these advances have yet to be widely disseminated. Creoles, for example, were once dismissed as degenerate forms of European languages, but

they have now become central to our view of the human capacity for language. In another development, recent research has sought to pursue genetic relationships between language families far beyond those currently established. These controversial proposals are now in the forefront of debate and open new perspectives on the history of human language.

LANGUAGE DIVERSITY IN TIME AND SPACE

The diversity of human language may be compared to the diversity of the natural world. Just as the demise of a plant species reduces genetic diversity, and deprives humanity of potential medical and biological resources, so the extinction of a language takes with it a wealth of culture, art, and knowledge. The avoidance registers of Australian aboriginal languages, for example, were used in speaking to "taboo" relatives with whom contact was to be kept to a minimum. The vocabulary of these "mother-in-law languages" is highly restricted, forcing the use of very general, rather than specific, terms and raising some fascinating questions: How do people communicate with such restricted languages, and how do children learn to use them? how do they reflect or reinforce the social relationships involved? We can barely begin to answer these questions because the mother-in-law languages have all but disappeared. Even in the case of those aboriginal languages which are still spoken, the avoidance registers have been lost, together with the traditional lifestyle, and our knowledge of them is based on elderly speakers' memories.

The Indo-European languages, now spoken by half the world's population, dominate both Western countries and their views of language. French, Russian, and Hindi, all Indo-European languages, differ in many respects, yet they represent only a small part of the range of diversity of the world's languages. In terms of the number of native

THE TOP TWENTY LANGUAGES

In terms of the number of native speakers, twelve of the top twenty languages belong to the Indo-European family, many spread by colonial expansion, as in the case of English, Spanish, and Portuguese.

Mother tongue speakers (millions)

1	Chinese	1,000	11	French	70
2	English	350	12	Punjabi	70
3	Spanish	250	13	Javanese	65
4	Hindi	200	14	Bihari	65
5	Arabic	150	15	Italian	60
6	Bengali	150	16	Korean	60
7	Russian	150	17	Telugu	55
8	Portuguese	135	18	Tamil	55
9	Japanese	120	19	Marathi	50
10	German	100	20	Vietnamese	50

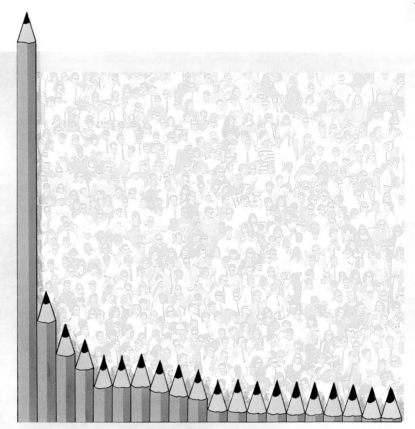

speakers, 12 of the top 20 languages (*see above*) belong to the Indo-European family, many spread by colonial expansion as in the case of English, Spanish, and Portuguese.

Linguistic diversity can be appreciated by any attempt to learn a second or foreign language. A common experience on encountering an unfamiliar language is incredulity that anybody could speak a language so different from one's own. For an English-speaker, this linguistic culture-shock might be provoked by a language where the verb comes at the end of the sentence (such as Japanese), or a tone language which uses pitch to distinguish words (such as Chinese). The scientific study of this range of diversity is called language typology, the study of language types. Some basic typological notions will be used in this book, especially in describing language families and features common to certain regions. The basic word-order typology, which focuses on the order of subject, verb and object, is important. It has been found that all six of the logically possible

BASIC WORD ORDER

Word order type		Example languages
SVO	"cows eat grass"	English; Finnish; Chinese; Swahili
SOV	"cows grass eat"	Hindi/Urdu; Turkish; Japanese, Korean
VSO	"eat cows grass"	Classical Arabic; Welsh; Samoan
VOS	"eat grass cows"	Malagasy (an Austronesian language of Madagascar); Tzotzil (a Mayan language of Central America)
OSV	"grass cows eat"	Kabardian (a language of the northern Caucasus)
OVS	"grass eat cows"	Hixkaryana (a Carib language of Brazil)

ARCTIC OCEAN

FRENCH AND
NATIVE AMERICAN

ENGLISH AND
NA - DENE

*This fish sign is
recognized worldwide as a
symbol of Christianity.*

*Totem poles were
carved heraldic
devices; they could
be mortuary poles,
memorial poles, or
house-posts.*

NORTH
ATLANTIC
OCEAN

PACIFIC OCEAN

SPANISH AND
NATIVE AMERICAN

PORTUGUESE AND
NATIVE AMERICAN

SOUTH
ATLANTIC
OCEAN

LANGUAGES OF THE WORLD

The classification of languages into families is still being developed: the Papuan languages of New Guinea may belong to five or more different families, while the Austric and Amerind groupings are recent proposals which remain the subject of debate. Such long-range groupings would reduce the world's languages to as few as 15 super-families. A few languages, such as Basque and Burushaski, which are shown on the detailed maps for each region, still defy classification. As the world map indicates, the Indo-European languages are the most widely represented family, spoken by around half the world's population.

*The Incas had no
written language so they
used knotted strings
called quipu to record
every aspect of their
daily life*

EURASIAN LANGUAGE FAMILIES
INDO-EUROPEAN
URALIC
ALTAIC
CHUKOTKO-KAMCHATKAN
CAUCASIAN (3 FAMILIES)
AFRICAN LANGUAGE FAMILIES
AFRO-ASIATIC
NILO-SAHARAN
NIGER-CONGO
KHOISAN

AMERICAN LAN
ESKIMO
NA-DEN
OTHER
SOUTHEAST AS
DRAVID
SINO-TI
AUSTRI
PAPUAN
AUSTRA

ARCTIC OCEAN

RUSSIAN

GEORGIAN

MONGOLIAN

ARMENIAN

KOREAN

JAPANESE

GREEK HEBREW

CHINESE

ABIC

TIBETAN

BURMESE

PACIFIC OCEAN

LAO

THAI

KHMER

The world's earliest printed book, the Dharani Sutra, dating before 751, is buried in a pagoda at the Pulak temple in South Korea.

MALAY

AMHARIC

SWAHILI

INDIAN OCEAN

MALAGASY

ENGLISH, AFRIKAANS

("AMERINO")

MAORI/ENGLISH

AUSTROASIATIC

Art is central to Aboriginal life. It connects the past with the present, evokes the powers of ancestors, and expresses the relationship between the people and the land.

iNwadi are "love letters" woven in colored beads by Zulu maidens and given to their loved ones as symbols of their love and devotion.

21

word orders occur (*see page 19*). The first three are overwhelmingly more frequent, reflecting the universal tendency for the subject to precede the object.

Although not all languages can be classified in this way (Hungarian has a very free word order and potentially allows all six possibilities), one order predominates in most languages. Word order also tends to be a common feature across geographical regions, shared by neighboring languages which may not be genetically related: for example, both the Indic and the Dravidian languages of India belong to the SOV (subject-object-verb) type. Alongside the charting of diversity, there is a search for language universals, statements which hold true for all languages. All languages have consonants, for example, and all distinguish between nouns and verbs. Implicational universals identify the properties which go together: one proposed implicational universal is that, if a language places the adjective before the noun (as in "black sheep"), the numeral is also placed before the noun ("five sheep").

Another point of similarity in the midst of diversity is that languages appear to be of approximately equal complexity. There are no simple languages – even pidgins and creoles have their complexities, while sign languages prove to be just as complex as spoken ones.

Chinese is the world's most widely-used language, with some 1,000 million native speakers. Until recently, it was mistakenly thought to be grammatically simple, because it lacked the inflections of many European languages.

Languages which appear simple in one respect inevitably prove to be complex in others. Chinese, for example, was once thought to be grammatically simple because it lacked the endings (inflections) of many European languages. The complexity of Chinese sentence structures, however, is just beginning to be appreciated, and the language can express the same concepts, such as time and hypotheticality, as Indo-European verbal inflections do. One feature of Chinese which looks superficially simple is reduplication, the doubling of a word or syllable. This may look like English "baby-talk" (*ma-ma, choo-choo*), but this doubling serves a variety of purposes. It can not only intensify the meaning of a word, but also downplay it: *kàn* ("look"), *kàn-kàn* "take a look." In addition to these two functions, which are very common in the world's languages, Chinese reduplication also has some specific grammatical functions, such as forming adverbs and quantifying words: thus *màn* ("slow") becomes *màn-màn* "slowly"; *rén* ("person") becomes *rén-rén* ("everyone").

Linguists generally believe that languages possess the same expressive power: even if a language lacks the vocabulary for, say, a certain field of science, the necessary words can readily be created or borrowed. Similarly, all languages have literature and poetry, whether written, oral, or signed, and its extent or quality depend on the creativity of the culture and its artists, rather than on the language itself.

LANGUAGES AND DIALECTS

How do we distinguish between a language and dialects of a single language? The answer often seems obvious: Dutch, German, Danish, and Norwegian are separate languages, while Cockney and Glaswegian are dialects of English, and Swiss and Bavarian are dialects of German. This obvious answer, however, is based on political rather than on linguistic realities. Many native speakers of English

THE SHEEP AND THE HORSES:

A PROTO-INDO-EUROPEAN FABLE

In perhaps the most ambitious of reconstructions, the nineteenth-century German linguist Schleicher composed a fable in reconstructed Proto-Indo-European. A more recent version, by the historical linguists Lehmann and Zgusta, runs as follows:

Gʷerēi owis, kʷesyo wlhnā ne ēst, ekwōns espeket, oinom ghe gʷrum woghom
hill-on sheep whose wool not exist horses saw,   one   heavy   load
"On the hill a sheep which had no wool saw some horses, one pulling a heavy load,

weghontm, oinom-kwe megam bhorom, oinom-kwe ghmenm ōku bherontm.
pulling,   one-also   great   burden   one-also   man   fast   bearing
one bearing a great burden and another carrying a man at speed.

Owis nu ekwomos ewewkʷet: "Kēr aghnutoi moi ekwōns agontm nerm widentei."
sheep now horses-to said   "heart pains me horses driving man seeing"
The sheep said to the horses: "My heart pains me seeing man driving horses".

Ek'wōs tu ewewkʷont: "Kludhi, owei, kēr ghe aghnutoi nsmei widntmos: nēr, potis,
horses then said   "listen sheep heart   pain us seeing   man   master"
The horses said: "Listen, sheep, our hearts pain us when we see how man, the master,

owiōm r wlhnām sebhi gwermom westrom kʷrneuti. Neghi owiōm wlhnā esti."
sheep's wool himself warm clothing makes And-not of-the-sheep wool is
makes the sheep's wool into a warm garment for himself. And the sheep has no wool."

Tod kekluwōs owis agrom ebhuget.
this hearing sheep field fled
On hearing this, the sheep ran off into the plain."

By separating the roots from inflections, we recognize such words as *owis* "sheep," (compare "ewe"), *wlh-nā* "wool," *e-speket* "see" (compare "inspect"), *oin-om* "one," *moi* "me" and *bher-ontm* "bearing."

Many of the reconstructed forms resemble Latin (*ovis* "sheep," *equus* "horse") or Greek (*mega* "very big," *aner* "man"). These languages are closer to the Proto-Indo-European of around 2500 BC represented by the fable.

The syntax reconstructs Proto-Indo-European as an SOV language, also resembling Classical Latin. While it is now thought that the linguistic reconstruction relies too heavily on Sanskrit, and it seems unlikely that the Indo-Europeans had domesticated horses at this time, the fable helps to bring the science of reconstruction to life.

The endings suggest both a nasal consonant ([n] in German, [m] in Gothic and Norwegian), and a labiovelar one ([v] in English, [f] in German and Norwegian). This evidence allows us to reconstruct a Proto-Germanic root *finv-* or *fenv-* (the asterisk marks it as a reconstruction). This can be compared with other Indo-European words:

Greek	Sanskrit	Latin	Breton	Polish
pente	*páñca*	*quinque*	*pempe*	*pięc*

With knowledge of sound correspondences (*f* in Germanic corresponds to *p* elsewhere as a

	Hungarian	Chaozhou	Ryukyuan	Hausa	Akkadian	Dyirbal
	(Uralic)	(Chinese)	(Japanese)	(Chadic)	(Semitic)	(Australian)
min "what?"	*mi*	*mi?*	*mi*	*mè/mì*	*mīn*	*minya*

Resemblances between the same word in different languages are said to indicate a common "proto-world" language. However, this theory is controversial.

result of the set of sound changes known as Grimm's Law) a Proto-Indo-European form *penkwe* ("five") has been reconstructed. Using this method, it is possible to reconstruct aspects of Proto-Indo-European inflections and even aspects of its syntax. The elaborate case systems of the early Classical languages (and of conservative Indo-European languages such as Lithuanian) suggest that Indo-European had around eight cases for nouns: nominative, vocative, accusative, dative, genitive, instrumental, ablative, and locative. In the case of Indo-European, Classical texts from Sanskrit, Greek, and Latin provide intermediate forms between the proto-language and the modern forms, whereas for most other language families, such evidence is lacking and reconstruction calls for correspondingly more detective work.

LONG-RANGE COMPARISONS

In recent years there has been renewed debate about the classification of the world's languages and the extent to which it can be pursued. For many years it was accepted that the existence of certain families, such as Indo-European and Uralic, had been established beyond reasonable doubt, while other families, such as Ural-Altaic and Austric, were questionable. It was widely believed that the evidence was insufficient to allow their classification beyond the time depth of Indo-European history.

Recently, however, interest in distant relationships has revived. Joseph Greenberg, whose earlier work proposed the four African language families, has attempted controversially to group the indigenous languages of America into three great families, corresponding to three successive waves of migration: Amerind, Na-Dene, and Eskimo-Aleut. The Na-Dene language family of America may be related to Sino-Tibetan, and even to Caucasian languages. Greenberg has also proposed a vast Eurasiatic family, viewing the Indo-European, Uralic, and Altaic families as distantly related. Basic vocabulary such as the pronouns *me* ("I") and *te* ("you"), which occur widely in Indo-European, Uralic, and beyond, may provide evidence according to some linguist. Such similarities which stretch beyond established groupings may point to long-range relationships.

As an extreme case, "global etymologies," which reach back to a "proto-world" language have been proposed for some items such as body parts and kinship terms. The words for "one" and "finger," for example, are said to go back to a common "proto-World" root *tik* (reflected in the word "digital"). Some grammatical items such as the question words *kin* ("who?") and *min* ("what?") are also proposed *(see example above).*

Skeptics suggest other possible explanations for these resemblances. Some sounds are symbolic: the widespread use of nasal sounds in words expressing negation, for example, might be due to an intrinsic or natural association, and the *mi(n)* pattern might have arisen independently for similar reasons, perhaps involving a reflex opening of the mouth. Another difficulty is distinguishing whether a shared word is the result of common inheritance or more recent borrowing. Finally, it needs to be demonstrated that the similarities are more pronounced than would be expected simply by chance. Given these difficulties, it seems unlikely that such proposed long-range groupings as Amerind or Eurasiatic will be established or refuted by linguistic criteria alone.

Language classification is becoming an interdisciplinary field, with attempts to match archeological evidence and genetic and

peoples from Eurasia, making hypotheses about American language families and their connections to Sino-Tibetan at least plausible.

LANGUAGE CONTACT

A recurrent theme in this book is contact between adjacent languages and its effects. No language exists in a vacuum: even geographically isolated languages such as Basque in the Pyrenees and Burushaski in the Himalayas have been influenced by the surrounding languages. Although English and

The Norman Conquest of England in 1066, depicted here in the Bayeux tapestry, was the start of nearly a millennium of close contact between the English and French, which has had a profound influence on the vocabulary of both languages.

anatomical analyses of human populations with linguistic classifications. Naturally, racial and linguistic boundaries do not necessarily match. However, the long-range linguistic classifications seem broadly consistent both with population genetics and with archeological evidence of the spread of human populations. Archeological findings suggest that America, for example, may have been populated as recently as 12,000 years ago by

French are related only distantly through the Indo-European family tree, the contact between them in the centuries since the Norman Conquest of England has led to much shared vocabulary. Similarly, Chinese and Japanese are related not through a common origin but by cultural contacts, leading to the borrowing of much Chinese vocabulary together with the Chinese writing system.

Language contact takes a number of forms

which have come to be more fully understood in recent research. In particular, borrowing occurs when languages come into contact for trading purposes and through bilingualism. Language shift occurs when speakers of one language come to speak another over the course of several generations. Borrowing affects primarily vocabulary, while language shift can have deeper effects on the structure of the language and often leaves clear marks in the grammar.

BI- AND MULTILINGUALISM

It has been estimated that around half the world's population is bilingual or multilingual. While relatively unusual in countries such as France, Britain, and the U.S.A., bilingualism is the norm in many parts of the world – Thailand, for example, is home to some eighty languages. In areas such as India, West Africa, and Papua New Guinea, it is common for individuals to speak a local language, a regional language, and a colonial language: in the Cameroon, for example, most people speak two or more African languages, and the educated also speak French. This does not necessarily lead to discord, as harmoniously multilingual countries such as Switzerland and Thailand demonstrate.

While bilingualism has sometimes been

CODE-MIXING

Code-mixing/switching is a colorful feature of bilingual societies and individuals. Mixing of Spanish and English is common in North American Hispanic communities: the following examples are typical.

"...those friends are friends from Mexico que tienen chamaquitos." [who have little children]

"All of a sudden I started acting real curiosa [strange], you know."

Such mixing occurs out of linguistic necessity, when the speaker cannot think of the words in the original language, but also for reasons of identity.

In Hong Kong, where most of the population speaks some English, those who are fluent in both Cantonese and English mix the two in a characteristic way which marks them as more or less bilingual.

This mixing is also found in Cantonese texts, as in the popular novel *Diary of a Yuppie*. The text uses English names (*Angie*), adjectives (*happy*) and half-digested idioms (*in another word* for "in other words"). The letter *D* is used to represent the Cantonese word dī meaning "a bit" and the colloquial verb *mit* "tear," for which no standard Chinese character exists, is written phonetically.

Angie 一邊 mit 面膜，一邊就住唔發脾氣，佢怕有皺紋，佢話：「超，我想客觀啲同你分析啫！」
「客觀？你係我老婆，你唔係要嚟客觀，係要嚟主觀嘅！你要識得欣賞你老公！」
Angie 答案係「我欣賞你咁單純！」
又過份咗叻！即係話我幼稚！我用個指甲鉗指住 Angie 話：「你一直睇小我！」
Angie 好「叻」，即刻調轉嚟講：「In another word，我係鼓勵緊你！」

A facsimile of a page from the popular Cantonese novel, Diary of a Yuppie, *clearly illustrates the mixing of Cantonese and English.*

seen as a handicap, linguists have accumulated evidence that, in addition to the obvious practical advantage of enabling communication with a wider range of cultures, bilingualism also offers cognitive advantages. It certainly raises awareness of language: bilingual children, for example, are aware that the names we give to things are largely arbitrary, so that a horse could equally have been called a dog. Bilingual education is seen as an important means of promoting cultural integration, at the same time preserving the use of minority languages and their associated cultural traditions. For these and other reasons, linguists are almost unanimous in their support for bilingual education and oppose legislation attempting to enforce monolingualism, such as laws making the use of English in the workplace compulsory.

LOAN WORDS AND BORROWING

All kinds of language contact give rise to "loan words," foreign words adapted and added to the vocabulary of the "borrowing" language (the terms are misleading in that the words are rarely returned to the "lending" language). English is full of loan words reflecting spheres of cultural influence, as in the case of French *cuisine* (*see map, pp. 32–3*), or the word *zero,* from Arabic mathematics. Expressions such as "lose face" and "long time no see!" are loan translations from Chinese, derived by translating separately each part of the corresponding Chinese expressions.

While English has long welcomed loans and continues to do so, some languages have resisted them as a threat to linguistic purity. French is protected by the *Académie Française* and the French government has introduced legislation to outlaw the use of English words (franglais) in official media. Computer terminology, for example, is created in French to avoid borrowing (*l'ordinateur* "computer, " *le logiciel* "software").

More extensive contact, especially when bilingualism is widespread, gives rise to structural borrowing in which not only

Contact between speakers of different languages, for example in a multi-ethnic society such as the U.S.A., can lead to the introduction of foreign loan words into the dominant language.

North America
abalone: *Costanoan*
pecan: *Illinois (Algonquian)*
pemmican, persimmon: *Cree (Algonquian)*
sockeye (salmon): *Salish*

Europe
halibut, pickle: *Dutch*
chowder, soup, sauce, mackerel: *French*
almond: *Greek via Latin and French*
asparagus: *Greek*
cucumber: *Latin*
gulash: *Hungarian*
sherry: *Spanish*
whisky: *Gaelic ("water")*
vodka: *Russian ("water")*

EUROPE

MIDDLE EAST

NORTH AMERICA

AFRICA

South America
barbecue, maize, potato: *Taino (Arawakan)*
avocado, guacamole, tomato, cocoa, chocolate: *Nahuatl*
cashew, tapioca: *Tupi via Portuguese*
jerky: *Quechua*
papaya: *Carib, via Spanish and Portuguese*

SOUTH AMERICA

Africa
banana: *Wolof/Fulani*
yam: *Wolof/Fulani via West Indian creoles*
okra: *possibly Akan (West African) via West Indian creoles*

Middle East

jasmine, spinach: *Persian via Arabic*

pistachio: *Persian via Greek*

alcolhol, albacore, artichoke, kebab, saffron, sherbert, tamarind: *Arabic*

coffee: *Arabic via Turkish*

caviar: *Turkish*

cinnamon: *Hebrew*

endive: *Egyptian via Greek*

India

chutney, kedgeree, samosa: *Hindu/Urdu*

curry, congee: *Tamil*

mango: *Tamil via Malay and Portuguese*

orange: *Sanskrit via Persian, Arabic, and Spanish*

sugar: *Sanskrit via Persian and Arabic*

SOUTH EAST ASIA

GASTRONOMIC LOAN WORDS

Food names are among the most easily borrowed items, partly for reasons of fashion and prestige. The Norman Conquest of England introduced the French terms "pork" and "beef", which replaced the Germanic words. Many loan words have been assimilated so that their foreign origins are not obvious. The word "hamburger" (German: "[sausage] from Hamburg" has been mis-analyzed as being a combination of "ham" and "burger", giving rise to words such as "cheeseburger". In addition to the hundreds of French loans, some everyday food names come from exotic sources:

chocolate (Nahuatl, via Spanish and French)

tomato (Nahuatl, via Spanish)

ketchup (Cantonese: "tomato-juice")

mango (Tamil, via Portuguese)

tea (Amoy Chinese)

chutney, kedgeree (Hindi)

kebab (Arabic)

One of the words given as evidence for a long-distance relationship between Indo-European, Uralic, and other language families is the root madw- "honey" (as in English mead, a drink made from honey):

Sanskrit (Indo-European)	Russian (Indo-European)	Hungarian Uralic)	Tamil (Dravidian)	Etruscan (unclassified)
mádhu	med	méz	mattu	ma`θ

Although these resemblances are striking, this is the kind of word which could easily be borrowed, in which case the forms would not be evidence of a genetic relationship. The word maθ "mead", for example, is not sufficient to show that Etruscan is related to the Indo-European languages.

Southeast Asia

ketchup, kumquat, lychee: *Cantonese*

tea: *Amoy Chinese (*char *is from Mandarin)*

sago, mangosteen: *Malay*

vocabulary but aspects of grammar are adopted. After Danish immigrants settled in Britain in the eighth and ninth centuries, for example, the influence of their Norse on Old English led to the borrowing of the pronouns "they," "them," "their," the form "are" of the verb "be," and the spread of phrasal verb constructions such as "pick up."

LANGUAGE SHIFT AND SUBSTRATES

The substrate phenomenon occurs as a result of language shift, when speakers of language A adopt language B, whether for cultural, political, or other reasons. Naturally, the first generation to adopt language B will be bilingual and will mix the two languages, as in the case of Cantonese and English in Hong Kong. Their use of B will show some features of A. The children of this generation will become native speakers of B, but retain some of the A-like features – a substrate derived from language A. An example of language shift occurred when the Franks, a Germanic tribe, colonized northern France and shifted to speaking French. They brought to their French the verb-second rule, familiar to learners of German, resulting in the inversion of subject and verb in questions such as *Que voulez-vous?* ("what do you want?"). The result is a Germanic substrate which distinguishes French from the other Romance languages.

Language shift is happening in many parts of the world today. In Scotland and Ireland, the shift from Gaelic to English continues, leaving some marks such as the construction

Lothair I (795–855), emperor of the Franks, a Germanic tribe who colonized northern France and, under their emperor Charlemagne (r.768-814), controlled an area stretching from Denmark to Rome.

"he's after drinking" meaning "he's been drinking" in Irish English. In California, many Hispanic families and communities are shifting from Spanish to English, and in Central America, from native American languages to Spanish. Successive generations of immigrants to North America – Norwegian, Polish, Hungarian – have discarded their languages for English, often with only surnames betraying their ancestry. In fact, language shift is now the principal way in which languages become extinct.

LINGUISTIC AREAS

As an extreme case of language contact, the languages of an area may come to share similar characteristics regardless of their genetic affiliation. A well-known example is the Balkan *Sprachbund*, the German term meaning a "bundle of languages" sharing common features. Unlike most of the surrounding languages, Greek, Romanian, Bulgarian, and Albanian lack an infinitive form of the verb – most have a suffixed definite article (Romanian *om-ul* "the man"), and an unusual case system in which one form serves as both subject and object and another as either dative ("to") or genitive ("of"). Such similarities result from a combination of contact influences, bilingualism, and language shift, which have taken place over a long period of coexistence. In the case of the Balkans, successive migrations following the conquests and colonization of the Ottoman Empire led to widespread bilingualism. Similar situations are found in South and Southeast Asia: the use of tone, for example, is an areal feature of Southeast Asia which is not associated with any one language family.

OVERVIEW

Part Two examines the language families of the regions of the world. Since it is not feasible to give the locations and affiliations of all 6,000 or so languages, the family trees and maps show only major languages or those specifically mentioned in the text. The book is organized primarily by geographical area, and secondarily by language families. Since they rarely coincide completely, the two kinds of classification, geographical and linguistic, need to be carefully distinguished: the terms European languages and Indo-European languages, for example, refer to two distinct sets of languages. European languages are merely those which

happen to be spoken in Europe, and include Uralic languages such as Hungarian, Finnish, and Estonian as well as the isolated Basque; the Indo-European languages are a family of related languages, and not merely those of India and Europe as the name might suggest.

Part Three traces the origins and development of writing systems. Part Four considers the prospects for the survival of languages and linguistic diversity.

ROMANIAN
lup-ul "the wolf"
lup-ul-ui "to/of the wolf"

BULGARIAN
žena-ta "the woman"
na balgarija "to/ofBulgaria"

ALBANIAN
mik-u "the friend"

GREEK
tu anthrópu "to/of the man"

THE BALKAN LINGUISTIC AREA

The Balkan languages belong to four different families of Indo-European. Nevertheless, they have come to share several features which are otherwise unusual, including a suffixed definite article and a case form which functions as both dative (to) and genitive (of).

Europe and Eurasia

The Eurasian land mass is home to the Indo-European, Uralic, and Altaic families, together with several obscure and isolated languages of uncertain origin. The Indo-European languages form the world's most widely distributed language family; it is also the best understood thanks to a long history of recorded texts. On the other hand, the Caucasus' "mountain of tongues" has the region's greatest linguistic diversity, while the Altaic family has a remarkable uniformity of structure. In the Far East, Japanese poses its own unique puzzle.

A man in Hungarian costume asserts his national identity. Hungarian does not belong, like most European languages, to the Indo-European family but to the Finno-Ugric group.

he Eurasian linguistic area, consisting of Europe and northern and central Asia, is home to the Indo-European, Uralic and Altaic language families.

It has long been suspected that distant relationships exist between these families. The Nostratic and Eurasiatic hypotheses, for example, both seek to establish such genetic linkages, the former suggesting that Eurasiatic is itself a branch of a greater Nostratic family (*see box*). This hypothesis dates the spread of

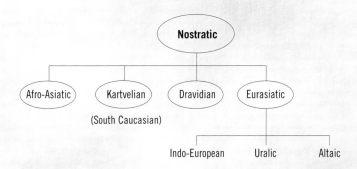

Nostratic

Afro-Asiatic — Kartvelian — Dravidian — Eurasiatic

(South Caucasian)

Indo-European — Uralic — Altaic

The evidence for a relationship between Eurasian language families begins with similarities in the pronouns (first person *me/mi*, second person *te/ti*), and extends to a wide range of vocabulary items, such as the verb root *man-* "live" (as in the Latin-based word *mansion*):

Indo-European	Dravidian	Afro-Asiatic	Altaic
(Latin)	(Telugu)	(Hebrew)	(Mongolian)
manēre "live"	*manu* "live"	*?āmen* "remain"	*mana* "keep watch"

In some cases the meanings must be presumed to have changed substantially, making the relationship much more speculative:

Indo-European	Uralic	Dravidian
English *milk*	Hungarian *mell* "breast"	Tamil *melku* "chew"

these languages across Eurasia to the end of the last Ice Age, some 15,000 years ago.

While the three main Eurasian families share some similarities, exceptions are presented by the highly diverse Caucasian languages and by isolated languages without known living relatives: examples include Basque, which is spoken in

the French and Spanish Pyrenees, and Ket and Nivkh, which are spoken in Siberia.

THE INDO-EUROPEAN LANGUAGE FAMILY

The Indo-European family was recognized when a colonial judge, Sir William Jones, came across the Sanskrit language in eighteenth-century India. Sanskrit was extinct as a spoken language but still used for religious purposes. It clearly resembled Latin and Greek, not only in its vocabulary but also in its grammatical system and inflections. Jones concluded that all three ancient languages had "sprung from a single source," which had also given rise to Germanic and Celtic.

Following this discovery, the Baltic and Slavic families were added, together with Armenian and Albanian, single languages which represent distinct branches. More recently, the long-extinct Tocharian and Hittite languages have also been found to have sprung from the same single source. Tocharian appears in Buddhist writings from China's Xinjiang province, showing Indo-European's early eastward expansion, while Hittite, known from inscriptions in modern Turkey (ancient

Celtic

Brythonic — Goidelic (Gaelic)

Breton +Cornish Welsh — Irish +Manx Scots

Over half a million Welsh-speakers are served by bi-lingual Welsh-English signs, such as this signpost at Devil's Bridge Station on the Rheidol Railway in Dyfed.

Anatolia), has been identified as Indo-European's tenth branch.

CELTIC

The Celtic languages, spoken widely in western Europe in the first millennium BC, have been in gradual decline since Roman times, when Latin replaced Gaulish in France. They survive as minority languages in the northwestern extremities of Europe, the most vigorous being Welsh, with half a million speakers, and Breton, with almost a million.

Breton spread to Brittany from southwest England in about the seventh century AD. Cornish became extinct in the eighteenth century, and Manx, formerly spoken on the Isle of Man, died out in 1974, although both have since been revived from written records. Scots and Irish Gaelic survive on the Hebridean Islands of Scotland and along the west coast of Ireland.

The Celtic languages are characteristically of the VSO (verb–subject–object) type. In Welsh, for example, the verb normally comes first in the sentence: *Collodd Siôn ddwy bunt* (literally, "lost Sion two pounds," translated

LATIN AND ROMANCE

The Romance languages clearly show their Latin ancestry, with Italian especially close to Latin in its sounds and vocabulary; typologically, however, they are very different. They have lost the case inflections of Latin and have SVO rather than SOV word order. In many instances where Latin used inflected forms of the verb, the Romance languages use separate AUXILIARIES:

	Latin	Italian	
Perfect	canta-vi	ho cantato	"I have sung"
Passive	canta-tur	é cantato	"it is sung"

While Latin had three genders, the modern languages have two. Nouns denoting neither males nor females are assigned more or less arbitrarily to either masculine or feminine gender:

	Latin	Italian	
Masculine	homo "man"	uomo "man"";	vino "wine"
Feminine	domina "mistress"	donna "woman";	guerra "war"
Neuter	vinum "wine",		
	bellum "war"		

as "Sion lost two pounds"). Similarly, the noun comes before adjectives which modify it: *Bws coch mawr* (literally, "bus red big," translated as "a big red bus").

ROMANCE LANGUAGES

The Romance languages are derived from the " Vulgar Latin" of the Roman empire, which would have differed from the literary Latin of classical texts just as the English spoken around the British Empire differed from standard British English. Italian remains closest to Latin, while many of the other Romance languages have been subject to external influences: French by Celtic and German; Romanian by surrounding Slavic languages; and Spanish by Arabic. Among the minority languages, the Rhaeto-Romance tongues of the Swiss and Italian Alps are so distinctive that they cannot be accommodated as dialects of major languages. Occitan (Provençal) was spoken thoughout southern France, but is now restricted to remoter parts of Provence and the Massif Central. In Spain, Catalan and Galician, which have much in common with Occitan and Portuguese respectively, are increasingly recognized as separate languages. Moldavian is a dialect of

Romanian which was written in Cyrillic script in the times of the Moldavian Soviet Socialist Republic. Dalmatian, a Romance language spoken on the Adriatic coast of Croatia until the nineteenth century, is now extinct.

GERMANIC LANGUAGES

The oldest records of Germanic, apart from the few Runic inscriptions, come from Gothic. Known largely from parts of a fourth-century translation of the New Testament, Gothic was still spoken around the Black Sea in the sixteenth century, but became extinct soon afterwards. English, German, and Dutch are the main representatives of the western branch of Germanic Frisian, which is spoken on the North Sea coast of Holland and Germany and on the neighboring offshore islands, is akin to

Sir William Jones, who first recognized the Indo-European language family.

THE INDO-EUROPEAN LANGUAGES

The Indo-European is the largest established language family in the world. The tree shows only major languages, others being listed in the sections devoted to each sub-family. Extinct languages are shown with the symbol +.

Within the Indo-European family, some groups are more closely related than the conventional family tree model implies: the Italic branch, to which Latin belongs, is particularly close to Celtic, presumably due to their close proximity in pre-Roman times.

Arctic Ocean

ICELANDIC
- REYKJAVIK

KEY
- CELTIC
- ROMANCE
- GERMANIC
- SLAVIC
- BALTIC
- OTHER INDO-EUROPEAN
- URALIC
- ALTAIC
- ISOLATES

SAAMI

SAAMI

SAAMI

FINNISH

SWEDISH

NORWEGIAN

OSLO

STOCKHOLM

Baltic Sea

■ HELSINKI

■ TALLINN

ESTONIAN

LATVIAN

RIGA ■

Atlantic Ocean

SCOTS GAELIC

North Sea

DANISH

COPENHAGEN

RUSSIAN

LITHUANIAN

VILNIUS ■

■ MINSK

BELARUSIAN

IRISH

FRISIAN

AMSTERDAM

BERLIN

WARSAW

ENGLISH

DUTCH

SORBIAN

POLISH

KIEV ■

WELSH

LONDON ■

BRUSSELS

FLEMISH

GERMAN

LUXEMBOURG

PRAGUE

CZECH

UKRAINIAN

SLOVAK

BRETON

PARIS ■

VIENNA

BRATISLAVA

BUDAPEST

KISHINEV ■

FRENCH

Bay of Biscay

BERNE ■

RHAETO-ROMANCE

SLOVENIAN

LJUBLJANA ■

HUNGARIAN

ZAGREB ■

CROATIAN

RUMANIAN

BUCHAREST ■

Black Sea

SERBIAN

SARAJEVO

GALICIAN

BASQUE

FRENCH

ITALIAN

ROME ■

BULGARIAN

MACEDONIAN

ALBANIAN

ISTANBUL

CATALAN

SARDINIAN

TURKISH

MADRID ■

SPANISH

GREEK

PORTUGUESE

LISBON ■

ITALIAN

ATHENS ■

Mediterranean Sea

THE LANGUAGES OF EUROPE

Most of the indigenous languages of Europe belong to the Indo-European family. There are the following exceptions: Finnish, Saami, Estonian, and Hungarian (all Uralic languages); Turkish (Altaic); and Basque, an isolated language without known relatives. The divisions between national languages suggest clearer boundaries than actually exist. Divergent dialects of Italian or German are not always mutually intelligible, while closely related languages such as Norwegian and Swedish are.

the Anglo-Saxon brought to Britain after the departure of the Romans, and is thus the closest continental relative of English.

Afrikaans developed from the Dutch of seventeenth-century settlers in South Africa, where it is spoken by over half the white population and by many of mixed European and African descent. It has undergone some simplification but remains partially intelligible to Dutch-speakers. Yiddish, spoken by Jews of Central and East European extraction, is also considered a Germanic language; although it has adopted much vocabulary from Slavic and other sources, its grammar displays characteristically Germanic features.

The mainland Scandinavian languages, Swedish, Norwegian, and Danish, are mutually intelligible to some extent. Swedish is also spoken in Finland, and much of the population is bilingual in Swedish and Finnish (a Uralic language). Together with some varieties of Norwegian and Serbo-Croatian, Latvian, and Lithuanian, Swedish is one of the few European languages with tone: different "tonal accents" distinguish pairs such as *bur-en* "the cage" and *buren* "carried."

The most conservative Germanic languages are Icelandic and Faroese, preserved by remoteness and a proud tradition of resisting international influences. While other European languages all use versions of "telephone" and "radio," Icelandic uses *sími*

WORD ORDER IN GERMANIC LANGUAGES

Most Germanic languages are not easily classified as SVO or SOV. Instead, they have a general rule that the verb comes second in a main clause:

German	Swedish
Gestern war ich zu Hause.	*I dag kommer jag inte*
Yesterday was I at home	today come I not
"I was at home yesterday"	"I'm not coming today."

While Old English was a typical Germanic language in this and other respects, Modern English preserves only relics of this rule:

"Along came a procession of cows."

"Never have I seen such a range of talent in one place."

(from the word "thread") and *útvarp* (literally "throw-out") for these devices. The system of four cases is also more fully preserved than in other Germanic languages. Thanks to this conservatism, the medieval sagas, epic poems in Old Norse, are still comprehensible to Icelandic speakers.

THE BALTO-SLAVIC LANGUAGES

The Baltic and Slavic families are closely related branches of Indo-European. The two Baltic languages, Lithuanian and Latvian, compete with Russian in the former Soviet republics (Estonia, the third Baltic state, belongs linguistically to the Uralic group). The Balto-Slavic languages are especially interesting for their conservative nature, which makes them useful in the reconstruction of Indo-European. While most Indo-European languages have lost the verb

Afrikaans, seen here on a bi-lingual sign, is based on seventeenth- century Dutch, and is spoken by half the white population of South Africa.

Germanic

West	North	East
English	Icelandic	+Gothic
Frisian	Faroese	
Dutch	Norwegian	
German	Swedish	
Afrikaans	Danish	
Yiddish		

PASOP VIR SEEKOEIE

BEWARE OF HIPPOPOTAMUS

and noun endings characteristic of Latin and Greek, the Baltic languages preserve complex case systems and in addition have developed tonal distinctions.

The Slavic languages, divided into western, southern, and eastern branches, are also conservative, are inflectional, like Latin and Greek, and their nouns have up to six cases. A characteristic and complex feature of Slavic grammar is the division of verbs according to aspect: the "perfective" form indicates a complete action, usually expressed by a prefix as in *ja pro-chital knigu* "I've read the book (and finished it)."

The recent political changes in eastern Europe have enhanced the status of several Slavic languages. Following the breakup of Czechoslovakia, for example, Czech has become the language of the Czech Republic, and Slovak that of Slovakia. In the former Yugoslavia, the relatively minor differences between Croatian and Serbian are now emphasized by the different writing systems: Serbian, like Russian, Ukrainian, and Bulgarian, is written in Cyrillic script, while Croatian, like Slovenian and the West Slavic languages, is written in a Roman alphabet. This distinction in turn reflects the historic division of Slavic peoples between the Eastern Orthodox and Catholic faiths. Similarly,

Ukrainian and Belarusian are now languages of independent states, although they are mutually intelligible with Russian. Upper and Lower Sorbian are minority languages, each with its own written form, spoken in eastern Germany near the Czech border.

The Slavic languages have a reputation for being difficult to pronounce. Asking for an ice cream (*zmrzlina*) in Czech, and even saying "hello" in Russian (*zdrávstvyjte*) are not the easiest accomplishments for an English speaker. The main sources of this difficulty are consonant clusters not found in English. These languages also use certain unfamiliar consonants, such as the labiovelar glide ł in Polish (for example, *Wałęsa*) and the trilled post-alveolar *r* in Czech (for example, *Dvořak*). Additional distinctive Slavic features are the palatalized or "soft" consonants, produced by raising the tongue to the roof (palate) of the mouth. In Cyrillic script they are shown by the soft sign Ь as in Russian Братъ (*brat*) "to bring," as opposed to Брат (*brat*) "brother."

In the Balkan region are two isolated sub-families of Indo-European: Greek and Albanian. Greek has been spoken in the Mediterranean since at least the fourteenth century BC, indicated by the Linear B inscriptions from the Minoan civilization of Crete (c. sixteenth century BC). Greek, especially the archaic language of the Homeric poems which date back to the seventh or eighth centuries BC, is one of the oldest sources for Indo-European. The differences between

Tablets found at the Cretan palace of Knossos date to the fourteenth century BC. Their inscriptions are written in Linear B , an archaic form of Greek. The tablets were used to record all aspects of the administration of the royal household.

modern and ancient Greek are far less drastic than the differences between English and Old English. Modern Greek is also spoken on Crete and Cyprus as well as in immigrant communities in America, Australia, and elsewhere.

There are some four million Albanian-speakers in Albania itself, in the Serbian province of Kosovo, and in Albanian settlements in Greece and southern Italy. The Balkan languages share several common features as a result of intense contact and bilingualism (*see Part One*).

Armenian is spoken in eastern Turkey and in the southwestern Caucasus. Until the post-Soviet establishment of Armenia, the Armenian people lacked a homeland, and many emigrated to the U.S.A. and elsewhere. Their language, while influenced by neighboring Persian and Turkish, has retained some Indo-European features: it is thought to be the only preserve of the so-called ejective consonants now reconstructed as a hypothetical feature of the Indo-European proto-language.

INDO-IRANIAN

Indo-Iranian is the largest Indo-European sub-family, with languages spoken in Iran, Afghanistan, India, and Pakistan. The ancient languages of the Indic and Iranian groups, Sanskrit and Avestan, provide valuable clues to the reconstruction of Indo-European.

The Iranian languages are spoken in southwestern Asia and the Middle East.

Romanies, or gypsies, are scattered throughout Europe, having migrated from northwest India from about the 9th century onwards. They maintain a nomadic way of life, and speak Romany, a language belonging to the Indic branch of the Indo-European family.

Persian, the national language of Iran, is also spoken in Afghanistan, together with Pashto. Kurdish is spoken in parts of Turkey, Iraq, Iran, and Syria, Ossetic in the northern Caucasus, Tajik in Tajikistan, surrounded by Turkic languages. The Baluchi and Pashto languages extend eastwards into Pakistan.

The Indic languages are spoken in South Asia (*see Part Two, Chapter 2*), with the exception of the Gypsy language, Romany, which exists in many forms throughout Europe. Some of these have become mixed, like Anglo-Romani, which uses a predominantly English vocabulary.

BASQUE

Basque, spoken in Spanish and French territory at the western end of the Pyrenees, is an isolated language; many inconclusive attempts have been made to link it with other families, especially the Kartvelian group of the Caucasus which it resembles in its grammatical structure. It is likely that other Basque-like languages were spoken more widely in western Europe before the Roman conquest: the French province of Gascony bears a Basque name, and the Gascon dialect shows many clear traces of Basque influence.

BASQUE AS AN ERGATIVE LANGUAGE

Basque is one of the few European languages with an ergative case system, the others being languages of the Caucasus. The "ergative" case is a special form for the subject of a transitive verb:

TRANSITIVE	INTRANSITIVE
Ni-k neska ikusten dut.	*Ni etorri naiz.*
I-ERG. girl see AUX.	I come AUX.
"I see the girl."	"I have come."

The subject of the first sentence, *ni* ("I"), has the suffix *-k* marking the ergative case, while the object *neska* ("the girl") is not marked for any case, just like the subject of the intransitive sentence, *ni*. This contrasts with the accusative system found in Indo-European languages such as Latin, Russian, and German, where the object of a transitive verb ("girl") is marked with a special case (accusative), leaving the subject of both transitive and intransitive verbs ("I") in the nominative case. While rather less numerous than the accusative type, ergative languages are widespread, especially in the Caucasus, the Far East, South Asia, America, Australia and the Pacific.

URALIC LANGUAGES

The Uralic family derives its name from Russia's Ural mountains, the presumed homeland of the proto-Uralic language. Uralic languages were formerly widespread in Eurasia, and left their mark on the Baltic and Slavic languages which replaced them in many areas. Most of the languages are now spoken in northern Russia, Siberia, and the Baltic region, while Hungarian was brought to Hungary by the Magyars in about the ninth century.

The Finno-Ugric group includes three national languages of Europe: Hungarian, Finnish, and Estonian. Finnish and Estonian, spoken on opposite sides of the Baltic, are closely related and Estonian became a national language when Estonia gained its independence from the U.S.S.R. in 1989. Saami is spoken by the nomadic Lapps of northern Scandinavia and the Kola peninsula in Russia. The Ugric branch to which Hungarian belongs has been separated from

The western end of the Pyrenees is a region inhabited by the Basques, a people of unknown origin. They speak Basque, which bears no proven relation to any other known language.

the Finnic branch for some 3,000 years, and Hungarian shows only distant traces of its relationship to Finnish and Estonian:

Hungarian	Finnish	Estonian	
három	*kolme*	*kolm*	"three"
szem	*silmä*	*silm*	"eye"

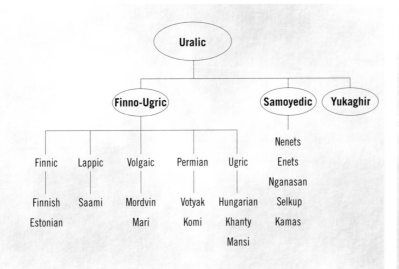

Outside Hungary, Hungarian is also spoken by substantial minorities in Transylvania (Romania) and Slovakia, reflecting the borders before World War I. Mansi, Khanty, and Mari are spoken by minorities in northern Russia and northwestern Siberia.

The Samoyedic languages, spoken by around 30,000 inhabitants of Siberia, are more distantly related to the Finnic and Ugric languages. Yukaghir, spoken much farther east in Siberia (*see box*), shares certain features with Samoyedic and the Uralic languages, but its genetic relationship to them is uncertain.

The Uralic languages are well known for their complex case systems (15 in Finnish, 17 in Hungarian) which represent spatial meanings like "onto" and "away from" as well as serving

grammatical functions, such as indicating the direct and indirect objects of the verb. While, compared to Latin's six cases, this seems highly complex, the forms taken by case endings are very regular and generally predictable.

Another typical Uralic feature is vowel harmony, a rule according to which a word can contain only a certain type of vowel; to meet this requirement, suffixes change their form according to the vowels of the word to which they attach. This is the one respect in which the Hungarian case forms are irregular: for example the suffix *-on* becomes *-en* in a *hegy-en* ("on the hill") and *-ön* in a *föld-ön* ("on the ground").

ALTAIC LANGUAGES

The Altaic languages of Eurasia are spoken by traditionally nomadic peoples over a large area in the dry steppe climate, from Turkey to northeastern Siberia. Like the Uralic languages, they are named after their presumed mountain

YUKAGHIR "WRITING"

Yukaghir is spoken in one of the world's harshest climates, and much of our knowledge of it comes from intellectuals exiled to Siberia who studied the local language and culture to relieve boredom. Among their discoveries are the pictorial "letters" whose meanings were to be guessed at, as in a game of charades.

The "love letter" represents two households and several characters shown as pine trees. A girl (c) is thinking of her sweetheart (b) who is living with a Russian woman (a). The crossed lines represent discord within the households. There is another man (d) interested in the girl, supposedly a warning to (b). Although the drawings are not regarded as true writing because they do not directly represent any aspect of the Yukaghir language, they are comparable to native American pictographs as symbolic representations in a pre-literate culture.

requiring each word to contain the same type of vowel. One of its uses in Manchu is to distinguish male and female, or *yin* and *yang* words: *eme* ("mother"), *hehe* ("woman"), and *emhe* ("mother-in-law") are all *yin* words, while *ama* ("father"), *haha* ("man"), and *amha* ("father-in-law") are all *yang*.

LANGUAGES OF THE CAUCASUS

The Caucasus, with its vast number of languages located in a small territory, has long attracted the attention of linguists. In the early 1800s, Russian missionaries, ethnographers, and even generals started collecting data on the languages of the area, and their discoveries have become an important foundation on which studies continue to rely. There are over forty spoken languages belonging to three distinct families, and the phrase "Caucasian languages" denotes a purely geographical grouping. The three main families are Kartvelian, Abkhaz-Adyghean, and Nakh-Dagestanian. In the surrounding lowland areas, Turkic (Azerbaijani and Kumyk) and Indo-European languages (Armenian, Ossetic) are also spoken (*see map*).

The Kartvelian family includes Georgian, Laz, Svan, Chan, and Mingrelian. Georgian has a long and well-established literary tradition whose earliest documents date back to the fifth century AD. Kartvelian languages are known for their complex morphology and voice systems.

The Abkhaz-Adyghean family of the northwestern Caucasus includes Abaza, Abkhaz, Adyghe, Kabardian or Circassian, and Ubykh. Ubykh used to be spoken in Turkey but is now considered a dead language; its last known speaker, from whose expertise three generations of linguists were able to benefit, died in 1992. The remaining languages of the family use writing systems based on Cyrillic.

Abkhaz-Adyghean languages are famous among linguists for their inordinately complex system of consonants (some experts distinguish 80 in Ubykh and 69 in the Bzyb dialect of Abhkaz), and for their extremely limited number of vowels (2-3). As vowels undergo reduction in speech (for instance, Kabardian *c'əχ°əf* – "a good person" may be pronounced as *c'χ°f*), some linguists have even described these languages as having no vowels at all. Several languages of this family are characterized by ergativity, (*see p. 45*).

Most of the languages of the Nakh-Daghestanian family are also ergative. These include Chechen, Ingush, Avar, Chamali, Tsez, Lak, Dargwa, Lezgian, Tabasaran, Archi, Tsakhur, and others. The largest languages are Chechen with close to a million speakers, and Avar and Lezgian with around 400,000 each. For a while, Tabasaran was known to linguists as the language with the world's richest case system. Indeed, all languages of this family have extensive systems of cases, primarily due to the abundance of locatives expressing

An Armenian villager from Karabagh represents just one of the up to 50 different ethnic groups and nationalities dispersed across the Caucasus region. Language is inseparable from ethnic identity, and is aggressively maintained by peoples who may owe more loyalty to clan and family than nation or region.

Nakh-Daghestanian

Nakh

Daghestanian

Nakh	Daghestanian			
Chechen				
Ingush	Tsez	Avar	Lak	Lezgian
Tsova-Tush	Hunzib	Andi	Dargwa	Tabasaran
	Beshta	Chamali		Archi
				Tsakhur

spatial relations (in Tsez there are 42). Cases are formed agglutinatively, and each case form includes a special suffix denoting the position of the reference point ("on," "under," "near, " "behind"). This suffix can in turn be followed by another suffix expressing motion ("to," "towards," "from") in relation to the reference point. Overall, the Tsez system is capable of expressing the following concepts by means of locative case markers: "in a hollow object" (e.g., a room), "in a mass among," "on a horizontal surface," "under," "at, by, near," "to," "from," "towards (a distant point)," "away from (a distant point)," and "through."

In the Nakh-Daghestanian family, Avar, Chechen, Lezgian, Tabasaran, Lak, and Dargwa are written languages which currently use Cyrillic alphabets (some formerly used Arabic script). Another language of the family, Udi, is linked to Old Udi or Caucasian Albanian, a written language of the sixth–tenth centuries which is found on ceramic fragments and stone tablets; the deciphering of Caucasian Albanian documents is far from complete.

The origins of the Caucasian languages remain mysterious. The two northern families, Abkhaz-Adyghean and Nakh-Dagestanian, may be distantly related. The Dene-Caucasian

hypothesis links them in turn with the Na-Dene languages of North America and with Sino-Tibetan.

The Caucasian languages also seem the most plausible of the many proposed relatives for Basque.

THE FAR EAST

The languages of the Far East do not form a single family, but are subdivided into two separate families and several isolated languages including Ket (see above), Yukaghir (possibly Uralic), and Nivkh. The number of people speaking these languages is dwindling, and the study of them undertaken by Russian and Soviet scholars in the nineteenth and twentieth centuries became a salvage operation. Ket, spoken along the Siberian Yenisey river, is partly inflectional, resembling the languages of the Caucasus more than those of Siberia. Nivkh is spoken by some 2,000 people living along the river Amur and on Sakhalin island.

The Eskimo-Aleut language family includes Asiatic Eskimo and Aleutian and extends over two continents, Asia and America. Varieties of Eskimo (also known as Inuit, Yupik, or Inuktittut) are spoken as far away as Greenland. In the Far East, due to intense contact, a mixed language known as Copper Island Aleut developed with Aleutian vocabulary and Russian grammar but, this is

An engraving depicts Eskimos in an Arctic landscape. The Eskimo-Aleut language family is found over a vast area, stretching from Siberia to Greenland.

now practically extinct.

The Chukotko-Kamchatkan family includes Alutor, Itelmen, Kerek, Koryak, and Chukchi. All these languages have undergone significant influence from Russian and the numbers of their speakers have decreased. Chukchi is probably the most robust, with about 12,000 remaining.

Languages of both the Eskimo-Aleut and Chukotko-Kamchatkan families are characterized by ergativity (where the subject of a transitive sentence is marked differently from the subject of an intransitive sentence, which is marked in the same manner as the object in a transitive one), as well as by agglutination and complex verbal categories. An unusual feature found in some languages of both families is incorporation, a process whereby a word (usually a verb) forms a compound with its

TYPOLOGY OF LANGUAGES

According to their morphology (word structure), languages can be classified into four basic types: isolating, agglutinative, fusional (inflectional), and polysynthetic. The classification is based on three essential criteria:

(1) does a word divide into smaller meaningful parts (morphemes)? (2) if so, are the boundaries between these component parts clear?

(3) does each component express a single meaning?

• If the answer to the first question is negative, we are dealing with an ISOLATING language, where even grammatical concepts are expressed by separate words which do not divide into smaller units. Chinese and Vietnamese are both examples of this type; in Mandarin *ta bu hui yong dao chi fan* translates literally as "he no can use knife eat rice," ("He doesn't know how to eat with a knife.")

• In an agglutinating language, words divide into smaller units (morphemes) with clear boundaries between them, and each grammatical meaning is expressed by a separate morpheme; for example, in Japanese *tabe-sase-rare-ru* translates as "can cause someone to eat"; *tabe* means "eat", *sase* "cause", *rare* "can" and *ru* marks the present tense.

• In an inflectional language, the boundaries between morphemes are fuzzy, and morphemes can express more than one grammatical meaning, as in Latin *pluribus* where the ending *-ibus* indicates both plurality and either Dative or Ablative case (as in the federal motto *e pluribus unum* "out of many, one").

• In a polysynthetic language, several morphemes are put together to form complex words which can function as a whole sentence, as in Chukchi *tə-meyŋə-levtə-pəɣt- ərkən*, literally "1stperson-big-head-ache-ing" ("I have a fierce headache").

Little was known in Europe of the peoples or languages of the Far East until Marco Polo, a Venetian merchant, travelled overland to China (1271–75). His account of his Asian travels became famous throughout Europe although recent research suggests that he never actually went to China himself.

object and modifiers but retains its original function in the sentence. Incorporation results in the creation of long, internally complex words. For example, the English sentence "Let's play ball all through the night," consisting of seven words, is rendered as a single, long compound word in Chukchi: *mən-nəke-ure-qepl-uwičwen-mək* (literally, "let-us-night-long-ball-play-we").

Ainu is a virtually extinct language formerly spoken on the northernmost Japanese island of Hokkaido and Russia's Sakhalin peninsula, where a few speakers may remain. Although some Ainu culture persists on Hokkaido, its people now speak only Japanese. Ainu is more distinct from Japanese and from Korean than the latter two languages are from one another. Its origins pose a problem; it may be an outlying Altaic language, separated from Japanese and from Korean by as many as 10,000 years. The Ainu had a rich oral literature which allows us a glimpse into their past. The archaic language of Ainu epic poems shows that, like Chukchi, it allowed a noun to be incorporated into a verb, as in *ney ta cise-kar-as* (literally, "There we house-made," or "We made a house there.")

Incorporation is not exclusive to languages of the Far East; it is also common in languages of the Americas and of Australia. Since some of these can express what is normally a sentence by a single compound word (as in the Chukchi

example above), they have been characterized as "polysynthetic" (*see page 53*).

JAPANESE AND KOREAN

Japanese is one of the world's major languages, ranking ninth in numbers of speakers at around 120 million. In terms of both its language and its culture Japan is one of the world's more homogenous countries, dominated by a single national language, although regional dialects differ considerably in pronunciation and may even be mutually unintelligible. Ryukyuan, with some 900,000 speakers on Okinawa and the surrounding islands, is considered a separate language as it is not mutually intelligible with Japanese.

The origin of Japanese is among the most disputed questions of language history. On the one hand, much of Japanese grammar resembles that of Altaic languages such as Mongolian and Manchu. On the other hand, in its use of prefixes and its sound system with a limited set of consonants and a preference for open syllables, Japanese resembles Austronesian languages, which are thought to have originated in the area of Taiwan (*see Part Two, Chapter 4*); certain words also support the Austronesian connection. These two hypotheses can best be reconciled in terms of a mixture of Altaic and Austronesian elements.

Korean is spoken on the Korean peninsula, in the neighboring Chinese province of

A 19th(?)-century engraving of a Mongolian shaman. This vast region of central Asia is inhabited chiefly by peoples who speak Altaic languages of the Turkic and Mongolic families.

HONORIFICS

One of the most striking, and for foreigners most difficult, features of Japanese and Korean is their honorific system. All languages have ways of showing politeness, such as the *tu/vous* contrast in French and similar distinctions in most European languages. Japanese and Korean are unusual in the extent to which politeness is encoded in the grammar by the various forms of the verb. Politeness to the person to whom one is speaking is shown in Japanese by the suffix *masu*:

Taroo-ga	*sono*	*tegami-o*	*yomu*	"Taroo reads that letter"
Taroo-SUBJ	that	letter-OBJ	reads	(neutral)
Taroo-ga	*sono*	*tegami-o*	*yomi-masu*	"Taroo reads that letter"
Taroo-SUBJ	that	letter-OBJ	reads-POLITE	(polite to addressee)

The Japanese honorific system also allows the speaker to show respect for a person referred to in a sentence. Respect for the subject of the sentence is expressed by a more complex form of the verb with the prefix *o-*:

Sensei-ga	*sono*	*tegami-o*	***o**-yom-i*	***ni nat-ta***
teacher-SUBJ	that	letter-OBJ	HON-read-HON-PAST	

"The (honorable) teacher read that letter"

Similar honorific forms are used in Korean, where the ages of the speaker and addressee are especially important, in accordance with the Confucian principle of respect for one's elders.

The influence of western culture on Japan and South Korea is reflected in fashion and street culture, as well as in the language – it is becoming fashionable to use English loan words rather than existing vocabulary.

Heilongjiang and on the island of Cheju, which possesses a distinctive dialect. The post-war political division of North and South Korea, like the separation of East and West Germany, has led to differences in language policy: the North Korean government has conducted purification campaigns to eliminate Chinese words and the use of Chinese characters.

Japanese and Korean are remarkably similar in structure: they are both agglutinating languages with SOV word order, the verb being placed strictly at the end of the sentence. There are also complex honorific forms which indicate respect to those spoken or referred to. Although these similarities are striking, they owe much to shared cultural developments, and it is not clear that the two languages are genetically related.

Both Japanese and Korean have borrowed extensively from Chinese, and both languages were first written with Chinese characters: Japanese script remains a combination of Chinese characters (*Kanji*) with syllabic systems, while Korean is now written largely in *Han'gul*, a unique form of phonetic script devised by King Sejong in the fifteenth century. In recent years Japanese has absorbed some English vocabulary, known as *gairaigo* ("foreign-coming language"): for example, *jīnzu* ("jeans"), *fitto suru* ("fit"), *furesshu na* ("fresh"), *repooto suru* ("report"). Since corresponding Japanese words exist in most cases, these loan words reflect fashion as much as need. They are distinguished by being written in the angular *katakana* script, rather than in the cursive *hiragana* syllabary used for native Japanese forms.

Part *2*/2

South and Southeast Asia

In South and Southeast Asia multilingualism is a way of life, and as a result there has occurred much remarkable linguistic convergence. The Indo-European family extends into South Asia where it meets the Dravidian and Austro-Asiatic languages. In Southeast Asia several language families have mingled in the shadow of China. The various forms of Chinese, one of the region's many tone languages, have more native speakers than any other language in the world; it is perhaps also the language most widely misunderstood.

Tibetans from China's least populated region. The Tibetan language, with about 4 million speakers, has a literary tradition dating back to AD 600.

The languages of South and Southeast Asia reflect the region's cultural antiquity and heavy population density. Although there are numerous language families, they are less diverse than might be expected, often sharing features resulting from contact between speakers over the course of several generations.

The South Asian languages have SOV word order, with retroflex consonants, sounds which are produced by turning up or curling back the tip of the tongue under the hard palate. The Southeast Asian languages belong to the isolating type, where grammatical

The Indian subcontinent is separated from the rest of Asia by the Himalayan mountain range. In the Himalayan region the Indo-Iranian and Tibeto-Burman language families meet, while Burushaski is the sole survivor of an earlier family.

concepts are expressed by separate words which do not divide into smaller units. These languages have few inflections, many noun classifiers, and use tone to distinguish words. Regional features tend to obscure the genetic relationships between the languages, which sometimes remain unclear.

INDIC AND DRAVIDIAN LANGUAGES

South Asia is dominated by two language families, Indo-Iranian and Dravidian, with much smaller groups speaking Munda and Tibeto-Burman. The Indo-Iranian branch of the Indo-European family extends through much of India, Pakistan, and Bangladesh as well as most of Sri Lanka and the Himalayan kingdom of Nepal.

In India and Pakistan, the Indic languages have come into contact with the Dravidian languages, from which they have acquired features such as retroflex consonants and strict verb-final word order. The Dravidian languages in turn have borrowed Indic vocabulary. Tamil has many loan words from Sanskrit, such as *pādam* "foot" (related to *pedal* from Latin). Some Tamils have tried to purge their language of these "foreign" words.

The main Indic languages spoken in India are Hindi, Urdu, Punjabi, Sindhi, Bengali, Gujarati, Marathi, Bihari, and Assamese. Hindi

Indo-European
- **Indo-Iranian**
  - **Iranian**
    - Farsi
    - Pashto
    - Baluchi
    - Kurdish
    - Ossetic
    - Tajik...
  - **Indic**
    - Hindi/Urdu
    - Punjabi
    - Sindhi
    - Gujarati
    - Marathi
    - Bihari
    - Bengali
    - Sinhalese
    - Nepali ...

Dravidian
- Brahui
- Telugu
  - Malayalam
  - Kannada
  - Tamil
  - Gondi ...

This family tree shows the two main language families of south Asia. Refer to the tree on page 40 to see how they connect with other Indo-European families.

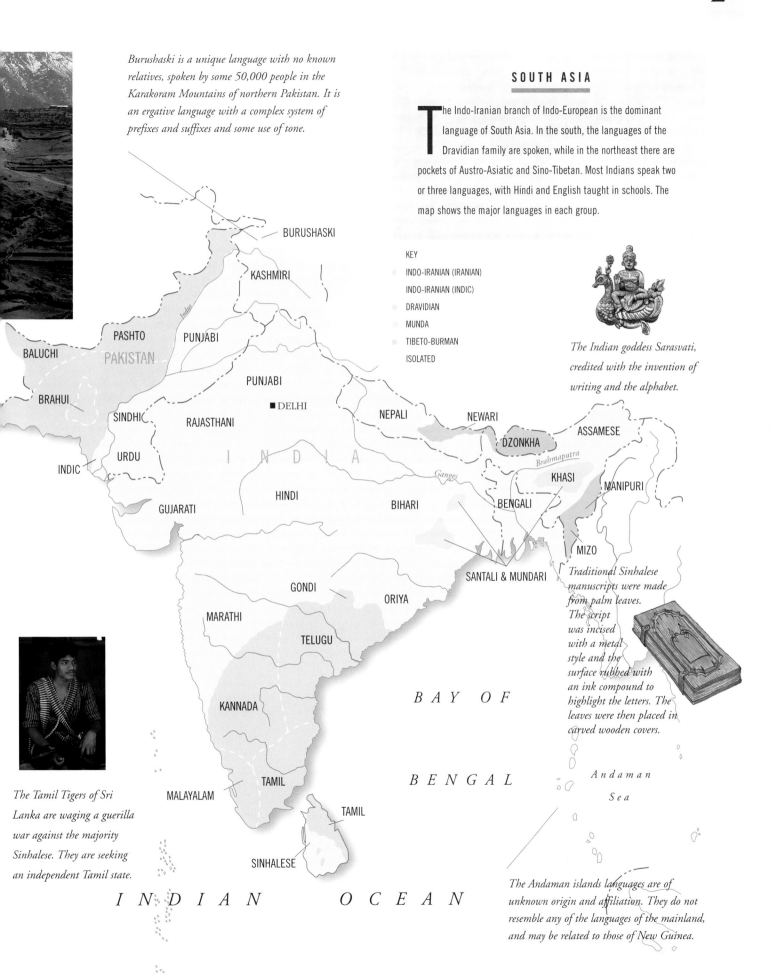

Burushaski is a unique language with no known relatives, spoken by some 50,000 people in the Karakoram Mountains of northern Pakistan. It is an ergative language with a complex system of prefixes and suffixes and some use of tone.

SOUTH ASIA

The Indo-Iranian branch of Indo-European is the dominant language of South Asia. In the south, the languages of the Dravidian family are spoken, while in the northeast there are pockets of Austro-Asiatic and Sino-Tibetan. Most Indians speak two or three languages, with Hindi and English taught in schools. The map shows the major languages in each group.

KEY
INDO-IRANIAN (IRANIAN)
INDO-IRANIAN (INDIC)
DRAVIDIAN
MUNDA
TIBETO-BURMAN
ISOLATED

The Indian goddess Sarasvati, credited with the invention of writing and the alphabet.

BURUSHASKI

KASHMIRI

PASHTO
PUNJABI
BALUCHI
PAKISTAN
PUNJABI
BRAHUI
DELHI
NEPALI
NEWARI
ASSAMESE
SINDHI
RAJASTHANI
DZONKHA
URDU
I N D I A
Brahmaputra
INDIC
Ganges
KHASI
MANIPURI
GUJARATI
HINDI
BIHARI
BENGALI
MIZO
SANTALI & MUNDARI

Traditional Sinhalese manuscripts were made from palm leaves. The script was incised with a metal style and the surface rubbed with an ink compound to highlight the letters. The leaves were then placed in carved wooden covers.

GONDI
ORIYA
MARATHI
TELUGU

B A Y O F

KANNADA

B E N G A L

Andaman Sea

TAMIL
MALAYALAM
TAMIL

The Tamil Tigers of Sri Lanka are waging a guerilla war against the majority Sinhalese. They are seeking an independent Tamil state.

SINHALESE

I N D I A N   O C E A N

The Andaman islands languages are of unknown origin and affiliation. They do not resemble any of the languages of the mainland, and may be related to those of New Guinea.

SANSKRIT

Sanskrit underlies the languages of South Asia as Latin does those of western Europe. It represents, albeit in a somewhat artificial literary form, the ancestor of the Indic languages, and its vocabulary has spread widely throughout languages as far east as Thailand and Laos, just as Latin vocabulary has infiltrated English and other European languages. Its cultural significance, again like that of Latin, derives from religious use: the name Sanskrit means "purified". Sir William "Oriental" Jones, who identified the Indo-European language family, described it memorably: "a wonderful structure; more perfect than the Greek, more copious than the Latin, and more exquisitely refined than either." For example, where Latin had six cases, Sanskrit had eight:

Nominative	*devas*	"God"	Dative	*devāya*	"to God"
Vocative	*deva*	"O God"	Ablative	*devāt*	"from God"
Accusative	*devam*	"God"	Genitive	*devasya*	"of God"
Instrumental	*devena*	"by God"	Locative	*deve*	"with God"

Sanskrit is typically written in the Devanāgarī script ("script of the city of the gods") containing the root *deva-*, as in "divine"). Dating from as early as 1500 BC, the Sanskrit texts represent crucial evidence in the reconstruction of Indo-European. Among the famous works of Sanskrit literature are the Vedas, the epic *Ramayana* and Panini's writings on grammar, in which many concepts of modern linguistics are pre-figured.

क्लिद् to become wet	क्लिद्यति क्लिद्यते	चिक्लेद	क्लेदिष्यति / क्लेत्स्यति	क्लेदयति
क्लिश् to be afflicted	क्लिश्यति क्लिश्यते	चिक्लिशे	क्लेशिष्यते	क्लेशयति
क्षम् to bear	क्षाम्यति क्षम्यते	चक्षाम	क्षमिष्यति / क्षंस्यति	क्षमयति
क्षुध् to be hungry	क्षुध्यति क्षुध्यते	चुक्षोध	क्षोत्स्यति	क्षोधयति
क्षुभ् to tremble	क्षुभ्यति क्षुभ्यते	चुक्षोभ	क्षोभिष्यति	क्षोभयति

An extract taken from a Sanskrit manual for high schools, showing conjugations of various verbs. Although only now used for religious purposes, Sanskrit is one of the official languages of India.

and Urdu, the official languages of India and Pakistan, are essentially dialects of a single language and share a common form, Hindustani, promoted by Gandhi as a unifying force. Some Indians resisted the imposition of Hindi/Hindustani, however, and English has been retained as a *lingua franca*. Faced with some 200 indigenous languages, India follows a three-language policy, whereby children learn Hindi and English as well as a local language at school.

Although Urdu is the official language of Pakistan, larger numbers of Pakistanis speak other Indic languages such as Punjabi and Sindhi or the Iranian languages Baluchi and Pashto. Burushashki, isolated in the Karakoram mountains of northwest Pakistan,

is unrelated to any other known language. In the Himalayan kingdom of Nepal, the main languages are Nepali, of the Indic family, and Newari, of the Tibeto-Burman, while in nearby Bhutan, Dzongkha, a form of Tibetan, is the *lingua franca*. In Bangladesh, Bengali, one of the major Indic languages, predominates.

The Dravidian languages are concentrated in southern and eastern India, though the isolated Dravidian language, Brahui, which is found in Pakistan, suggests that they were spoken throughout the region before the Indo-European expansion. They are agglutinating languages with numerous consonants and as many as eight case forms. The major Dravidian languages are Kannada, Malayalam, Tamil and Telugu; each has its own established literary

Head of a golden Buddha statue from Thailand. Buddhism was founded nearly 2,500 years ago in northeast India by Siddharta Gautama (563–483 BC). The doctrine then spread throughout South and Southeast Asia, bringing many Sanskrit loan words to the languages of Thailand and Cambodia.

tradition and each is the official language of an Indian state. In Sri Lanka the Indic language Sinhalese coexists uneasily with the Dravidian Tamil.

The Munda languages are found in the highland regions of northeastern India. They are distantly related to Southeast Asian Vietnamese and Khmer, but have been influenced by the surrounding Indic languages. The main examples are Santali and Mundari.

SOUTHEAST ASIA

Mainland Southeast Asia constitutes a distinct linguistic area: most languages have SVO word order and belong to the isolating type, where most words consist of a single syllable. Many of these languages are also known for their use of tone as a distinctive feature, whereby the pitch at which a syllable is pronounced indicates its meaning: in Mandarin *zhū* with a high tone means "pig," *zhǔ* with a fall-rise means "lord." Typical tone patterns are pitch levels (high, low, or mid-) and contours (falling or rising, fall-rise or rise-fall). Tones can also involve voice quality, as in Burmese which has a "creaky sound", and Hmong with its "breathiness."

Chinese and Indian cultures, with their Confucian and Buddhist belief systems, dominate the languages of Southeast Asia. Chinese loan words are found in most languages of the region, and Sanskrit ones in

A Tamil tea-picker from Sri Lanka. A Dravidian language, Tamil is spoken in both Sri Lanka and in the southeast Indian state of Tamil Nadu.

Thai and Khmer. Chinese writing is, or has been, used to write non-Chinese languages such as Vietnamese, Japanese, and Korean, while scripts of Indic origin are used for Thai and Tibetan.

MON-KHMER

Together with the Munda languages of northeastern India, the Mon-Khmer languages form the Austroasiatic family. Their scattered distribution suggests that they were once spoken over a wide area of mainland Southeast Asia, but were split by the movement of Tai speakers southward. Tai is the name of a language family to which Thai belongs.

Vietnamese and Khmer, the latter spoken in Cambodia, are the best-known languages in this group. Mon, the language of an ancient civilization of Thailand, is now spoken in

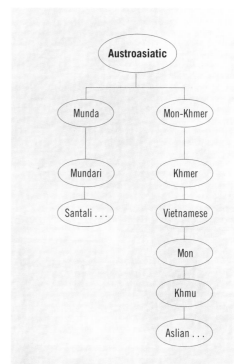

Family tree of the Austroasiatic family. The individual languages are distributed over a wide area of the Southeast Asia mainland.

Dong woman in traditional costume.

MAINLAND SOUTHEAST ASIA

The mainland Southeast Asian languages belong to four families: Tibeto-Burman, Tai-Kadai, Mon-Khmer, and Hmong-Mien. Though numerous, the languages are of a similar type due to long proximity and nearly all use tone. In Laos, languages of all four families are spoken, typically at different elevations: the Hmong, for example, live in mountain areas.

CHINA

MIAO

CHINESE
(YUE)

ZHUANG

YAO

MIAO

YAO

Red

Black

HANOI

MIN

LAI

WA

SHAN

LOLO

KHMU

HMONG

LI

MINNAN

YAO

BURMA

BURMESE

KAREN

Irrawaddy

LAO

VIENTIANE

South
China
Sea

Ping

Yom

THAILAND

LAOS

THAI

Mekong

RANGOON

MON

KAREN

VIETNAM

Indian Ocean

BANGKOK

KHMER

CAMBODIA

Mekong

PHNOM PENH

VIETNAMESE

Gulf of Thailand

PAK TAY

KEY

- TIBETO-BURMAN
- SINITIC
- HMONG-MIEN
- TAI-KADAI
- MON-KHMER

A traditional Hmong house.

A Zhuang mother and child from the city of Nanning in Kwangsi Chuang Autonomous region, southern China. The Zhuang language has its own romanized script; in 1982 there were 13 million Zhuang-speakers.

southern Myanmar (Burma), northeast Thailand, and along the border between China and Vietnam. The Aslian languages are spoken in inland peninsular Malaysia.

Although similar in type to Chinese and the surrounding Tai-Kadai languages, the use of tone is not typical of Mon-Khmer: the tones of Vietnamese seem to have developed relatively recently, under the influence of Chinese and/or Tai languages. Many Mon-Khmer languages have a distinction of register, some vowels being pronounced with a low "creaky" voice, rather than of tone.

TAI-KADAI

This family includes two standard languages, Thai and Lao, which are spoken in Thailand and Laos respectively. The Tai languages are thought to have originated in southwest China, and are still spoken by many of the minority peoples of this area; Zhuang, with its own romanized script, has the most speakers (around 13 million in 1982: the Zhuang

people also have an Autonomous Region in the province of Guangxi). The Kam-Sui languages of China's Hunan and Guizhou provinces differ more radically than Zhuang from Thai and Lao. The Li and Be languages are indigenous to Hainan island, although Hainan has since been settled by both Yao and Chinese speakers. Shan, a minority language of eastern Myanmar, is also of the Tai family.

The Tai-Kadai languages were once believed to belong to the Sino-Tibetan family because they share some vocabulary and similar sound systems with southern Chinese dialects such as Cantonese. These similarities are now seen as the result of borrowing and language shift, whereby speakers of the Tai-Kadai languages came to adopt Chinese, bringing to it features of their original languages. The Tai-Kadai group are all tone languages: standard Thai has five tones, Lao six, while Kam-Sui languages have as many as 15 tones. They are SVO languages but unlike Chinese, modifiers come after the noun, as in *phaasăa thay* "the Thai language" (the word *phaasă*a is a loan from Sanskrit). Thai writing, which is based on the Indic script used for Sanskrit, includes special markers for tones.

HMONG-MIEN (MIAO, YAO)

These are languages of minority groups in China and Thailand who have suffered a

Tai-Kadai family tree. These languages share some vocabulary and similar sound systems with southern Chinese dialects. However, this is not because they are related, but due to borrowing and language shifts.

THE AUSTRIC HYPOTHESIS

This hypothesis links the main language families of Southeast Asia, with the exception of the Sino-Tibetan family.

The inclusion of the Austroasiatic family is debated among proponents of the hypothesis; the main difficulty is finding a distinction between the effects of contact and genetic relationships. Some evidence comes from similar INFIXES and from roots where Austronesian has two syllables, of which Mon-Khmer preserves the first and Tai-Kadai the second:

Proto-Austronesian	Proto-Mon-Khmer	Proto-Kam-Thai
*mata "eye"	*măt "eye"	*taa "eye"

history of oppression. Their remaining speakers now number about 5 million, mainly dispersed in mountainous areas of southern China. The largest group, the Miao, are found mostly in the southwestern provinces Guizhou and Guangxi, and in adjacent areas of Vietnam, Laos, and Thailand. The Yao live in Guangxi and Hunan and in parts of Laos and Thailand, with a small population also on the island of Hainan.

The She people, in small communities near the coast of Fujian and Guangdong, have mostly shifted to Chinese: only a few She communities in southeast Guangdong preserve their language, while using the surrounding Hakka dialect of Chinese to communicate with outsiders. This gradual "Sinicization" of the minority groups in southern China has been happening for centuries.

The Hmong-Mien languages are tonal and use SVO order, with Miao being especially close to the Tai-Kadai languages in structure, suggesting either extensive contact or a distant genetic relationship, as assumed in the Austric hypothesis. Hmong is a language of the Miao group spoken in Thailand and Cambodia. It has several writing systems including a unique semi-syllabic script, said to have been revealed to its originator in a divine vision. In recent years Hmong speakers, refugees from the wars in Vietnam and Laos, have settled in the U.S.A, Australia, and France. The two main varieties, "Green" and "White" Hmong, are named after the colours of traditional women's dress.

SINO-TIBETAN

This family is spoken across China and in much of Southeast Asia. There are over a billion speakers – more than any family other than Indo-European. In addition to the many

CLASSIFIERS

In Thai, as in Chinese and most Southeast Asian languages, each noun is assigned a classifier which denotes a class of items or a distinctive feature of the item the noun refers to, for example:

khon	"person"	(people, except royal and sacred ones)
tua	"body"	(animals, except sacred ones such as elephants)
lêm	"point"	(sharp and pointed objects, for example needle or sword)
khan	"objects with handles"	(for example fishing rod or plough)

The classifiers are used, not unlike articles in European languages, when a noun is counted or otherwise modified:

lûuk săam **khon**	child three "person"	"three children"
nók **tua** yày	bird "body" big	"the big bird"

THE LANGUAGES OF CHINA

Chinese has spread across China at the expense of the Altaic languages of the remote north and northwest, and the Tai and Miao-Yao languages, which are spoken by ethnic minorities in the moutainous southwest of China. The number of speakers of these minority languages is steadily declining, as the peripheral areas of China become absorbed into mainstream Chinese culture. Nevertheless, the minority languages have left their imprint on local varieties of Chinese, which are as different from each other as individual Romance or Germanic languages in Europe.

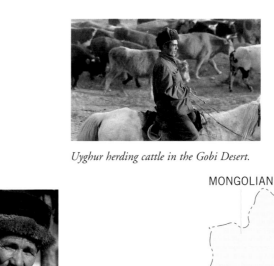

Uyghur herding cattle in the Gobi Desert.

Muslims are a minority group in China.

MONGOLIAN

KAZAKH

UYGHUR

TURK

TAJIK

TIB

KEY

MON-KHMER

TIBETO-BURMAN

ALTAIC

INDO-IRANIAN

TAI-KADAI

MIAO-YAO

CHINESE

*Indian
Ocean*

K'uei-hsing, god of examinations, is shown standing on the head of a turtle in this c. seventeenth-century Chinese figurine. He wields a brush which he will use for recording the list of successful entrants.

The Uighurs of Northwest China are an Islamic people, speaking a Turkic language. Their main city, Kashgar, was an important trading post on the Silk Road.

A selection of the brushes, paints, dyes, and wax seals which form part of the equipment of a skilled Chinese calligrapher.

She tribeswoman having her hair dressed.

Chinese New Year is traditionally celebrated with dragons – a symbol of good luck.

varieties of Chinese, Tibetan, and Burmese, the family includes a number of lesser-known minority languages, spoken mostly in southwest China and Tibet. The main branches of Sino-Tibetan are shown below.

The Bai language, with over a million speakers in Yunnan province, is thought to be a distant relative of Chinese; although similar to the neighboring Yi languages in many respects, its word order is SVO, like Chinese, rather than SOV like most of the Tibeto-Burman branch.

Due to the cultural unity of the Chinese people and its standard written form, "Chinese" is often regarded as a single language, both inside and outside China. However, it encompasses an enormous range of dialects, which divide into eight main groups,

each as different from the others as the languages within each branch of Indo-European. Cantonese, for example, differs from Mandarin as much as Italian differs from French or Swedish from German. Dialects from different groups are mutually unintelligible: even within a dialect group, such as Wu or Yue, speakers of one rural dialect may fail to understand speakers of another, though Shanghainese and Cantonese are widely understood within these cities' spheres of influence. The Min dialects of the southeast coast are especially diverse, with some features reflecting the influence of Tai, Miao-Yao, and the Austro-Asiatic languages that were spoken in southern China formerly.

Mandarin Chinese is the official language of the People's Republic of China, where it is

SINO-TIBETAN FAMILY

The languages in this family are spoken in China and Southeast Asia. This tree shows the main branches of the family. Chinese divides into eight main dialect groups. Mandarin is the official language of the People's Republic of China, Xiang is spoken in Hunan province, Gan in Jiangxi province, Hakka is spread over the south and southeast, Wu is spoken in Zhejiang province and includes Shanghainese, Northern Min includes Fuzhou, Southern Min includes Xiamen, Taiwanese and Chiu Chow, Yue (Cantonese) is spoken in Guangdong and Guangxi provinces.

A public health announcement is written on a blackboard; of the 50,000–80,000 characters used at one time or another in Chinese writing, 8,000 are still in use, and a knowledge of 1,000 characters is needed for a basic reading knowledge of the language.

termed *Putonghua* meaning "common speech," and of Taiwan, where it is called *Guoyu* ("national language"). Mandarin Chinese has more native speakers than any other language – approaching one billion – and it is widely understood as a second language in most of Chinese territory. Written Chinese, based on Mandarin, is often used by speakers of different dialects and even languages, but while this can overcome some problems – as when Chinese-speakers "draw" characters in the air to confirm their names – Chinese writing is far from universal. The traditional characters, still used in Hong Kong, Macao, and Taiwan, have been simplified in the People's Republic, sometimes beyond recognition. Many dialects use additional characters of their own: writing in Hong Kong, for example, employs some 200 non-standard characters to represent Cantonese words. As a result of these differences, mainland Mandarin-speakers may have difficulty reading a Hong Kong newspaper and vice versa. Variations in grammar, vocabulary and usage between

LANGUAGES OF TAIWAN

The indigenous languages of Taiwan are Austronesian; about seven are still spoken by minority groups in the central mountains and on the east coast. In the seventeenth century the island was settled by Chinese who spoke a southern Min dialect of the Xiamen area. The Japanese occupation from 1895–1946 imposed Japanese. The Kuomintang regime, forced from mainland China onto Taiwan by the Communists in 1950, imposed Mandarin as the national language (*Guoyu*) at the expense of the Min dialect (*Taiyu*). With the relaxation of the political climate the local dialect has regained some of its status and Taiyu can now be heard beside Mandarin on the radio, in film, and in popular songs.

A Taiwanese street scene in Kaohsiung city. A history of invasion has imposed three major languages on the Taiwanese: Japanese, the Min dialect of Chinese and Mandarin.

South and Southeast Asia

HAINAN

The large tropical island of Hainan, a province of China in the South China Sea, is home to languages from four different families: the indigenous Li and Be languages, belonging to the Tai-Kadai family; Yao, a Hmong-Mien language whose speakers were supposedly brought to Hainan to subdue the Li; Chamic languages belonging to the Austronesian family; and Chinese. The local southern Min and Yue dialects are gradually giving way to Mandarin as the island develops.

China

Hainan

dialects also impede comprehension.

Cantonese, the dialect of the southern port city of Canton (Guangzhou), is spoken in most of Guangdong and Guangxi provinces, in Hong Kong, Macao, and in the Chinese communities of North America and around the world. The majority of Chinese living in Southeast Asia (Thailand, Vietnam, Malaysia, Singapore, and the Philippines) speak southern dialects such as Cantonese, Hakka and Chiu Chow.

THE STRUCTURE OF CHINESE

Chinese is one of the clearest examples of an isolating type of language. One feature of this type is that instead of endings indicating grammatical categories, the grammatical concepts are expressed by independent words, called particles. Thus the possessive relation is expressed by the particle *de* as in *wǒ de fángzi* ("my house"); the pronoun *wǒ* has the same form, whether it means "I," "me," or "my." The verb has no tense forms, but aspect is indicated by particles such as the progressive *zài* for example *tā zài chī fàn* "She's eating" (literally, "she at eat rice").

Tone, the use of pitch to distinguish words, is a feature of almost all forms of Chinese. The four tones of Mandarin Chinese, for example, give four completely different meanings to the same syllable:

High level Rising Dipping Falling
fān "sail" *fán* "trouble" *fǎn* "turn" *fàn* "rice"

A Buddhist monastery in the Tibetan city of Lhasa. Tibet was invaded by Communist Chinese in 1950 and traditional religious institutions were banned under Chinese rule. There are about 4 million Tibetan-speakers; the language is written in scripts of Indic origin.

HONG KONG

Cantonese is the dominant language of Hong Kong, with minorities also speaking other Chinese dialects such as Chiu Chow, Hakka, and Shanghainese. Mandarin is increasingly used, symbolizing the reunification with China, while English is the language of education and international trade. Bilinguals mix elements of Chinese and English by, for example, inserting English verbs with the Cantonese suffixes indicating aspect attached to them:

*Léih **present**-gán mātyéh a?*

"What are you presenting?"

*Léih bōng ngóh **keep**-jyuh nī dī lā*

"Will you keep these for me (for a moment)?"

This represents a relatively simple system: in some varieties of Chinese there are as many as eight tones, which may change according to where the word comes in a sentence.

TIBETO-BURMAN

The Tibeto-Burman branch of Sino-Tibetan is separated from the Sinitic (Chinese) branch by around 6,000 years. Comprising eight or nine families and 250–300 languages, it is comparable to Indo-European in size and time depth, but the languages are much less well known. They are spoken primarily in China, where 16 are recognized minority languages, in Myanmar, Nepal, Bhutan, and in northeastern India. Many of them are tone languages, like Chinese, but with SOV word order and sometimes with an ergative case system.

Tibetan and Burmese are the major languages, with around 4 million and 22 million speakers respectively.

Both are written in scripts of Indic origin and possess long literary traditions, going back to around AD 600 for Tibetan and AD 1100 for Burmese. Most other Tibeto-Burman languages have far fewer speakers, the most important being Newari in Nepal, Dzhongkha in Bhutan, and Manipuri in India.

Tibeto-Burman minority languages include the Yi (Loloish) group, with some 5 million speakers in the highlands of southwestern China, and across the borders into Burma and Thailand; of these, Lisu and Lahu have been extensively studied.

The Karen group, spoken by minority peoples in eastern Burma and adjacent areas of Thailand, have SVO word order, unlike most Tibeto-Burman languages, and were probably influenced by neighboring Tai languages.

SINGAPORE

Singapore is a melting pot of cultures, with four official languages: Malay (Austronesian), Tamil (Dravidian), English, and Mandarin. The majority Chinese population speaks a variety of Chinese dialects including Hokkien, Chiu Chow, Hainanese, Cantonese, and Hakka. The government has promoted Mandarin as a means to unify the Chinese population, while English is used between the ethnic groups, in education and business. Singapore English is often mixed with Malay and Chinese elements, such as particles ending the sentence:

A: " One boy, one girl ... going to have some more?"

B: "No! I willing to stop **lah**! Family planning **lah**! No poin[t] more kids **lah**, because we thin[k] of working **ah**, so we have not time with the kids **lah**."

Africa and the
Middle East

The origin of language may lie in sub-Saharan Africa with the emergence of modern humans. The present Bantu languages of the region include those of the Zulus and the Shona and *lingua francas* such as Swahili, while the Khoisan languages of the Bushmen, renowned for their "click" sounds, have long been in decline. The Semitic languages of North Africa are of a unique structure, notably reflected in the Arabic writing systems.

A Nigerian woman in the capital, Lagos. The main ethnic groups in Nigeria are the Hausa, Fulani, Yoruba and Ibo, who together make up 65% of the population.

Recent research suggests that the people of the world can be divided in terms of their genetic make-up into just two groups: broadly, native peoples of central and southern Africa, and everyone else.

Moreover, linguistic research has shown that the languages spoken by the African peoples belong to three families, none of which has any known relationship to any other language family in the world.

North Africans, however, belong genetically with Europeans and some Asian populations. The languages of these peoples may belong to a single superfamily such as Nostratic (see below).

Many scholars also now believe that mankind originated in Africa, and that all living humans must trace their descent from an original African population.

LANGUAGE FAMILIES PAST AND PRESENT

Africa is split by two great physical features, the Sahara desert and the mountains of Ethiopia. Crossing these has always been enormously difficult. North of this divide there are written records going back thousands of years; to the south written records go back only a few hundred years, and few of these are in the native languages of the region, but rather in the languages of foreign traders and invaders. For knowledge of earlier times we

GENETIC GROUPS AND LANGUAGES

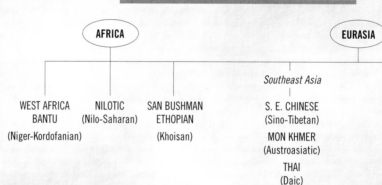

AFRICA

| WEST AFRICA BANTU | NILOTIC | SAN BUSHMAN ETHOPIAN |
| (Niger-Kordofanian) | (Nilo-Saharan) | (Khoisan) |

EURASIA

Southeast Asia

S. E. CHINESE (Sino-Tibetan)
MON KHMER (Austroasiatic)
THAI (Daic)
INDONESIAN MALAYSIAN PHILIPPINE POLYNESIAN MICRONESIAN (Austronesian)
MELANESIAN NEW GUINEAN (Indo-Pacific)
ABORIGINAL (Aboriginal)

North Eurasia

ETHIOPIAN BERBER, N. AFRICAN S. W. ASIAN (Afro-Asiatic)
IRANIAN EUROPEAN SARDINIAN INDIAN (Indo-European)
S. E. INDIAN (Dravidian)
LAPP SAMOYED (Uralic)
MONGOL TIBETAN (Sino-Tibetan)
KOREAN JAPANESE SIBERIAN (Altaic)
ESKIMO (Eskimo-Aleut)
CHUKCHI (Chukchi-Kamchatkan)
S. AMERIND C. AMERIND N. AMERIND (Amerind)
N. W. AMERIND (Na-Dene)

RELATIONSHIPS

Recent research has suggested that the genetic classification of human populations broadly matches the family relationships which can be reconstructed among languages. Although many aspects of the classification are controversial, and many cases exist where populations have mixed or switched language groups, the two classifications concur on the primary split between sub-Saharan Africa and the rest of the world.

AFRICAN PEOPLES C.8,000 BC

Studies of African prehistory have identified five populations, assumed to correspond to four surviving language families: North Africans correspond to Afro-Asiatic, West Africans to the Niger-Congo family, Nilotic peoples to Nilo-Saharan and Bushmen to Khoisan. Although there are still pygmy peoples, their original languages are extinct and they now speak Bantu languages brought by West Africans as they moved south and east.

must rely on archeology, oral traditions, and the hypothetical reconstructions of linguists based on the living languages of the present.

One study of African history has proposed a grouping of African peoples about 10,000 years ago (*see map below*).

Contrast this with the map showing the present day distribution of African language families (*see page 77*). Each language family can be correlated with one of the population groups shown below: Afro-Asiatic with North Africans, Niger-Congo with West Africans, Khoisan with Bushmen and Nilo- Saharan with Nilotics.

Undoubtedly the greatest change in the map on page 77 results from the eastward and

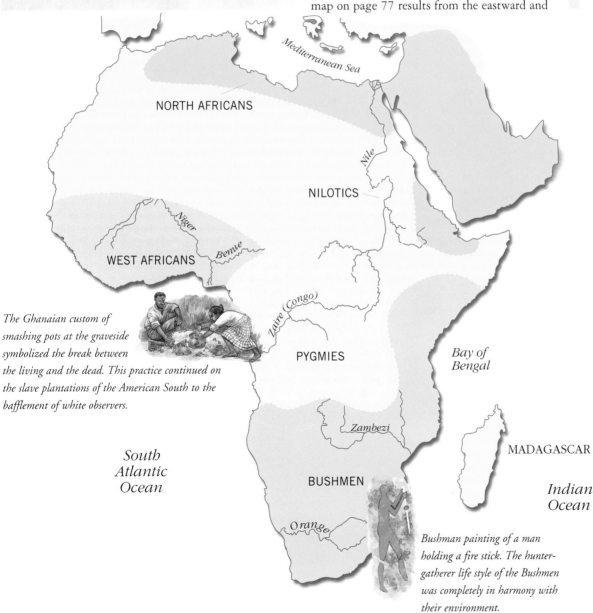

The Ghanaian custom of smashing pots at the graveside symbolized the break between the living and the dead. This practice continued on the slave plantations of the American South to the bafflement of white observers.

Bushman painting of a man holding a fire stick. The hunter-gatherer life style of the Bushmen was completely in harmony with their environment.

southward expansion of the West African peoples. The pygmies were surrounded and few now remain as identifiable populations. The Bushmen were pushed to the south and then engulfed by European settlement and by the resulting conflicts between Europeans and the descendants of the original West African migrants.

Though there are still pygmy peoples, there are no known pygmy languages. As for the Bushmen, few remain, and even fewer speak their ancestral languages.

CLICK SOUNDS

Click sounds are a characteristic of the Khoisan languages, some of which have up to 80 different types. Clicks are used in many languages, for example as interjections or indicators of disapproval, but what makes them remarkable in Khoisan is their use as ordinary sounds, equivalent in function to other consonants as constituents of words.

Clicks are best known to the world through the Bantu languages of South Africa, which are thought to have borrowed them from Khoisan-speakers, probably through intermarriage. Some readers may have heard the click song of the South African singer Miriam Makheba, in which the clicks sound like an accompaniment to the words of the song but in fact are intrinsic to the lyrics.

Zulu and Ndebele each have three basic click sounds: the dental (like the English "tsk, tsk"), the lateral (made from one side of the mouth, often used in English to call a large animal like a horse), and the palatal (a cork-popping sound made by placing the tongue against the roof of the mouth and sucking). These are written 'c', 'x', and 'q' respectively. In the following examples the letters standing for clicks are capitalized.

iCala	fault
iXaXa	frog
iQanda	egg

More complicated clicks can be made by combining 'c', 'x', or 'q' with one of two different nasal sounds, or with an almost simultaneous 'k' or 'g'. The result is a total of 15 different click sounds.

In the Khoisan languages themselves there are other basic clicks – such as the bilabial click, which is a kissing sound – and further possibilities for combining with other sounds.

In 1959 Miriam Makheba's Xhosa click song was a U.S. hit. An exiled figurehead of the anti-apartheid movement, she returned to South Africa in 1991.

Today the languages of the former European colonial powers are widely used in African countries. Some native languages, such as Swahili in East Africa and Fulani in West Africa, are also used as *lingua francas*.

NILO-SAHARAN

This family still remains close to the position it occupied 10,000 years ago. It comprises 100 or so languages in three branches: Songhai, a single language, and two language groups Saharan and Chari-Nile. As can be seen on the map on page 77, Songhai is isolated from the other branches.

Few languages in this family have even a million speakers; the languages are often very different from one another and many have been little studied.

KHOISAN

Most languages of this family are completely or nearly extinct. Only Damara in Namibia has a significant number of speakers (163,000, about 10 percent of the population). In 1990 it was standardized as a national language and renamed Khoekhoe.

AFRO-ASIATIC

The most important of the Afro-Asiatic languages is Arabic, spoken in one form or another by more than two hundred million people. Arabic and Hebrew are great cultural languages, and the languages of two of the

BERBER

SEMITIC

Mediterranean Sea

BERBER

BERBER

SEMITIC

SEMITIC

Nile

SAHARAN

SONGHAI

CUSHITIC

ATLANTIC

CHADIC

MANDE

GUR

Niger

KHORDOFANIAN

Benue

KWA

CUSHITIC

ADAMAWAN

CHARI-NILE

Zaire (Congo)

BENUE-CONGO

Bay of
Bengal

MADAGASCAR

South
Atlantic
Ocean

Zambezi

Orange

Indian
Ocean

*Most Moroccan potters
are illiterate so they are wary
of copying Koranic texts.
Instead they simulate
Koranic calligraphy.*

*The Ekoi tribe of Nigeria
used the same patterns for
traditional hair styles as
they did for their pottery.*

*The traditional color of Zulu pots is black. A decorated
grass lid keeps the contents cool and free of insects.*

CURRENT DISTRIBUTION OF AFRICAN LANGUAGE FAMILIES

The current African language map shows the
expansion of the Benue-Congo-speaking peoples from
West Africa, at the expense of the Khoisan languages
of the Bushmen and the now extinct languages of the
pygmies. Nilo-Saharan languages are spoken in more
inaccessible areas of Central Africa, often surrounded by
Afro-Asiatic or Niger-Congo languages, while Khordofanian
is an eclave of some 30 languages, related to the Niger-
Congo family, spoken in the Sudan.

KEY

NILO-SAHARAN

KHOISAN

NIGER-CONGO

AFRO-ASIATIC

great religions of the world. Hebrew, which for many centuries had no home but survived as the religious language of the Jewish diaspora, has found new life in Israel, where it has become the country's national language.

Consonants and Vowels in Arabic

The distinctive sounds of the Arabic language are the pharyngeals proper, pronounced at the back of the throat, and a whole range of sounds spoken with pharyngealisation.

The Afro-Asiatic languages are well known for the extent to which vowel changes are used in the formation of words. Vowel changes are used in English too, but only to a limited extent: for example the plural of "foot" is not "foots" but "feet."

A verb in Arabic generally has three sets of forms: present, past, and present participle; many verbs also have past participle forms. This is not unlike English where the verb "kick" has the present forms "kick," and "kicks," the past form "kicked," the present participle "kicking," and the past participle "kicked." Here are four examples, one from each set for the Arabic verb meaning "to write:"

1. *ti-ktib*   she writes   present
2. *katab-it*   she wrote   past
3. *kaatib*   writing   present participle
4. *ma-ktuub*   written   past participle

The prefix *ti-* and the suffix *-it* of the first two words mean "she." The prefix *ma-* of the last word is used with past participles.

Grammarians often say that what is common to a set of words when the affixes are removed is the root. So in English if we remove the affixes from "kick," "kicks," "kicked," and "kicking" we are left with the root "kick." But in the case of the four Arabic words it is not as simple. If we remove the affixes we are still left with the four different forms *ktib, katab, kaatib,* and *ktuub*.

In fact the only thing that is common to all four forms are the consonants "k," "t," and "b:" "kt-b" in (1) and (4), and "k-t-b" in (2) and (3), where the hyphens stand for the missing vowels. Because these consonants are all that the four different forms have in common, they are regarded by grammarians as constituting the root in each of these words. Thus the root is often written simply as *ktb*.

Of course *ktb* is a strange, "discontinuous" root, for its consonants never occur next to one another, but are separated by one or two vowels. In each word the vowels are also regarded as expressing a meaning of their own. In the second word the vowels are "- a - a -" (now using hyphens to stand for the missing consonants), and this vowel pattern expresses the past tense; similarly the vowel pattern "- - i -" expresses the present tense in the first word, "- aa - i -" the present participle in the third word, and "- - uu -" the past participle in the fourth.

These Arabic verbs thus each contain two meaningful but discontinuous word parts, the consonants expressing the root meaning and the vowels expressing a grammatical meaning:

ktb	"write"
- - i -	the present tense
- a - a -	the past tense
- aa - i -	the present participle
- - uu -	the past participle

Is there anything like this in English? Yes: two hundred or so irregular verbs take the past tense or the past participle forms by using a different vowel. For example we have "swim, swims, swimming" but "swam" and "swum." However, there is only one vowel in each word which changes; there are only two forms (past tense and past participle) which change; and there is only a small number of such verbs. By contrast, in Arabic more than one vowel in a word may change; each set of forms has its own vowel pattern; and such word formation is normal and widely used.

Not only verbs but also nouns and other word classes show a similar use of roots consisting of consonants which alternate with vowel patterns which express other meanings. In Arabic the plurals of nouns are often formed by alternating the consonants of the root with one vowel pattern in the singular, and another in the plural. For example the noun *xalifa* (the loan word "caliph") has as its plural *xulufu*. Thus the parts of these words are:

xlf "caliph"   the discontinuous root
- *a - i - a*   the singular part
- *u - u - u*   the plural part

There are nouns derived from verbs, so that in addition to the patterns of the verb, there are further patterns for the noun. From the verb "write" derives the noun "book" with the same root consonants, giving *kitaab* as the singular, and *kutub* as the plural.

ktb   "book"
- *i - aa -*   singular
- *u - u -*   plural

This account of consonant roots may be relevant to an understanding of early Semitic writing systems discussed in Part Three of this book. In these writing systems only the consonants were written, and the reader was left to infer the vowels from the context. This, as we have seen, means that the reader is always given the roots, but may be left without any explicit indication of numbers and tenses.

NIGER-CONGO

There are more than 200 million speakers of languages in this family, and more than 900 languages, of which only the most important are shown. The sub-groups stretch from southern and central Africa (Benue-Congo),

A village meeting in Niger, which was part of French West Africa from 1883, and gained independence in 1960. The official language of Niger is French.

along the coast of West Africa (Kwa) to the Atlantic coast (Atlantic), then back along the edge of the Sahara (Mande, Gur, Adamawan). Finally there is an isolated group in the east called Khordofanian.

Half of the Niger-Congo speakers belong to the Bantu subgroup of Benue-Congo which covers much of central and southern Africa. Many of these are important as national

Students at a Koranic school, in Zinder, southern Niger. Over 80% of the population of Niger is Muslim, a religion introduced to the region by Arab traders, whose trans-Saharan caravan routes brought great wealth to the West African empires of Mali and Sohghay in the fifteenth and sixteenth centuries. Arabic is still spoken widely across North Africa.

languages, but few are spoken by large numbers of people.

The word "Bantu" means "people," and the group was given this name because of the occurrence of this, or some similar word, in most of the languages of the group. We are fortunate to have a major comparative study of the Bantu languages, the result of a lifetime's work by Malcolm Guthrie.

Three languages in particular are referred to more extensively in this chapter: Fulani in the north, Shona in the center, and Zulu in the south of Africa.

Fulani speakers are found all across West Africa from the Atlantic coast to beyond the eastern border of Nigeria. Two of the main groups are found in the east of Nigeria and in Cameroun.

As can be seen from the table, Shona has the largest number of native speakers of any Bantu language. It is principally spoken in the central African republic of Zimbabwe, as well as in Mozambique. There are several major dialects; in Harare, the capital of Zimbabwe, the dialect is called Zezuru.

In the south, Zulu is a major language, and is closely related to Xhosa, its even more southerly neighbor. In the nineteenth century a group of Zulus broke away from the main Zulu nation and headed north to what is now Zimbabwe, where they established an independant state. Their king – Lobengula – and his capital Bulawayo (now a great city of southern Zimbabwe), are known to British history under the heading "Matabele wars." These Zulus called themselves "amaNdebele," anglicized as "Matabele." In this chapter both people and language are termed "Ndebele." Ndebele is often referred to as a separate language, but is mutually intelligible with Zulu spoken 700 miles to the south.

TONE FOR LEXIS AND GRAMMAR

Tone is an important mechanism found in hundreds of Niger-Congo languages. Differences of pitch are used to distinguish both word meanings and grammatical patterns. Most African languages south of the Sahara are tonal in this way, with the relative pitch of a word's syllables being fixed, either high or low.

Hausa, from a non-tonal family, uses tone, perhaps acquired through contact with neighbors. Fulani, on the other hand, has lost its tones, as has another important language, Swahili, which is spoken more than two thousand miles away in Kenya and Tanzania. It is even possible for some dialects of the same language to have tone, and some not. The Ndau dialect of Shona spoken in Mozambique has no tones, but the other Shona dialects do.

To illustrate a typical Niger-Congo tone language, we shall describe some of the

MAJOR LANGUAGES OF SUBSAHARAN AFRICA

The table below lists national languages with more than 5 million speakers.

LANGUAGE	NUMBER OF SPEAKERS (in millions)	COUNTRY
AFRO-ASIATIC LANGUAGES		
1 Hausa	25	Nigeria, Niger
NIGER-CONGO NON-BANTU LANGUAGES		
KWA GROUP		
2 Akan	6.7	Ghana
3 Yoruba	24.2	Nigeria
4 Igbo	20.2	Nigeria
ATLANTIC GROUP		
5 Fulani	10.7	Nigeria (and other countries)
NIGER-CONGO BANTU LANGUAGES		
6 Gikuyu	5.0	Kenya
7 Rwanda	7.6	Rwanda
8 Rundi	5.1	Burundi
9 Kongo	5.0	Congo, Angola, Zaire
10 Luba Lulua	6.5	Zaire
11 Swahili	6.0	Tanzania
12 Makua	6.0	Mozambique
13 Chewa/Nyanja	8.2	Malawi
14 Shona	9.2	Zimbabwe
15 Zulu	7.0	Republic of South Africa
16 Xhosa	7.0	Republic of South Africa

The major languages of central and southern Africa belong to the Bantu family. Some are used widely as second languages: Swahili is an official language of Tanzania and Kenya and also serves as a lingua franca in neighboring countries.

West Africa is home to several hundred languages, mostly belonging to the Niger-Congo group but not to the Bantu family. An important exception is Hausa, belonging to the Chadic branch of Afro-Asiatic.

characteristic features of one language in which tone is used extensively – the Zezuru dialect of Shona. A dash is written beneath each low-toned vowel and a slash beneath each high-toned vowel:

> *havabike*   they don't cook
> - / - /

Stems and affixes have to be distinguished, because the tones which a word has are determined partly by the stem, and partly by the affixes. The word above is divided into a stem and affixes thus:

prefix	prefix	stem	suffix
ha	*va*	*bik*	*e*
-	/	-	/
not	they	cook	(present tense)

Shona and all the Bantu languages are quite unlike English since they never have a lone verb stem used as a word. In English the stem "cook" is used as a word in all kinds of contexts, but there is no Bantu word which consists of just a stem, such as *bik* in the example above. This means that in the Bantu languages every word with a word stem also has at least one affix.

There are over 600 Shona verb stems with the same phonetic shape as *bik*, that is having a consonant-vowel-consonant structure, and there are many more longer ones. If we keep the affixes the same, we can substitute these stems for *bik* in the structure above. For example:

> *ha va bik e*   they don't cook
> *tem*   strike
> *tor*   take

But there are only two different tone patterns:

> 1.   *ha va bik e*
>   - / - /
> 2.   *ha va tor e*
>   - / / /

Since the stem itself has a low tone in 1 but a high tone in 2, all the stems with pattern 1 are called low stems, and all the stems with pattern 2 high stems. There are no exceptions;

every verb stem is either low or high. It is the same with longer stems: there are only two patterns, and every verb is used with either the one or the other. If we compare the two words above, it is clear that we could still distinguish their meanings without tonal variations, because their constituent sounds differ.

However if there were two stems with exactly the same three sounds, then the tone could be a way of marking a difference. In fact in Shona and other Niger-Congo languages, there are a number of stems with the same sounds, but one a low stem and one a high stem. Two such stems are

> 1.   *par* (low)   to offend
> 2.   *par* (high)   to scrape

If these stems are used with the above affixes, they form two words with the same consonants and vowels, but with different tone patterns. Here, only the tone gives the meaning; without tone, the two words would be pronounced identically:

> 1.   *ha va par e*   they don't offend
>   - / - /
> 2.   *ha va par e*   they don't scrape
>   - / / /

One count of verb stems having a consonant-vowel-consonant structure in the Karanga dialect of Shona lists 634 different stems. But there are only 31 pairs of stems which differ solely in tone like *par* (low) and *par* (high). Shona verb stems are listed in dictionaries with their tone properties, called "lexical" tone. In Karanga verbs, for example, lexical tone distinguishes meanings for about 10 percent of stems. In other stems the differences are redundant, and meanings can be distinguished without lexical tone.

A second important use of tone in Bantu languages, usually called the "grammatical" use, is to distinguish different meanings of two or more words, where all the words have the same stem, and the affixes all have the same consonants and vowels. For example:

A school in Malawi caters for refugees from the civil war in neighboring Mozambique. Chewa, the language of one of the main ethnic groupings, shares official language status with English, a legacy of the period when Malawi was a British colony, from 1891 to 1964.

va no bik a	they cook	
/ - - -		
va no bik a	the ones who cook	
- / - -		

In these words *no* and *a* together express a present tense meaning. Pairs or triplets of words like this are very common. In the Niger-Congo languages grammatical tone is more extensive and important than tone used to distinguish the meanings of stems.

Characteristically in Niger-Congo languages, the lexical and grammatical uses may be combined so that three words or more can be distinguished by tone alone. This is illustrated by a final example of four Shona words with just two different stems, and with the same affixes as the previous examples:

1. *va no par a*   they offend
    / - - -
2. *va no par a*   the ones who offend
    - / / /
3. *va no par a*   they scrape
    / - / /
4. *va no par a*   the ones who scrape
    - / / /

(1) and (2) have different grammatical tones, (1) and (3) have different lexical tones, (1) and (4) have different lexical and grammatical tones, and similarly for the remaining pairs.

NOUN CLASSES AND AGREEMENT SYSTEMS

The Niger-Congo languages are famous for two related features: a large number of noun classes and an extensive agreement system.

In most Bantu languages a noun typically begins with a prefix which marks its class. When a noun is used in a sentence, the words which agree with the noun also have a prefix similar in form to that of the noun. In any sentence most of the words are either nouns or words that agree with nouns, so that a majority of the words of the sentence will have one of these prefixes.

European languages like French or German do, of course, have noun classes. But

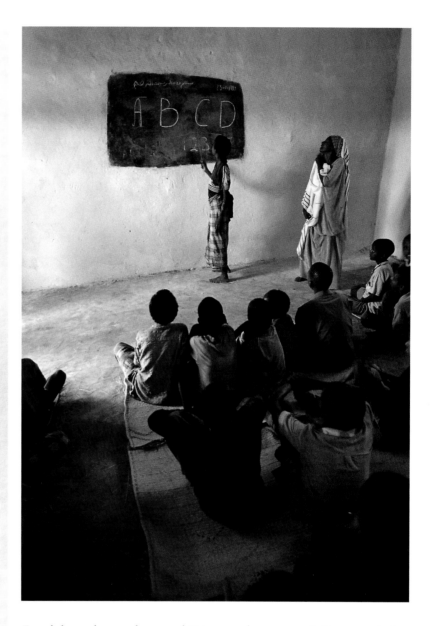

French has only two classes and German only three. Compared to European languages the noun classes of Niger-Congo languages are much more numerous, and the agreement between nouns and other words is not only more extensive but is expressed in a much clearer way.

The noun classes of Ndebele – spoken in Zimbabwe – are given on page 84 as an example of such a system. In all the examples a prefix is separated from the remainder of the word by a hyphen.

There are 16 different prefixes in Ndebele. One noun illustrating each prefix is listed alphabetically in the table on page 84. Three

Children at a school in Somalia. Although the entire population is ethnic Somali, clan-based rivalries have nevertheless led to years of violent civil war. During this period the infrastructure has almost totally broken down, and schools are only now beginning to reopen.

SINGULAR AND PLURAL PREFIXES

One important function of the prefixes is to mark singular and plural nouns. The table below shows all the possibilities for prefixes in Ndebele. A singular prefix need not always pair with the same plural prefix. The table below right shows Ndebele noun classes.

PREFIX PAIRS

Nouns with Singular Prefix		Nouns with Plural Prefix		Translation
i	- yezi	ama	- yezi	cloud(s)
i*	- bheka	ama	- bheka	baker(s)
in	- doda	ama	- doda	man, men
in	- komo	izin	- komo	cow(s)
isi	- lwane	zi - l	wane	lion(s)
u*	- seko	izin	- seko	custom(s)
u	- khokho	o	- khokho	ancestor(s)
um	- fazi	aba	- fazi	woman, women
um	- Ndebele	ama	- Ndebele	Ndebele(s)
um	- fula	im	- fulu	river(s)

Just two prefixes "*ubu*" and "*uku*" are never paired.

ubu	- khulu	bigness
uku	- pheka	cooking

With some stems a singular or plural prefix occurs alone.

Singluar Prefixes:

i	- zulu	rain
i*	- tiye	tea
isi	- Ndebele	the Ndebele language
u*	- Nkulunkulu	God
u	- chago	milk
um	- khathi	sky
i*	- tiye	tea

Plural Prefixes:

ama	- zolo	dew
im	- thombo	yeast
izi	- khihli	sour milk
izin	- yembezi	tears

NOUN CLASSES

Noun			Translation
1	aba	- fazi	women
2	ama	- yezi	clouds
3	i	- yezi	cloud
4	i*	- bheka	baker
5	im	- fula	rivers
6	in	- komo	cow
7	isi	- lwane	lion
8	izi	- lwane	lions
9	izin	- komo	cows
10	o	- khokho	ancestors
11	u	- khokho	ancestor
14	u*	- seko	custom
12	ubu	- khulu	bigness
13	uku	- pheka	cooking
15	um	- fazi	woman
16	um*	- fula	river

prefixes have the same form but different grammatical properties, so they are distinguished by marking one with an asterisk and one without; thus prefix *i-* is different from prefix *i*-*. In other Bantu languages the corresponding forms are often different.

NOUN CLASSES AND THEIR MEANINGS

It is natural to wonder if there is any property common to all of the nouns with the same prefix, and some generalizations can be made: nouns with prefixes *aba-* or *um-* refer to people; nouns with prefixes *um*-* or *im-* do not refer to people; and almost all nouns with prefixes *uku-* or *ubu-* are abstract.

Names, nations, and denominations are just three examples of how meaning can determine the prefixes used with a particular stem. If other names need to be created, or other denominations or nationalities need to be named, they take the same prefixes as all other previous words of similar meaning.

NON-BANTU NOUN CLASSES

Not only Bantu, but many other Niger-Congo languages have complicated class and agreement systems. In this chapter Fulani is used to illustrate such a non-Bantu language.

In Ndebele the noun class markers are prefixes, but in Fulani they are found as suffixes. We see a similar difference of position in closely related languages like English and Norwegian, where the definite article comes before the noun in English but after it in

Norwegian. There are 18 noun classes in Fulani and one example of each is given in the table on page 86. They are listed in the alphabetical order of the suffixes, each of which identifies a different noun class, just as each different prefix identified a different noun class in Zulu or Ndebele. The letters *B* and *D* stand for implosives, ʔ is a glottal stop, N̲ is like the "ng" of "singer" and n̲g like the "ng" of "finger. "

Just as in Ndebele there are singular and plural prefixes, in Fulani there are singular and

NDEBELE NAMES

People's names are all found with the prefix *u-*: *u-Mako*, for example, is borrowed as "Mark." Since names usually identify individuals, the plural *o-Mako* may mean "Mark and the people with him." Ndebele given names often derive from nouns, adjectives, or verbs which describe the parents' feelings or circumstances at the child's birth.

For girls

u-Jabulani	Rejoice
u-Linda	Take-care (of the village till father's return)
u-Sakhile	We-have-made-a-good-home
u-Senzeni	What-have-we-done
u-Sithembil	We-are-hopeful
u-Sibahle	We-are-beautiful
u-Thandiwe	She-is-loved (that is by God, because she survived difficult times)
u-Thokozile	We-are-happy (to have a child)

For boys

u-Themba	Hope
u-Zenzo	Things (happened when he was in the womb)

For both

u-Zibusiso	Blessings (are given us by God)

The Ndebele prefixes for neighboring or foreign peoples are *um-* (singular) and *ama-* (plural): *um-Khalanga*, "a Kalanga," *ama-Amelika*, "Americans."

NDEBELE ANIMAL NAMES

A list of sample Ndebele animal names indicates that it is difficult to discover a property common to all the animals with the same prefixes:

Prefixes	Translation	Stem			
i ama	caracal	*duha*	*isi izi*	lion	*lwane*
	cheetah	*hlosi*		mongoose	*tsikibololo*
	jackal	*khanka*		water buck	*dumoka*
	polecat	*qaqa*	*u o*	bat	*malulwane*
	rat	*gundwane*		rhinoceros	*bhejane*
	roan	*thaka*		shrew	*tswebe*
	wild cat	*gola*		spring hare	*mayelani*
in izin	baboon	*dwangu*	*um im*	antelope	*ziki*
	buffalo	*nyati*		hare	*vundla*
	eland	*pofu*		reed buck	*tshwayeli*
	elephant	*dlovu*			
	giraffe	*tundla*			
	hippopotamus	*vubu*			
	leopard	*gwe*			
	wildebeest	*konkone*			

Makishi dancers entertain tourists at the Victoria Falls in Zimbabwe. The two main ethnic groupings in Zimbabwe are the Ndebele in the north and the Shona, who outnumber the Nedebele by about four to one, in the south.

FULANI NOUN CLASSES

Stem	Suffix	Translation
laam	- *Be*	chiefs
loo	- *De*	storage-pots
Bow	- *Di*	mosquitoes
laam	- *Do*	chief
Biraa	- *Dam*	milk
nood	- *a*	crocodile
njar	- *am*	a drink
les	- *di*	country
yiit	- *e*	fire
nyor	- *go*	cover-mat
taador	- *gol*	girdle
nyala	- *hol*	calf
ngas	- *ka*	hole
daN	- *ki*	grass shelter
loo	- *nde*	storage-pot
Ɂen	- *ndu*	breast
Dem	- *ngal*	tongue
hottoll	- *o*	cotton

FULANI SECONDARY SUFFIXES

	Singular	Plural	
Primary suffixes	*laam - Do*	*laam - Be*	chief(s)
Secondary suffixes:			
Diminutive	*laam - ngel*	*laam - kon*	petty chief(s)
Augmentative	*laam - nga*	*laam - ko*	mighty chief(s)

SHONA SECONDARY PREFIXES

	Singular	Plural	
Primary suffixes	*mu-komana*	*va-komana*	boy(s)
Secondary suffixes:			
Diminutive	*ka-komana*	*tu-komana*	little boy(s)
Double diminutive	*ka-mu-komana*	*tu-va-komana*	tiny little (boys)

plural suffixes. In both, the number of singular affixes (8 and 16 respectively) is greater than the number of plural ones (6 and 3), with the ratio higher in Fulani. This occurs in many languages: more differences are marked in the singular than in the plural. It is more important, it seems, to distinguish between single entities, than between grouped ones. In Fulani one singular suffix (-*Do*) and one plural suffix (-*Be*) are always paired together, and nouns with these refer only to people: *laam-Do*, "chief," *laam-Be*, "chiefs." All of the other 15 singular suffixes must pair with one of the two remaining plural suffixes -*De* or -*Di*: *loo-Nde*, "storage-pot," *loo-De*, "storage-pots," and *Bow-ngu*, "mosquito," *Bow-Di*, "mosquitoes."

SMALL THINGS AND BIG THINGS

Fulani illustrates another common Niger-Congo feature: there are special "diminutive" and "augmentative" suffixes for indicating smallness and bigness, or importance and unimportance. These "secondary suffixes" replace the nouns' normal "primary" ones:

This is the only important way in which the Fulani noun class system differs from that of Ndebele and Zulu. But many Bantu languages work similarly, with the suffixes of Fulani becoming prefixes. This is the case in Shona, for example. Here, however, there is a further twist: the secondary prefixes not only replace the primary ones, but may also be added to them. Some secondary prefixes from the Karanga dialect of Shona are shown in the table above.

Special diminutive forms are found in many languages around the world, but augmentatives are rarer. In English we find diminutives like duckling, gosling, and princeling, but the -ling suffix is used with very few words, and there is no generally-used diminutive. Secondary prefixes make a noun class system more complicated, and some Bantu languages have even more secondary prefixes than those noted above, but they also generate an increase in expressive and creative possibilities by allowing the formation of new words.

AGREEMENT MARKERS AND PRONOUNS

A group of words which can replace a single noun in a sentence is a noun phrase. In a noun phrase the noun is the most important word, about which the other words, or "modifiers," give further information. English nouns have different forms for the singular and the plural, and there are just two modifiers, "this" and "that," which change respectively to "these" and "those." We say that these modifiers "agree with" the nouns for number. But in English no other modifiers change in this way.

In Bantu languages the situation is quite different. In fact most of the words which modify nouns change when the noun changes. Just as nouns have an affix which shows their class, so the modifiers too have an affix which shows their noun's class, the class affix of the modifier being determined by the class affix of the noun. In the following four noun phrases of Ndebele, the prefix of the adjective is different for each different noun prefix; in Ndebele all the modifiers commonly follow the noun and there are no words for "the" or "a."

um-fazi	*om-khulu*	the big woman
aba-fazi	*aba-khulu*	the big women
i-yezi	*eli-khulu*	the big cloud
isi-lwane	*esi-khulu*	the big lion

The adjective stem is *khulu* which means "big." The class affixes of the modifiers are called "agreement markers." In the examples the agreement markers are shown in bold type.

If instead of an adjective we use the word for "my" then we will see that once again the agreement markers change when the noun changes. The Ndebele words for "my" all begin with an agreement marker.

um-fazi	*w-ami*	my woman
aba-fazi	*b-ami*	my women
i-yezi	*l-ami*	my cloud
isi-lwane	*s-ami*	my lion

Another thing that can be seen from these examples is that the agreement markers are not always exactly the same with different modifiers, although they often are. In these four words for "my," every agreement marker is different from the corresponding agreement marker with the adjective stem *khulu* given earlier, though there is usually some recognizable similarity of form between the agreement markers which occur with the same noun prefix.

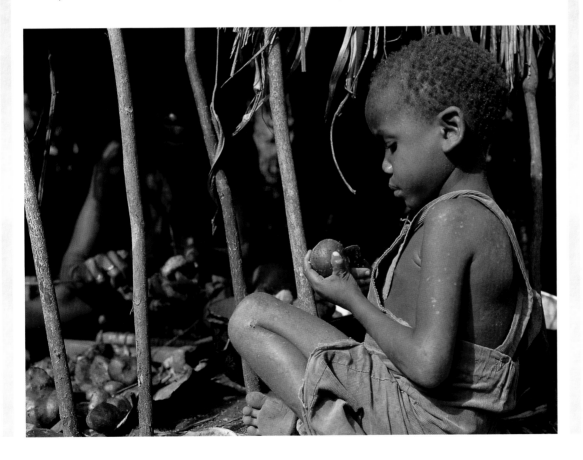

A small boy in the forests of Zaire. Most of Zaire's ethnically diverse population is of Bantu origin, descendants of the Bantu pastoralists who migrated from the West African coast to South and East Africa between 500 BC and AD 500.

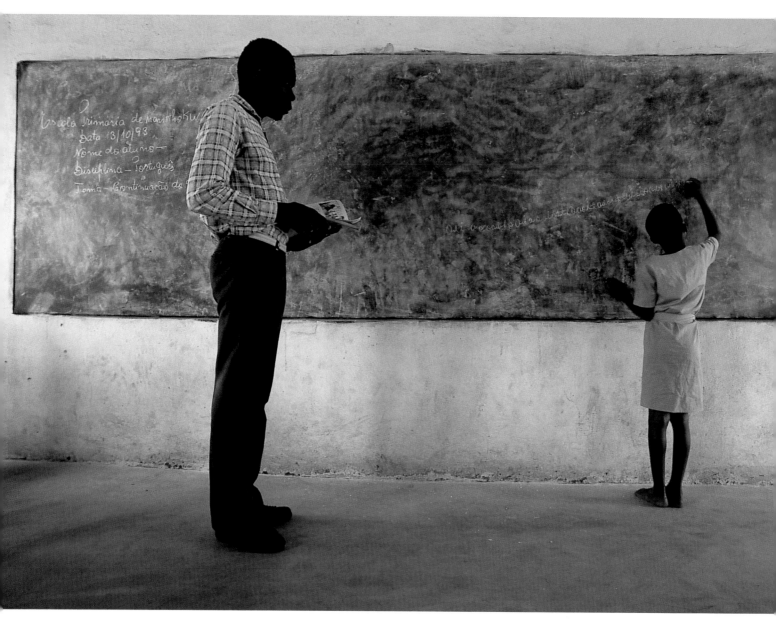

A class in Senegal, where the literacy rate is currently 38%. Senegal's many ethnic groups are associated with clearly-defined geographical regions, although inter-marriage is reducing the potential for ethnic tension.

When we translate a Bantu noun and its modifiers, the prefix and the agreement markers are not translated; they simply identify the noun's class. Similarly, in a sentence with a subject and a verb, the verb's agreement marker is not translated. For example in the sentence *Um-fazi u-pheka*, "the woman cooks," the agreement marker *u* is not translated. However, if the subject is omitted, the verb functions like a complete sentence in English and the agreement marker is now translated by the English pronoun "she:" *U-pheka*, "She cooks."

In the same way, we may omit the noun from an adjective-plus-noun combination and translate the agreement marker as the English pronoun "one:" *um-fazi om-khulu*, "the big woman," or *om-khulu*, "the big one."

Agreement markers regularly have this double function: when the noun is present they are just agreement markers, but when the noun is absent they take on the role of a pronoun.

Noun class and agreement markers together constitute the famous and distinctive class and agreement system which, in its expressive clarity and its ubiquity, probably makes the Niger-Congo languages unique.

It is often said that languages differ in the way they categorize the world. We shall briefly discuss some characteristic properties of African languages in relation to sex, relatives, and the ways people walk.

Most languages of sub-Saharan Africa mark no distinction between males and females in their pronominal (pronoun-like) forms. The Shona sentence *Unobika* means either "He is cooking" or "She is cooking." The pronominal is the first letter *U,* and there are no equivalents to the English pronouns "he" and "she." Of course it is the same with many other language families. In Mandarin, *Ta shi wode pengyou* means "he/she is my friend," with "Ta" meaning either "he" or "she."

In Africa the kinship systems are very different from those of Europe, and the differences are seen in the languages. In Ndebele, for example, there are three distinct words each for "mother" and "father:"

u-baba	my father
u-yihlo	your father
u-yise	his father
u-mama	my mother
u-nyoko	your mother
u-nina	his mother

An individual may also have more than one father or mother since your father's brothers are also your "fathers," and your mother's sisters are also your "mothers." These "fathers" and "mothers" can be distinguished from your natural mother and father by using the additional epithets "small" for brothers and sisters younger than your father or mother, and "large" for older ones, giving the terms listed above.

Our last example illustrates the complexity of African vocabulary. In Shona there are more than two hundred different words for walking, just a few of which are listed opposite.

NDEBELE KINSHIP TERMS

Ndebele	Literal Translation	English
u-baba	my father	my father
u-baba (omncinayane)	my (little) father	my uncle
u-baba (omkhulu)	my (big) father	my uncle
u-mama	my mother	my mother
u-mama (omncinyane)	my (little) mother	my aunt
u-mama (omkhulu)	my (big) mother	my aunt

SHONA WALKING WORDS

Shona Word	Translation
chakwair	walk with a squelching noise through a muddy place
chwakatik	walk making a noise of breaking sticks
dowor	walk for a long time on bare feet
donzv	walk with a stick
duduk	walk backwards
kokonyar	walk bent double with an arched back
kunzvur	walk about restlessly
mbey	walk all round an area
mbwembwer	walk with your body or buttocks shaking about
minair	walk with swinging hips
panh	walk a long way
pfumbur	walk raising dust
pushuk	walk with a very short dress
rauk	walk with long steps
rindimar	walk haughtily
seser	walk along with the flesh rippling
shwitair	walk naked or almost naked
svavair	walk huddled up with cold and wet
tabvuk	walk like a grasshopper with thighs so thin you seem to be jumping
vefuk	walk bent under a heavy load

Pacific

The Indo-Pacific region is home to the greatest diversity of languages on earth. The Philippines have 70 languages, Indonesia 200, and New Guinea and the Melanesian islands over one thousand. Here, the linguistic history is also that of the conquest of the Pacific: the evidence of Austronesian languages has helped researchers trace the prehistoric Polynesian mariners' odyssey to the ocean's remotest islands. The indigenous languages of New Guinea remain the least known in the world, and their history and inter-relationships still pose unsolved puzzles.

A monumental statue from Easter Island in the South Pacific. The main colonization of the Pacific took place between 4000 and 1000 years ago, but early Polynesian settlers did not reach remote Easter Island until about AD 400.

The number of Austronesian languages still remains a point of contention, primarily because linguists are still uncertain about differentiating separate languages from their dialects. This is in turn due to the lack of actual data on some Austronesian languages, particularly those spoken in New Guinea and certain islands of Indonesia. In other instances, political factors interfere with the identification of dialects or languages; the national languages Bahasa Malaysia (Malay), spoken in Malaysia, and Bahasa Indonesia (Indonesian), spoken in Indonesia, are sufficiently similar to be considered merely dialects of a single language (*see map*).

Similarities between the languages of Indonesia, Polynesia, and Madagascar were first noticed as early as the eighteenth century, but the first systematic classification of Austronesian languages was produced by the German scholar Otto Dempwolff in 1934–38.

INDONESIA AND MALAYSIA

The languages shown all belong to the Austronesian family, with the exception of the Aslian group. The national languages Bahasa Indonesia and Bahasa Malaysia (standard Malay) are spreading at the expense of local languages. Also spoken are southern Chinese dialects including Hokkien, Hakka, and Teochew, and Malay-based creoles.

A Javanese shadow puppet, representing the hero, Rama. The puppets are used in shadow plays to enact myths and legends, involving gods, giants, princes, and ogres.

The Southern Philippine languages, Sama, Bonggi, and Bajau, have spread to coastal areas of Borneo and Sulawesi.

Buffalo heads, which symbolize wealth, are carved on the doors of rice-barns in Sulawesi.

Malagasy, the Austronesian language of Madagascar, is thought to have originated in southern Borneo.

SHARED WORDS IN MODERN AUSTRONESIAN LANGUAGES

This table shows a sample of shared words (also known as cognates), including their hypothetical form in Proto-Austronesian.

Tagalog	Malay	Fijian	Samoan	Proto-Austronesian	English
dalawa	dua	rua	lua	*Duwa	"two"
apat	empat	vaa	faa	*e(m)pat	"four"
lima	lima	lima	lima	*lima	"five; hand"
anim	enam	ono	ono	*enem	"six"
manok	manu	manu-manu	manu	*manuk	"bird"
mata	mata	mata	mata	*mata	"eye"
daan	jalan	sala	'ala	*Zalan	"road"'
pandan	pandan	vadra	fala	*panDan	"pandanus"
niyog	nior	niu	niu	*niuR	"coconut"

This classification underwent a number of changes in the works of Isidore Dyen, Otto Chr. Dahl, Robert Blust, and others. The classification presented here is based on Robert Blust's proposal, according to which the primary division in Austronesian languages is between the languages of Taiwan (the so-called Formosan territorial grouping, which in turn is divided into the Atayalic, Tsouic, and Paiwanic groups) and all the remaining languages,

THE SETTLEMENT OF POLYNESIA

The acceptance of a primary division between the Formosan languages and the Malayo-Polynesian languages is consistent with archeological evidence indicating that Proto-Austronesian (the language from which

modern Austronesian languages descended) was spoken in and around Taiwan about five to seven thousand years ago. A combination of linguistic and archeological findings allows us to reconstruct to a certain extent the way of life led by speakers of Proto-Austronesian. They apparently relied on fishing and agriculture, and cultivated taro, yams, bananas, sugarcane, breadfruit, coconuts, and possibly rice. They kept pigs and probably dogs and chickens, but had no domesticated sheep, goats, or cattle. They made pottery.

They were in their element in their maritime environment, developing excellent navigational skills and using outrigger canoes for transportation, which to this day are found throughout the Austronesian-speaking area. It is these early navigational skills that played a crucial role in the expansion of Austronesian-speakers. The first waves of migration, which

The Polynesians sailed vast distances across the Pacific Ocean in outrigger canoes, stocked with plants and domesticated animals. The outrigger is kept to windward to provide balance and the canoe is sailed into the wind by tacking.

Pandanus is a widespread plant with useful leaves and edible fruits which can be stored after cooking, an important factor for sailors and inhabitants of infertile lands. The name itself is Austronesian, and is shared by languages as far west as Tagalog in the Philippines and as far east as Samoa.

CAROLINE ISLANDS
**CHAMORRO
PONAPEAN**

MARSHALL ISLANDS
MARSHALLESE

HAWAII

KIRIBATI
GILBERTESE

Traditional trading canoe.

SOLOMON
ISLANDS

TUVALU

FUTUNA

SAMOA
SAMOAN

VANUATU

TONGA
TONGAN

FIJI
FIJIAN

N
NI

NEW
CALEDONIA

DISTRIBUTION OF AUSTRONESIAN LANGUAGES

Area	Number of Languages*	Number of Speakers
Madagascar	1	8 million
Taiwan	10	220 thousand
Philippines	70	40 million
Interior Vietnam, Cambodia	7	700 thousand
Indonesia and Malaysia	300	130 million
Melanesia	350	1.2 million
Micronesia	12	200 thousand
Polynesia	20	700 thousand

* for some areas, approximate

MAORI

NEW
ZEALAND

*The languages to the east
outnumber those to the
west but have a very
small number of speakers,
because many of these
languages are spoken on
small isolated islands or
parts of islands.*

THE PACIFIC ISLANDS

The Polynesian languages arose in island Southeast Asia as a branch of the Austronesian family. Skilled seafarers, the Polynesians settled the inhabitable islands of the Pacific in a series of eastward migrations. Linguistic reconstruction together with archeological evdence help us to piece together the approximate routes and dates of settlement. Hawaii and New Zealand, for example, were settled relatively late and from eastern Polynesia, rather than directly from the west.

Tahitian has become the lingua franca of French Polynesia, with over 100,000 speakers.

MARQUESAS

The peoples of the Pacific islands used many unusual objects to represent money; stones, shells, pigs' tails, feathers. Feather money was made by overlapping scales of doves' feathers along a ribbon of string.

TAHITI
TAHITIAN

TUAMOTO

RAPA
RAPANUI

EASTER ISLAND

On Easter Island, the easternmost outpost of their culture, the Polynesians left not only statues but the Rongorongo script. Athough Polynesian seafarers may have reached South America, they left no linguistic evidence of their presence.

The peoples of the Pacific did not use metals until after the arrival of the Europeans. This suit of armour, from Kiribati, is made entirely of woven and stitched coconut fibre. Swords and daggers were made of carved wood, studded with sharks' teeth.

The pearl fishers of the Pacific region dive to great depths to find pearls embedded within the shells of clams or oysters lying on the sea-bed.

probably took place between 3000 and 2000 BC, were from Taiwan to the Philippines and on to the Moluccas. Sea-borne migrations then moved southeast, and Oceania was settled during the first millennium BC. Many settlers were either traders or young warriors for whom sailing to remote lands was part of the initiation into adulthood. The expansion of early Austronesian speakers into the islands of the Pacific Ocean is associated with a number of prehistoric cultures; one of the best known is the so-called Lapita. Distinctive Lapita pottery is found on numerous islands from New Guinea all the way east to Samoa.

The last expansion of Austronesian speakers was west to Madagascar, which was settled in the first millennium AD. The name

Madagascar is probably a distortion of the African placename Mogadishu, brought to Europe by Marco Polo. The Austronesian-speakers living on the island call themselves and their language Malagasy. While Malagasy is clearly an Austronesian language, it has borrowed heavily from the Bantu languages of Africa – the Malagasy had intense trade contacts with Bantu-speakers. For example, the name for chicken in Malagasy is *akoko*, a borrowing from the Bantu *-koko*. Like Bantu languages, Malagasy has all open syllables, whereas other Western Austronesian languages tolerate closed syllables.

Kublai Khan presents Marco Polo with a gold tablet. It is thought that Marco Polo, returning from his travels in the Far East, introduced the placename Mogadishu to Europe. It was then probably distorted to become Madagascar.

There are a large number of borrowings from Arabic in the languages of Malaysia and Indonesia, due to the early influence of Islam. There are also borrowings from the Indo-European languages of India, primarily through trade. Despite such borrowings, Austronesian languages remain strikingly similar in their core or basic vocabulary, the

vocabulary which is unlikely to be affected by cultural contacts or migrations.

AUSTRONESIAN LANGUAGE FEATURES

Despite the vast geographical area they span, Austronesian languages continue to have much vocabulary in common and to share many grammatical features. Many languages of the family have rather small inventories of both vowels and consonants, and Polynesian languages are the most economical in that respect. Hawaiian, for example, has only eight consonants (w, m, p, l, n, k, h) and the glottal stop, represented as ', for example, *'ala* in the table on p.91, and five vowels (a, i, u, e, o). Western Austronesian languages have several more consonants but make up for that by a four-vowel system (i, a, u, ə). This final vowel is similar to the sound of the last vowel in the English word "doctor." More complex consonant systems, found in Melanesia for example, are sometimes attributed to the influence of neighboring non-Austronesian

ALIENABLE AND INALIENABLE

POSSESSION

Alienable possession implies that an object can be transferred to another's ownership. Inalienable possession is viewed as an inseparable, indispensable characteristic of the owner. Inalienable possession includes such concepts as body parts, kinship terms, and some valuable items. In Samoan, for example, "my arm" (an inalienable body part) is expressed differently from "my biscuit" which could readily become someone else's biscuit:

le masi	*a*	*a'ue*
the biscuit	POSSESSIVE	me
"my biscuit":		

le lima	*o*	*a'u*
the arm	POSSESSIVE	me
"my arm"		

FOCUS CONSTRUCTION IN TAGALOG

Tagalog (also known as Pilipino) is one of the largest languages of the Philippines and its national language. In Tagalog the PREDICATE, which occurs at the beginning of a clause, can be followed by one or more nouns; one of the nouns is preceded by the particle *ang*, and this noun is the topic of the sentence (the information component that the sentence is about). Depending on the noun chosen as topic, the verb also changes its form. There are several possible ways of representing the situation "The woman will give the rice to the child" (the topic of each sentence is in **bold**):

mag-bibigay	**ang**	**babae**	ng	bigas	sa	bata
AGENT TOPIC-will give	TOPIC	woman	ARTICLE	rice	to	child

"The woman will give rice to the child."

i-bibigay	ng	babae	**ang**	**bigas**	sa	bata
OBJECT TOPIC-will give	ARTICLE	woman	TOPIC	rice	to	child

"The rice, the woman will give it to the child."
("The rice will be given to the child by the woman")

ibigy-an	ng	babae	ng	bigas	**ang**	**bata**
will give-GOAL TOPIC	ARTICLE	woman	ARTICLE	rice	TOPIC	child

"The child, the woman will give him/her the rice."
("The child will be given the rice by the woman")

languages. Open syllables predominate in Austronesian languages, and this tendency is apparent in well-known Polynesian names such as Ta-hi-ti, Sa-mo-a, Ho-no-lu-lu, u-ku-le-le, and a-lo-ha.

Austronesian languages make heavy use of agglutination. The technique of making new compound words by combining existing words allows Austronesian languages to create their own words for new concepts, rather than borrow such words. This tendency is apparent, for instance, in Malagasy, where the creation of native Malagasy words has long been preferred over direct borrowing. Often new words are extremely long, for example: *zava* "to be lit, illuminated" – *fahazavana* "illumination, brilliance" (*faha* is a nominal prefix expressing state) – *fahazavan-tsaina* "intelligence" (*saina* "mind"). Of course, this example is not intended to show that Malagasy never borrows words; it actually has quite a few borrowings,

from Bantu, Arabic, and later from French and English. Some French nouns were borrowed by Malagasy complete with an article, hence *latabatra* "table" (*la table*), or a preposition, hence *dipaina* "European bread" (*du pain*).

Reduplication (a full or partial repetition of a word) is a widespread phenomenon in Austronesian languages. As a result, these languages often have long words; for example, the Samoan word *mata* "unripe," is reduplicated to become *fa'amatamata* "raw." Reduplication is sometimes accompanied by a change in the initial sound of the reduplicated element; in Bolaang Mongondow (Indonesia) *bontat* "hack open, hack through" becomes *mo-montat* "cut open a new path through vegetation"; in Malagasy *hendratra* "startled" becomes *hendra-trendratra* "very scared."

Widespread Austronesian features include the distinction of inclusive first person pronouns (indicating the speaker and the

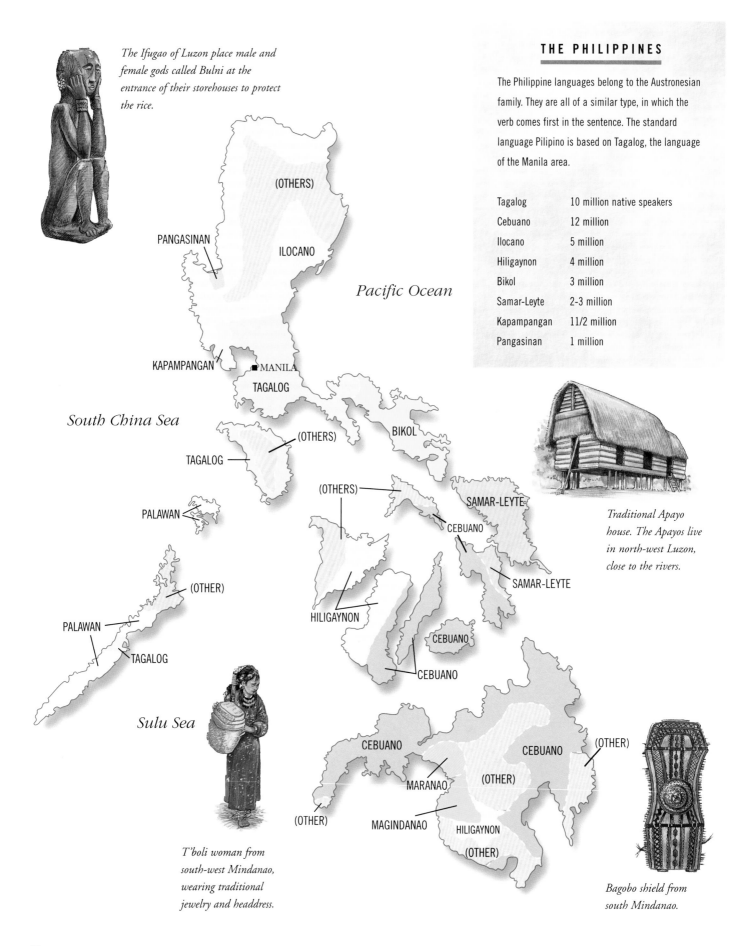

The Ifugao of Luzon place male and female gods called Bulni at the entrance of their storehouses to protect the rice.

THE PHILIPPINES

The Philippine languages belong to the Austronesian family. They are all of a similar type, in which the verb comes first in the sentence. The standard language Pilipino is based on Tagalog, the language of the Manila area.

Tagalog	10 million native speakers
Cebuano	12 million
Ilocano	5 million
Hiligaynon	4 million
Bikol	3 million
Samar-Leyte	2-3 million
Kapampangan	11/2 million
Pangasinan	1 million

Pacific Ocean

South China Sea

Sulu Sea

(OTHERS)

PANGASINAN

ILOCANO

KAPAMPANGAN

MANILA

TAGALOG

BIKOL

(OTHERS)

TAGALOG

PALAWAN

(OTHER)

PALAWAN

TAGALOG

(OTHERS)

SAMAR-LEYTE

CEBUANO

SAMAR-LEYTE

HILIGAYNON

CEBUANO

CEBUANO

CEBUANO

MARANAO

(OTHER)

CEBUANO

(OTHER)

(OTHER)

MAGINDANAO

HILIGAYNON

(OTHER)

Traditional Apayo house. The Apayos live in north-west Luzon, close to the rivers.

T'boli woman from south-west Mindanao, wearing traditional jewelry and headdress.

Bagobo shield from south Mindanao.

addressee or several addressees) and exclusive first person pronouns (indicating only the speaker(s) and excluding the people who are addressed). Pronominal suffixes mark the possessors of nouns (for example, in the Polynesian language West Futuna, *tupu*-u "your grandparent," *tupu*-na "his/her grandparent"). A distinction is also made between alienable and inalienable possession (possession which can be transferred as opposed to possession which cannot be transferred) (*see p.94*).

A number of Austronesian languages rely heavily on passive constructions; in Malagasy and Maori the percentage of passives in a narrative text can reach up to 70 percent (for comparison, the use of passives in scholarly English seldom goes beyond 6-8 percent and is even lower in spoken language). In addition to regular passives such as "The fish was caught" (by the fisherman), Austronesian languages use passive in requests (so-called "passive imperative").

Compare the following requests in Malagasy:

Manaraha	*ny*	*mpampianatra*
be-followed	the	teacher

"Let the teacher be followed."

Araho	*ny*	*mpampianatra*
follow	the	teacher

" Follow the teacher. "

The former request, which uses the passive imperative, is far more polite; the latter sounds more harsh and uncompromising and has to be used carefully.

Some Austronesian languages (for example, Motu and West Polynesian languages), are ergative, and scholars are still debating whether or not Proto-Austronesian was also ergative. Some languages demonstrate the so-called "split ergativity," where pronouns have

The Philippines has one of the highest literacy rates among the developing countries. The Philippines encompasses over 100 distinct ethnic groups, and over 70 languages are spoken. Chinese make up just 2% of the population but over 120 Chinese schools ensure that they retain their cultural and linguistic identity.

accusative marking and common nouns have ergative marking. Research has found that the use of the ergative form varies with social factors such as the relatonship between the speaker and hearer: the case marker is used more in formal situations than in the home, and more by men than by women.

West Austronesian languages and Philippine languages in particular are famous for their use of the so-called "focus construction," illustrated on p.95 by Tagalog examples. The Tagalog examples point to another interesting feature of Austronesian: a number of languages of the family have a verb-initial word order. In Tagalog and Maori, this order is VSO ("Caught the cat the mouse" rather than "The cat caught the mouse"); in Malagasy, it is VOS ("Caught the mouse the cat"); finally, in some languages (certain Fijian dialects and Samoan) it can be both VSO and

The rongorongo *script of Easter Island is thought to be an emulation of European scripts introduced by Spanish colonists. It was probably used as a memory aid or for decorative purposes, not for recording the Rapanui language of the islanders.*

VOS. As the list of languages exhibiting these orders shows, verb-initial orders in Austronesian languages are not confined to a single geographical location but are found in all parts of the area. These orders alternate with SVO and, more rarely, SOV (the occurrence of SOV in some Melanesian languages is explained by the influence of the neighboring Papuan languages).

Linguists have numerous opportunities to study such grammatical features of Austronesian languages, which are solidly

represented in modern languages of the family. Certain features, however, have almost disappeared and must be studied primarily through early grammars compiled by travellers and missionaries, or through comparative analysis of Austronesian languages. One such feature is distinct vocabulary subsystems (and probably some distinct grammatical elements) for different social castes. In Oceania, this is known as "the chiefs' language"; in speaking to or of chiefs, people had to use special words for "eat," "sleep," "walk," "dwelling," and so on. It is also possible that only chiefs were allowed to use some words, which were considered sacred and forbidden for the common man. This special vocabulary is still very much alive in Javanese, a Western Austronesian language.

Austronesian languages still pose a number of other puzzles. One question concerns remote relationships between this family and other languages of the world. There are various theories; a hypothetical link between the Austronesian and Austro-Thai family has been suggested, and a possible link between Austronesian and Japanese is also proposed. Another puzzle is Easter Island, a remote island in the South Pacific, famous for its enigmatic stone monuments and statues, dating to between AD 1000–1600. Current theories link the mysterious devastation of this island culture to the exhaustion of its ecology. Wooden boards found there exhibit the script known as *rongorongo*, which probably developed as a formal emulation of European writing (of which the Spanish treaty of annexation of 1770 was the most likely source). It is thought that the script was used for ornamentation or for mnemonic purposes, and was not used for writing down the Rapanui language spoken on the island. The link between the culture of Easter Island and South American cultures, proposed by the Norwegian scholar Thor Heyerdahl, seems implausible in the light of both archeological and linguistic evidence.

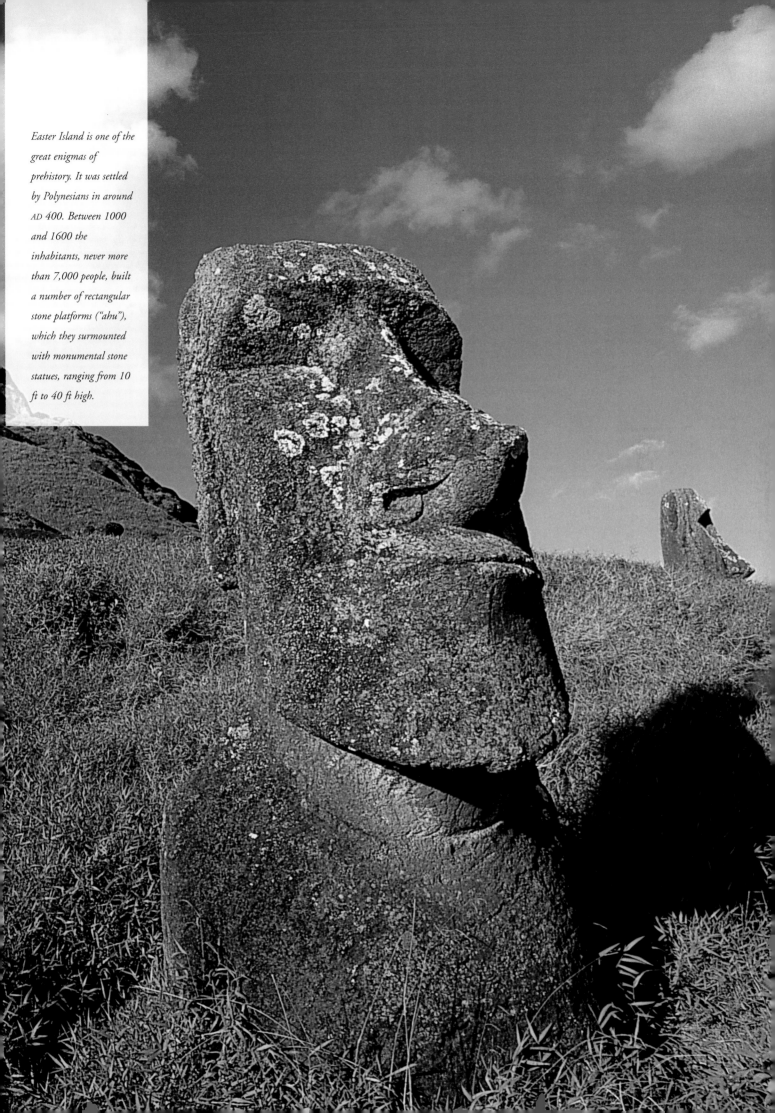

Easter Island is one of the great enigmas of prehistory. It was settled by Polynesians in around AD 400. Between 1000 and 1600 the inhabitants, never more than 7,000 people, built a number of rectangular stone platforms ("ahu"), which they surmounted with monumental stone statues, ranging from 10 ft to 40 ft high.

The Melanesian Islands are situated in the southwestern Pacific, and were so named by early explorers because of their inhabitants' dark skin (from the Greek *melas*). The largest land mass is vast, mountainous New Guinea, to the east of which lie the hundreds of smaller islands of the Bismarck Archipelago, the Solomons, Vanuatu, and New Caledonia (*see map*). The western limit of the Melanesian population is indeterminate, as there has been much intermixing with other populations, but a Melanesian element can be found throughout eastern Southeast Asia. To the east, the Fijians are apparently Melanesian in physical appearance, but have a culture and language which more closely resemble those of their Polynesian neighbors. At the northern tip of Australia, the Torres Strait Islanders appear to

be Melanesian physically, linguistically, and culturally, although as Australians their recent history has been different.

Human society is very ancient in Melanesia. Radiocarbon dating of prehistoric sites such as Kosipe in Papua have indicated 26,000 years of settlement, with some estimates ranging up to 40,000. This timespan corresponds to dates suggested for the peopling of the Australian continent. Indeed, until about 6,000 years ago, a land bridge connected New Guinea and the Australian land mass, whose populations were then continuous, and it is likely that the original migrations to Australia followed this route. Linguistic evidence supports this hypothesis, as links have been found between the languages of the Central Highlands and proto-Australian (*see Part Two, Chapter 5*).

For the linguist, the most remarkable feature of Melanesia is the extreme diversity of its languages. Vanuatu has a population of little over 150,000, but boasts 105 identifiable languages, making it the world's most linguistically diverse country, with one language for every 1,500 speakers. The Solomon Islands have similarly small language groups: nearly 90 languages are spoken by a population of about 300,000. According to the Summer Institute of Linguistics' latest survey, in Papua New Guinea there are over 860 languages in a population of less than 4 million. many of these are still undescribed or incompletely known to outsiders, so for this reason alone care must be taken when making universal generalizations about human language. For example, SOV languages nearly always have case systems, but the Haruai language in Papua New Guinea does not. Phonologically, some Chimbu languages of the New Guinea Highlands have the highly unusual "lateral velar affricate", which can be thought of as a kind of scraped "g" sound made with the side of the tongue, while the Rotokas language of the North Solomons (*see*

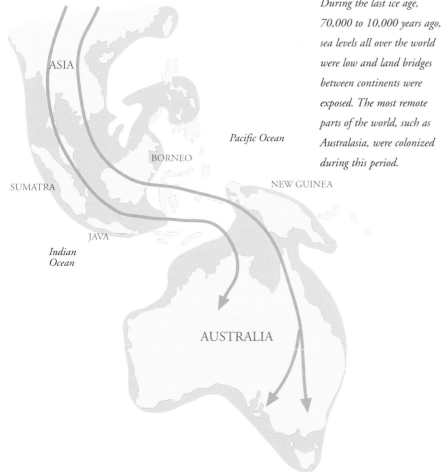

During the last ice age, 70,000 to 10,000 years ago, sea levels all over the world were low and land bridges between continents were exposed. The most remote parts of the world, such as Australasia, were colonized during this period.

ASIA

SUMATRA

JAVA

Indian Ocean

BORNEO

Pacific Ocean

NEW GUINEA

AUSTRALIA

The societies of Papua New Guinea remained small-scale due to preferred residence patterns and an ideology of equality which prevented large political units from emerging.

p.108) appears to lack distinct nasal phonemes, once thought to be universal.

Taking Papua New Guinea as an example, how do we account for this incredible diversity? Why should an area with only one-tenth of one percent of the world's population harbor almost one-sixth of the world's languages? The fragmentation is frequently explained in terms of the tribal groups' isolation by the mountainous, rugged terrain and by constant warfare, but for a number of reasons this cannot be the full story.

To begin with, the most populous language in Papua New Guinea is Enga, with approximately 160,000 speakers. Yet the Engans live in the Central Highlands in some of the most rugged and remote areas in the country, or indeed anywhere on Earth. On the other hand, the region of greatest linguistic diversity is probably Sepik, near the mainland north coast, where it is not unusual for villages to speak very different languages despite close proximity and easy social contact. The idea that before the Europeans' arrival, the tribal groups were unaware of outsiders, has been greatly exaggerated. Anthropologists and archeologists have clearly demonstrated that complex and extensive trading networks had already existed.

In many of these societies, great pride is taken in small cultural differences. It seems there is a tendency to emphasize linguistic peculiarities for the sake of identity, and over the millennia this has doubtless generated difference. The phenomenon of word taboo may also have been a contributing factor: in-laws, for example, are commonly forbidden to utter one another's names; similarly, those of the recently deceased may be taboo. Since personal names can also be ordinary words, alternatives may be substituted, creating an accelerated rate of change.

The late Don Laycock, who made a life-long study of Papua New Guinean languages, suggested that perhaps the problem should be approached from another direction. Instead of wondering why Melanesia has so many

Oceania is linguistically diverse, but the region is linked by many cultural traditions and beliefs; the veneration of deified ancestors and the worship of images of departed relations, such as this ancestral image from New Guinea, is widespread.

languages, maybe we should ask why the rest of the world has so few, or how some languages become established over such wide areas. Most of the conditions required to establish a dominant language – centralized political power, standardization, a writing system, and a literary tradition – were absent in Melanesia, and thus could not allow any one language to become pre-eminent.

THE LANGUAGES OF MELANESIA

The main division is between the Austronesian and non-Austronesian, or Papuan languages. The Austronesian languages are part of the huge group stretching from Madagascar in the west to Polynesia in the east. It is thought that Austronesian speakers moved through the southwestern Pacific some 3,000 years ago, although the details of these migrations are still being debated by linguists, archeologists, and pre-historians (*see pp.94–5*). Many of the Austronesian languages of the area have been in close contact over a long period with other non-Austronesian languages, and have been extensively influenced by them, becoming untypical of Austronesian languages as a whole. Indeed, some cases, like Maisin of the northeast Papuan coast, defy classification and are best described as "mixed languages."

The late arrival of the Austronesian languages in Melanesia is reflected in their distribution. Most are spoken by groups living in coastal or island locations, although there has been considerable penetration inland in northeastern New Guinea (*see map opposite*). Further east, as the uninhabited islands were

Women of the Yali tribe, Irian Jaya. Although the population of Irian Jaya is just 1.9 million, linguists have documented about 250 languages, many spoken by only a few thousand individuals.

MIXED LANGUAGES: THE CASE OF MAISIN

The Maisin language has caused problems for linguists as it shares features of both Austronesian and Papuan languages. It has alternatively been described as an Austronesian language strongly influenced by Papuan features, or as a Papuan language strongly influenced by Austronesian. Professor A. Capell, a life-long researcher of New Guinea languages, viewed Maisin as a "mixed language." However, this theory has been rejected by many linguists, as it does not fit the "family tree" model. Since little is still known about language mixing, this rejection may be premature, and it may be the model which eventually proves to be inadequate.

Other languages have also been described as mixed, such as Magori in southeastern Papua and the Reef-Santa Cruz family in the Solomon Islands. There may be some relationship to the processes of pidginization and creolization as described in Part Two, Chapter 7.

colonized, the whole of Polynesia became an Austronesian-speaking area.

PAPUAN LANGUAGES

Nearly all the languages of the Solomon Islands, Vanuatu, and New Caledonia are Austronesian, but the majority of those of New Guinea are not. The latter used to be classified simply as non-Austronesian languages, but recent research has shown that many are related as families, or more distantly as stocks, or phyla (*see opposite*).

CHARACTERISTICS OF PAPUAN LANGUAGES

As can be expected, with such an enormous group of languages there are few universal features. However, some generalizations can be made. Professor. W. A. Foley, one of the world's leading authorities on Papuan languages, has described in detail the phonology, morphology, and syntax typically found in the group.

Warrior from the highlands.

LANGUAGES OF NEW GUINEA

The map shows the languages mentioned in the text and the main language phyla that have been tentatively identified. Of the 750 or so Papuan languages (shown in green), Enga has the largest number of speakers, some 157,000. The Austronesian languages (shown in pink), scattered around the coast and on surrounding islands, arrived some 5,000 years ago and many have changed radically through contact with Papuan languages.

Mask used during ceremonies to mark the passage from boyhood to manhood. The grass skirt hides the person wearing the mask.

THE MAIN DIVISIONS OF PAPUAN LANGUAGES

Professor Stephan Wurm of the Australian National University coordinated much of the original research which led to the identification of what he termed "the Trans-New Guinea Phylum," a large group of some 500 languages occupying the major portion of New Guinea. Today, the term Papuan rather than non-Austronesian is preferred, highlighting the relationships between the languages. Other phyla, such as the Sepik-Ramu phylum, the Torricelli phylum, and the East and West Papuan phyla have been identified, and there are even some languages termed "isolates" for which no relationship with any other language can be demonstrated. Although a more refined classification of the languages is slowly emerging, many puzzles remain about the relationships between them, and much is lost in the mists of New Guinea's long prehistory.

Papuan Languages

Trans-New Guinea Phylum	West Papuan Phylum	East Papuan Phylum	Torricelli Phylum	Sepik-Ramu Phylum	Minor phyla & Isolates
507 languages	24 languages	27 languages	48 languages	98 languages	37 languages

Papuan languages usually have subject-object-verb (SOV) word order, or at least have the verb in final position. This is in contrast to many of the surrounding Austronesian languages, which typically have SVO order. The verb morphology may be complex (*see box below*), but the morphology of nouns is usually simpler, and restricted to some case marking. Dual pronouns are often distinguished to represent two people, for example "we two" and "you two," as well as the more familiar singular and plural. Within these broad

KIWAI VERBS

Languages of the Kiwai family are spoken around the delta of the Fly River in southwestern Papua by about 25,000 people. The verb morphology of Kiwai is one of the most complex in the world. Various prefixes, suffixes and infixes indicate subtle differences of tense, mood and aspect, and the number of agents or objects, as these examples from Island Kiwai demonstrate:

asidim-ai	"cover one object once"
asidim-o	"keep on covering one object"
i-asidim-ai	"cover more than one object once"
i-asidim-uti	"cover more than one object in separate actions"

Sometimes this process of agglutination can lead to very long verb forms. The most complex so far encountered are the following:

odi	"string a bow"
ri-mi-bi-du-mo-i-odi-ai-ama-ri-go	"in the remote future, they three will definitely string two bows at a time"
atate	"move, remove"
g-a-bi-duru-mo-iw-ar-atate-ai-ama-go	"in the near past they three had the habit of removing many, one at a time"

Fortunately, other aspects of the language, such as phonology and the structure of the noun phrase are not so complex.

generalizations, there is a multitude of individual grammatical features which makes the study of Papuan languages endlessly fascinating.

MULTILINGUALISM

How have the people of Melanesia adapted to such linguistic diversity? One way of overcoming the problems of communication has been a traditionally high rate of

multilingualism. It is still not unusual in Melanesia for people to have a working knowledge of four, five, or even more languages. Since many language groups only have a few hundred speakers, it is almost impossible for individuals to find marriage partners from within their own group. As a result, most children have parents who speak different languages, and as they grow up they may acquire more in communication with relatives from other groups. Adults may have widespread trading networks and acquire at least a working knowledge of their trading partners' languages. In some cases simplified trade languages emerged, such as a simplified Motu in the Gulf of Papua or simplified Yimas or Iatmul in the Sepik. More recently, other languages of wider communication have become established: mission *lingua francas*, Melanesian Pidgin, and the languages of European colonialism.

MISSION LINGUA FRANCAS

Missionaries were some of the earliest European visitors to Melanesia, and by the late nineteenth century, there was already a significant missionary presence in many coastal areas.

Often the missionaries would take an interest in the local languages with the aim of spreading the Christian message more effectively, and some of the earliest linguistic material from the region consists of word lists and sometimes grammar sketches prepared by the missionaries. In Papua New Guinea, a number of local vernaculars were

The Kiwai language family is based around the delta of the Fly River. There are about 25,000 speakers.

POROME: A LANGUAGE WITH
NO KNOWN RELATIVES

The Porome language isolate is spoken by some 1,000 people in a remote corner of the Gulf Province in western Papua. So far, it has not been linked with any of the other languages of the area. Its vocabulary and grammar are quite unlike the surrounding languages from the Kiwaian family. It has a number of unusual features, such as the presence of nasal vowels and absence of subject marking on the verb.

The origin of Porome continues to be one of the fascinating unsolved mysteries facing linguists in this part of the world. However, as more and better data become available, it is possible that relationships will eventually be established.

adopted as languages of wider communication for mission-related activities (*see map*). Even today, the Summer Institute of Linguistics, a Christian organization, carries out much of the field investigation of Papua New Guinea languages, as workers describe the grammars of local languages and cooperate with local language-speakers to produce vernacular versions of the gospels.

Melanesian Pidgin

While multilingualism may have been an adequate solution to the problems of Melanesian language diversity when communities were isolated, the twentieth century has seen an opening-up of the area, and new opportunities for travel. Laborers from the New Hebrides, the Solomon Islands, and the New Guinea islands were recruited to work on the plantations of Queensland and the Central Pacific, giving rise to the various varieties of Melanesian pidgin

(*see Part Two, Chapter 7*). Originally pidgin was a means of surviving in a multilingual plantation environment, but when laborers returned to their home communities it had immediate currency as a language of wider communication in areas where inter-tribal contact was increasing rapidly due to mission and government activity. The descendants of this early pidgin, Tok Pisin in Papua New Guinea, Pijin in the Solomon Islands, and Bislama in Vanuatu, are now firmly established as languages of national unity in the emerging democracies of the southwestern Pacific. A variety known as "Broken" is widely spoken in the Torres Strait in northern Australia, but has no official status.

HIRI MOTU

Another interesting development of a pidgin language is the case of Hiri Motu. Motu is a native Austronesian language spoken by people in 12 coastal villages near the capital city Port Moresby. Early missionaries attempted to learn Motu, but it was later apparent that what the locals taught them was just a simplified version. This supports the suggestion made by some theorists that "foreigner talk" is

Mission lingua francas developed in the nineteenth century as a means of communication between European missionaries and the local peoples. Most of the painstaking study and recording of Papuan languages was undertaken by missionaries.

important in the formation of pidgins. Later, a pidginized form of the language was used by the administration, especially the police, on patrols to other parts of Papua, giving rise to its alternative name, Police Motu. The somewhat romanticized name Hiri Motu is a reflection of the past trading activity of the Motuan people, who used a simplified form of their language on expeditions known as *hiri*, sailing large canoes westward to the Gulf of Papua, where they traded pots for sago. However, it is doubtful if the language used on such expeditions was in fact a direct ancestor of today's Hiri Motu, which is formally recognized as one of the country's official languages alongside Tok Pisin and English.

EUROPEAN COLONIAL LANGUAGES.

Like many other parts of the world, Melanesia has a complex history of colonization by outside powers, especially the nineteenth century Europeans. The western half of the island of New Guinea was colonized by the Dutch in 1828. In the late nineteenth century, Britain occupied the southern half of the mainland, first known as British New Guinea and later Papua. Germany took control of the northern half of the mainland and the islands of New Britain, New Ireland, and Bougainville. Following World War I, the whole of the eastern part of New Guinea and the adjacent islands came under Australian administration. In 1963 Dutch New Guinea became the Indonesian province of Irian Jaya.

The Solomon Islands eventually became a protectorate of Britain long after the Spanish, who originally claimed the discovery of the fabulous "Isles of Solomon" but failed to rediscover the location of their prize. The New Hebrides became a unique Anglo-French condominium under joint administration, while the French took New Caledonia, which remains a colony today. Thus English, French, German, Dutch, and more recently Bahasa Indonesia, came to be spoken in the region. The Solomon Islands gained independence in 1978, Vanuatu in 1980, and Papua New Guinea in 1975.

SURVIVAL OF MELANESIAN LANGUAGES

As communication, education, and modernization proceed, there is considerable pressure on many of the smaller languages of Melanesia. The use of English in education and of varieties of Melanesian Pidgin as national languages means that many children are failing to acquire their parents' traditional tongues, and since many have fewer than 500 speakers, their future is uncertain. The plight of the Susuami language (*see p.109*) is typical.

Some steps are being taken to promote language maintenance. The Summer Institute of Linguistics is doing much work on the grammars of local languages, other non-government organizations are involved in the promotion of vernacular literacy, and recent government policy in Papua New Guinea

---

THE SOUNDS OF ROTOKAS

Generally the phonology of Papuan languages is relatively simple compared with other language groups. It is quite common, for example, for there to be only five vowels. One of the Papuan languages of Bougainville in the North Solomons, Rotokas, has achieved fame in *The Guinness Book of Records* as the language with the world's smallest number of phonemes. It has 11, compared, for example, with the 44 in English. These 11 distinct sounds consist of 5 vowels and 6 consonants.

Vowels

a	e	i	o	u

Consonants

b	g	k	p	r	t

All Rotokas words are constructed from the above basic sound distinctions. This leads to a certain amount of repetition of the basic elements.

HIRI MOTU: A PIDGIN LANGUAGE FROM PAPUA

A pidginized form of the Austronesian language Motu was used on trading expeditions (*hiri*) to the Gulf of Papua. Later, the name Hiri Motu was applied to the language based on Motu used by the colonial administration in other areas of Papua. It was also sometimes known as "Police Motu." The following examples show how Hiri Motu is simplified as morphological features of Motu are omitted.

Motu	Hiri Motu
umui iboumuiai	*umui ibounai*
"you [plural] all"	"you [plural] all"
idia iboudiai	*idia ibounai*
"they all"	"they all"

In Hiri Motu, number and person inflections are lost and the general adverb *ibonai* is used with all pronouns.

Similarly, in "Pure" Motu, a distinction is made between *ruma ibounai* meaning "the whole house" and *ruma iboudiai* meaning "all the houses," while in Hiri Motu, *ruma ibounai* is used for both. A further example:

Motu	Hiri Motu
lau ese baina abia	*dohori lau abia*
"I [subject] I [future] get it"	"[future] I get"
ia ese baine abia	*dohori ia abia*
"he [subject] he future get it"	"future he get"

has increased emphasis on preservation of traditional cultural values, including languages. In several provinces vernacular pre-schools now teach initial literacy in the mother tongue before formal schooling begins. In spite of these encouraging moves, a number of small languages have disappeared in recent years, and many others must be considered to be under acute threat.

SUSUAMI: A MORIBUND LANGUAGE

Susuami is a language spoken in the resettlement village of Manki in the Upper Watut Valley in northeast New Guinea. In 1980 there were approximately 50 speakers, but already the language was threatened by a number of other languages spoken in the same village. Most of the other inhabitants of the village spoke the distantly related languages Hamtai or Angaataha, while many spoke Tok Pisin to communicate with outsiders. Marriage partners speaking half a dozen other languages were also living there.

By 1990, the number of Susuami speakers

had shrunk to about a dozen. Children were failing to acquire the language, even the children of the only married couple who were both native speakers of Susuami. The prognosis for this language, like many other Melanesian languages with fewer than 50 speakers, is gloomy indeed.

A complex colonial history has had an impact on the languages of the region. The map shows that the dominant colonial powers were Britain, France, Germany, and the Netherlands.

Australia

The aboriginal languages are a repository of ancient knowledge, myths, and traditions, many of which were lost with the colonial breakdown of aboriginal society. These languages are now known to be highly complex both grammatically and socially, with nuances and taboos reflecting the elaborate kinship systems of aboriginal communities. Today, their richness is belatedly being recognized, and attempts to halt their decline are underway. Bilingual education may offer a future for the aboriginal languages and culture which remain.

An Australian Aborigine in traditional body paint. Today, 66 percent of aboriginal peoples live in towns, and there is a danger that their long-established ways of life and unique languages will be lost.

VICTORIA

Bass Strait

KING ISLAND

ROBBINS
ISLAND

FLINDERS
ISLAND

CAPE BARREN
ISLAND

CLARKE
ISLAND

CIRCULAR HEAD

NORTH
WESTERN

NORTHERN   PORT
SORELL

Launceston

PIPER
RIVER

CAPE
PORTLAND

BEN
LOMOND

UNOCCUPIED

NORTH
MIDLANDS

TASMANIA

Derwent

MACQUARIE
HARBOUR

BIG RIVER

OYSTER
BAY

LITTLE
SWANPORT

Southern
Ocean

SOUTH

Hobart
SOUTH
EASTERN

WESTERN

BRUNY ISLAND

Tasman
Sea

TASMANIA

At least nine groups, speaking distinct languages, populated Tasmania before British settlement. In the 1830s, in an effort to put end to conflicts between aboriginals and settlers, the remaining native Tasmanians were moved to Flinders Island where, lacking a common language, they resorted to pidgin English and succumbed to western diseases. As an Aborigine who left the colony explained: "Too much sickness at Flinders at Pea Jacket Point. Too much dead man."

show great diversity. Some scholars have suggested that all the languages, Pama-Nyungan and non-Pama-Nyungan, are ultimately related and come from an ancestor called proto-Australian, probably spoken many thousands of years ago. This hypothesis is generally accepted, but has not been proven in detail (unlike, say, proto-Indo-European, which is the ancestor of most of the modern languages of Europe).

TASMANIAN LANGUAGES

The Tasmanian Aborigines suffered a terrible fate at the hands of the European settlers and were almost exterminated in a campaign of genocide backed by the British government. The people of Tasmania looked different from the mainland Aborigines, and their lifestyle was relatively simpler and adapted to the special requirements of their southerly environment. Archeological records indicate

that Tasmania was separated from mainland Australia by rising seas some 10,000 years ago (at the end of the last Ice Age) and remained socially and culturally isolated from the rest of the world until the Europeans arrived in 1804. The Tasmanians, for example, did not have domestic dogs, which were introduced to the mainland some 4,000 years ago.

The materials we have on the languages of Tasmania are fragmentary; they date from the last century and almost all were collected by amateurs who did a very poor job of recording in writing what they heard. However, the records indicate that there were at least nine separate communities living on the island when Europeans arrived, each speaking their own language. The nature of the languages

The island of Tasmania, located off the south coast of Australia, was discovered in 1642 by Abel Tasman, a Dutch navigator. It was taken over by Britain in 1803 and served as a penal settlement.

and their grammatical structure remains unknown, and we are also unable to tell if the Tasmanian languages were related to those spoken on the mainland.

Despite the appalling history of the European colonization of Tasmania, Aboriginal people continued to care for their traditions and preserve what knowledge remained; in 1972, for example, a linguistic researcher, Terry Crowley, recorded a lady in Hobart who taught him some words and one sentence that had been handed down for several generations, even though the language had not been used for daily communication since the 1830s. As in many areas of Australia, the Tasmanian people are working on recovering their lost languages and traditions.

Students at the Yirara Aboriginal College, Alice Springs. In 1972 the Australian government established bilingual education in the Northern Territory, and there are now about thirty bi-lingual programs.

TORRES STRAIT ISLAND LANGUAGES

The people living on the islands in the Torres Strait (between Australia and Papua New Guinea) are primarily Melanesian in origin. Two indigenous languages are spoken there: Kala Lagaw Ya is spoken by people in the western and central islands (including Saibai, Mabuiag, Masig, and Yam), while Meriam Mer is spoken on the eastern islands of Mer, Erub, and Ugar. Kala Lagaw Ya is related to the Aboriginal languages of the Pama-Nyungan group, while Meriam Mer is completely different and related to languages spoken on the coast of Papua New Guinea. Today, there are about 5,000 speakers of these languages. The Torres Strait island people, including sizeable communities who have migrated to mainland Queensland, strongly maintain their distinctive culture, especially its music, dance, and songs.

A third language, Broken or Blaikman Tok, is spoken in the Torres Strait islands and other neighboring areas. This creole has become the first language of most people under 50 years of age.

NEW LANGUAGES: PIDGINS AND CREOLES

When communities come into contact and they do not share a common language, the need to communicate can sometimes give rise to new languages. This has been the case in Australia, and pidgins and creoles have consequently developed. From the earliest days of settlement, Aboriginal people developed pidgin varieties of English to communicate with the settlers, who showed little interest in learning their speech. These basic languages use words, primarily from English, mixed with words from other languages in rudimentary sentence structures. An example is the following quotation from a Tasmanian Aborigine in an official government report: "Blackfellow no come back. Too much sickness at Flinders at Pea Jacket Point. Too much dead man. Blackman frightened like to crackenny [die] bust."

When a pidgin becomes widely used in a community and children begin to learn it as their first language it can develop into a creole, which is a full language with a developed grammatical system. This has happened in the northern part of Australia, where two creoles are now spoken by many thousands of Aboriginal people. Cape York Creole is spoken in the northern Cape York peninsula and the islands in the Torres Strait, where it is also called "Broken" or "Blaikman Tok". Kriol is spoken from the Kimberley region of Western Australia through into western Arnhemland in the Northern Territory. These two languages have a full grammatical structure that differs in significant ways from English and pidgin. In Kriol, for example, there are several ways to express "we" (as in Aboriginal languages): *yunmi* "we two, you and I," *mintupala* "we two, he and I," *mipala* "we all, including you," and *melabat* "we all, excluding you." The following comment from a Kriol-speaker, Ralph Dingul, who comes from Ngukurr on the Roper River in northeastern Australia, demonstrates the differences between Kriol and English:

La Ngukurr melabat garrim eitbala langgus. Wen naja traib wandim tok la dis traib, dei tok mijalb garrim Kriol. Jad impotan langgus im Kriol. Olabat gan sabi bla wanim olabat toktok. (" At Ngukurr, we have eight languages. When another tribe wants to talk to this tribe they talk to each other in Kriol. The important language is Kriol. They all can understand whatever they want to discuss.")

Bilingual education is now undertaken in Kriol at several centers in northern Australia and publication in the language has been established, including Bible translations, dictionaries, and school books.

STRUCTURE OF THE LANGUAGES

The pronunciation of Aboriginal languages shows a remarkable degree of similarity across the continent. Usually, just three to five vowels are distinguished, and a larger number of consonants. Most languages do not distinguish

WORD ENDINGS IN ABORIGINAL LANGUAGES

Word endings in the Jiwarli language of Western Australia are used to express fine shades of meaning:

ngatha parlirrinyja   "I returned"
ngatha jurla nhanyanyja   "I saw a tree"
ngatha ("I") is used for the subject of a sentence.

thuthungku ngathanha nhanyanja   "The dog saw me"
ngathanha (formed by adding the ending *nha* to *ngatha*) indicates "me" and is used for the object of a sentence.

All pronoun objects take this *nha* ending, as do words referring to human beings and animals (but not other things, which is why *jurla* "tree" has no ending in the example above).

For words other than "I," however, there is a difference in the form of intransitive subjects and transitive subjects (transitive subjects are the subjects of verbs like "hit" or "see" that require an object, intransitive subjects are the subjects of verbs like "go" or "fall" that do not take an object):
thuthu parlirrinyja   "The dog returned"
thuthu "dog" has no ending, but:
thuthungku ngathanha nhanyanyja "The dog saw me"
The ending *ngku* indicates a transitive subject.

jumangku thuthunha nhanyanja   "The child saw the dog"
thuthu takes the ending *nha*, to indicate a transitive object.

Typically, the ending selected varies according to the shape (pronunciation) of a word: in Jiwarli, words of two syllables take *ngku* for transitive subject, but words of three or more syllables take *lu*.

The subject and object of the sentence can always be identified by the form of the word, so word order is free:
thuthunha jumangku nhanyanyja   "The child saw the dog"
nhanyanyja thuthunha jumangku   "The child saw the dog"
Compare English "The child saw the dog" versus "The dog saw the child."

In addition to these endings, nouns and pronouns also take case endings to indicate location, direction and possession, as in Jiwarli:

thuthungka	"with the dog"
thuthurla	"to the dog"
thuthuparnti	"from the dog"
thuthuwu	"belonging to the dog"

It is possible to attach an ending before the case marker which expresses concepts like the number of items, as in *kutharra* ("two"), *martu* ("small group"), and *nyjarri* ("many"):

*thuthu**kutharra**rla*	"to the two dogs"
*thuthu**martu**rla*	"to the group of dogs"

Further subtle expressions of meaning are possible through the use of other suffixes, for example *jaka* "having", or *yirra* "'lacking."

between p and b, t and d, k and g, and ch and j. Although these sound different to European ears, Aboriginal languages have sounds that are part-way between each of these pairs; the result is that often there are two or more spellings in English for a single term because different people wrote down the word. (Thus the Arrente people of central Australia were formerly called both "Arunta" and "Aranda.") On the other hand, the languages often distinguish sounds which are not found in English, or use familiar sounds in unfamiliar ways. For example, all Aboriginal languages have a sound *ng* (as at the end of English "sing"); frequently words begin with this sound (such as *ngaya* "I" in many languages), creating a problem for English-speakers to copy. Most languages have two r sounds: a trilled r, as in Scottish English (written "rr" in modern spellings) and a glide r, as in American English (written "r" in modern orthographies). In languages of central, western, and northern Australia there are retroflex r-colored sounds reminiscent of those found in the languages of India; these are written as "rn" and "rt." Aboriginal languages do not normally have sounds such as s, z, sh, h, th, f, and v. Word forms are relatively straightforward and pronunciation and stress is quite rhythmical.

In their grammars Aboriginal languages show great use of word endings to express fine shades of meaning. Nouns and pronouns characteristically change their endings according to function (*see opposite*). Because of the existence of these endings, the order of words in a sentence is completely free. Word order in these languages is used for stylistic reasons to express emphasis

A seated Aborigine plays the didgeridu, a deep-toned wind instrument. The Aboriginal population of Australia is about 250,000; economically and socially marginalized, they still face severe discrimination. From the 1970s they have made an increasingly well-organized stand against land rights abuses, as well as championing their own civil rights. The status accorded Aboriginal languages has inevitably been an important part of this political agenda.

Central Australia is a vast area of arid semi-desert. It was occupied by European settlers on the basis that the land was terra nullius *(belonging to no-one). As a result of Aboriginal campaigns, the concept of* terra nullius *was rescinded in 1992.*

or contrast, not to indicate who does the action and who suffers it.

In northern Australian (non-Pama-Nyungan) languages, nouns and adjectives can take prefixes (elements attached before the word) and these indicate the class or gender of the noun. For example, in Kunwinyku (northern Territory) *na-* is masculine, *ki-* is feminine, *ma-* is plant, and *ku-* is neuter. In languages of the Kimberley region even more classes are distinguished.

Pronouns in Aboriginal languages also express contrasts not found in English. Typically, three numbers are distinguished: singular (one); dual (two); plural (three or more). To express "we" in the dual and plural forms, the languages make a contrast between including the person spoken to ("inclusive") and excluding that person ("exclusive"). Jiwarli has four forms for "we": *ngali* "we two including you," *ngaliju* "we two excluding you," *nganthurru* "we all including you," and *nganthurraju* "we all excluding you." In some languages the kinship status of the persons speaking can also be reflected in the choice of pronoun used.

A Mayali word can correspond to an English sentence:

abanyawoihwarrgahmarneganjginjeng

aban	*yawoih*	*warrgah*	*marne*	*ganj*	*ginje*	*ng*
"I-them"	"again"	"wrong"	"for"	"meat"	"cook"	"past"

"I cooked the wrong meat for them again"

Verbs also change their endings to express meaning differences, such as tense. In Jiwarli, for example, tense is expressed as follows: distant past *nhanyaartu* "used to see," recent past *nhanyanja* "saw," present *nhanyinha* "sees," and future *nhanyara* "will see." There is also an ending to express an order, as in *nhanyama* "see! look!" In addition, many Aboriginal languages have endings which express concepts that have no equivalent in European languages. For example, to express the purpose of an action ("in order to ...") the ending *ngku* is added if the same person does both actions, and *puka* if not: *ngatha mirlimirli mananyja nhanya*ngku "I brought the book to look at," but *ngatha mirlimirli mananyja nhurralu nhanya*puka "I brought the book for you to look at."

Among northern (non-Pama-Nyungan) languages verbs typically take prefixes that indicate the subject and object involved in the action, and often take other prefixes or suffixes that express ancillary information. Complex verb forms in these languages correspond to a whole sentence in a language such as English *(see below left)*.

These subtle grammatical distinctions give the languages great expressive power that is difficult to convey in translation, especially in the poetic language of mythology and songs.

Many people in Australia believe that Aboriginal languages are simple and have few words, but their vocabularies are in fact large and well developed. A recently published dictionary of Arrernte, for example, is over 750 pages long. The languages are able to express fine shades of meaning and have many words for describing the physical and social world in which the people live. Many specific terms are used for different species of flora and fauna, aspects of the landscape, parts of the body, kinship, and for those items used in people's daily lives. Terms for feelings and emotions are particularly well developed, as are words for different types of actions (the Jiwarli, for example, have three different words for "carry," depending on whether something is carried on the head, in the hand, or on the back). The languages have also developed ways of talking about the modern world, either by borrowing from English or by coining new combinations from old words (the Jiwarli call a dentist *yirrawa wiingkalji*, literally "tooth puller").

KINSHIP AND LANGUAGE

The core of Aboriginal traditional society centers on kinship relations; everyone in the community is classified as a relative through blood or marriage, and there are complex systems of referring to and addressing kin. In addition, rules of appropriate behavior are governed by the kinship system; in all communities, for example, a man must act in a restrained and respectful way towards his wife's mother. In some communities they must completely avoid one another and cannot speak. Contact with other relatives, such as between a man and his sisters, is also restricted and is typically registered by the use of a style of speech which indicates respect. These respect styles have the same grammatical structure as ordinary speech, but they use completely different words, often with more general and polite meanings. In some areas pronouns (words for "I" and "you," and so on) vary according to the nature of the relationship between the people speaking (much as French uses *tu* "you" for intimate friends and family, and *vous* for strangers).

Among the Adnyamathanha (South Australia) there are ten sets of pronouns distinguishing such kinship relations.

In some communities there are also respect styles connected with the rituals of male initiation; among the Panyjima of Western Australia, for example, men must use the *paathupathu* respect style in the presence of the man who initiated them.

In addition to kinship relations, Australian Aboriginal communities are also divided into social groups according to the marriage system. Among the Jiwarli of Western Australia there are four groups (called "sections" by anthropologists and "skins" by Aboriginal people): *panaka, karimarra, palyarri,* and *purungu.* A *panaka* man must marry a *karrimara* woman and their children will be *purungu;* a *karimarra* man marries a *panaka* woman and their children will be *palyarri.* These groupings are reflected in language; a *karimarra* man speaking to two other

PLAINS KANGAROO AND HILL KANGAROO

Here is a traditional story from the Jiwarli people of Western Australia told by the late Jack Butler. It deals with the time of the Ancestral Beings (called in Jiwarli ngurra pulharalapurra "when the earth was soft") and explains why the hill kangaroo and the plains kangaroo now live in different places:

Kurrpirli mathanma kumpaja wangkaarni ngana kumpayi parlungka ngana kumpayi parlkarrala. Mathanma wangkaja. Nhurra tharrpama nyirnta walhungka. Ngurntama nhurra nyirnta jumangka walhungka. Kurrpirli ngunha tharrpanyja ngurntayi walhungka ngunhi jumangka parlungka. Kurrpirli wangkaja. Nhaarrinyjarru. Nhurra ngarta ngurntinha jurungka. Kurrpirli wangkaja. Nhurra tharrpama ngurntayi. Pikurta tharrpanyja ngunhipa walhungka ngurntayi. Nhurra ngurntinha pirturarru warrirru mulku nhanyapuka manthartalu kurningurru nhurrampa. Nhurra kumpama parlunyungu. Ngunha wangkaja.

Ngaa. Nhurra yanama kumpayi. Kurrpirli wangkaja. Nhurra yanama pukartirarrila kumpayi parlkarrala malungka ngurntayi pukartila kujilarapirrila.

"Plains kangaroo and hill kangaroo were talking to one another about who would live in the hills and who would live on the plain. Hill kangaroo said: 'You go into the cave here. You lie down here in the small cave.' Plains kangaroo went in to lie there in the small cave. Plains kangaroo asked: 'What happened?' 'Your legs are lying in the sun' (replied the hill kangaroo). Plains kangaroo said: 'You go in to lie down.' Hill kangaroo went in there to lie in the cave. 'You are lying hidden so you won't be seen by men looking for you. You should live among the hills.' Hill kangaroo said: 'Yes. You go and live there. You go to live amongst the snakewood on the plain to lie in the snakewood and amongst the mulga trees.'"

European settlers borrowed Aboriginal words for the new plants, animals and landscapes they encountered in Australia. The word 'kangaroo' comes from Guugu Yimidhirr, spoken in the Cooktown region, and was recorded in the journals of Captain James Cook.

karimarra men will call them *kurtarra*, but if he is speaking to a *karimarra* and a *panaka* man he will say *ngathalkarra*. There are terms for all the other possible combinations of sections.

ORAL CULTURE

Each Aboriginal group has a store of myths, stories, and songs handed down by word of mouth from generation to generation. Much of the traditional mythology deals with the travels and actions of the Ancestral Beings, the ancestors of modern humans, animals, and plants. The Ancestral Beings lived long ago when the Earth was being formed (called "The Dreamtime" in

In the language of the Arrernte people of central Australia, aarwe-iltyinke *('rock wallabies with their tails tied together') is a game resembling cat's cradle. The designs represent parts of stories chanted by children (see below)*

Australian English), and through their actions they created the features of the landscape and established the customs and traditions that Aboriginal people follow today. Throughout Australia the land is covered with sacred sites, placenames, and names for geographical features that reflect these Ancestral actions; the mythology celebrates and retells the past and carries it through to the present. Some

of this knowledge is sacred and restricted to people who have been through ceremonies of initiation, while other stories and songs are known to all.

Complex song cycles, often many hundreds of lines long, also have their origins in the Ancestral Beings. In some areas song cycles and myths are shared by neighboring groups with each group owning its own particular section of the song or myth, traditions can then stretch for many hundreds of miles as the Ancestral Beings travelled from place to place, changing language and style as appropriate for the people whose country they travelled through. Individual Aboriginal people can know dozens of these myths and songs.

In some cases there is clear evidence that Aboriginal people handed down their stories and songs for many hundreds of generations. There are stories from Queensland of Ancestral Beings walking across dry land to what are now islands off the coast. It was in fact possible to walk to these places during the last Ice Age, some 10,000 years ago, when the sea level was lower than now, though it has not been possible since the sea levels rose. Similarly, in the Pilbara region of Western Australia people have a word for a dog-like animal whose description matches that of the *thylacine*, or Tasmanian tiger (rock engravings in this region also depict

Curlews wrestling at night

Running water

A well

Three eagles: mother, father and baby in the middle

SIGN LANGUAGE

I n many communities sign languages are used alongside the normal oral means of communication in two special circumstances: by hunters to signal messages silently so as not to disturb game, and much more widely, by women who are in mourning. A woman must spend a period of time in mourning after the death of her husband. During this period, she cannot travel about and is not allowed to feed herself or communicate in spoken language, so sign language is used by the women to communicate with one another. It consists of many hundreds of hand shapes and movements to signal words and meanings.

An example of sign language from the Arrernte people of central Australia is the sign for aherre 'kangaroo' which begins as a closed hand and moves to an open shape.

thylacines). This animal has been extinct on the mainland for many thousands of years, and survived until early this century only on the island of Tasmania.

As well as this type of oral literature there are also songs and stories of a more ordinary nature that deal with day-to-day matters – stories of love and hate and rivalries between people and groups, love songs, songs to make rain or increase animal and plant species, and curses to inflict pain and suffering on others. In many areas there are also stories and songs that report on the first contact with European settlers, from amusing anecdotes about the strange actions of the new arrivals to chilling details of massacres and murders carried out by the Europeans as they took away the land and livelihood of the original inhabitants.

LANGUAGE AND EDUCATION

In the early period of contact between Aborigines and Europeans, Aboriginal languages were used in some mission communities for church and school functions, and books, primers, and

Cave painting of the Wardaman people of northern Australia. About 50 of these people remain, now speaking mostly Kriol.

functions, and books, primers, and dictionaries were published in them. Many books were published in the language of the Diyari from Lake Eyre between 1870 and 1910, for example, but from around the turn of the century until 1972 Aboriginal languages in general were given a very minor role in community life. In 1972 the Australian government established bilingual education in the Northern Territory, and there are now around thirty bilingual programs operating in central and northern Australia, with children beginning school in their own languages and gradually being introduced to English (*see map*). The academic and social success of these programs has been widely demonstrated, as has their role in helping to stem the decline in the number of speakers of traditional languages. Aboriginal groups have also set up language centers throughout Australia to assist with the documentation and development of the languages, and to produce literacy materials. In areas where languages are under threat the centers assist in the preservation and revival of languages.

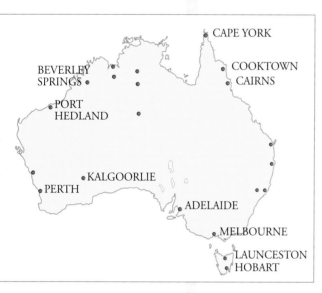

A number of Aboriginal language centers, set up to record and develop disappearing languages, are to be found throughout Australia.

Today, Aboriginal languages are used in education, publications, films, video, and in the media; the Central Australia Aboriginal Media Association, for example, broadcasts in four languages in Alice Springs, while Imparja television carries Aboriginal language material throughout central Australia. Aboriginal bands have also become popular among young people of all races, with some perfomers using traditional languages in their songs; the internationally-known band Yothu Yindi, for example, sings popular songs in Gumatj from

eastern Arnhemland (see World Wide Web http: //www.yothuyindi. com). In this way Aboriginal languages are facing the challenges of use in the modern Australian community.

ABORIGINAL WORDS IN ENGLISH

A striking feature of the English spoken in Australia is that it contains many words that originate in the Aboriginal languages. As the settlers established themselves they came across many new plants, animals, and features of the landscape that were unknown in Europe, and often borrowed a term from one of the local languages and adapted it into English. Often the pronunciation of the Aboriginal word has been altered somewhat in the process of borrowing (and sometimes the meaning also), but in many cases it is possible to discover which language the word has been taken from. Perhaps the most famous example is "kangaroo" which comes from Guugu Yimidhirr of the Cooktown region through the journal of Captain James Cook, who first saw these unique marsupials when he and his crew put in to the Endeavour River for repairs to their ship.

Aboriginal bands, such as Yothu Yindi, use traditional languages in their songs and have acquired a worldwide following.

BORROWINGS FROM ABORIGINAL LANGUAGES IN ENGLISH

The main areas where English has borrowed from Aboriginal languages are the following:

• names for animals, such as: barramundi, dingo, koala, wallaby, wallaroo, and wombat;

• names for birds, such as: brolga, budgerigar, currawong, galah, and kookaburra;

• names for plants, such as: bindi-eye, coolabah, gidgee, karri and mulga;

• features of the landscape and Aboriginal artefacts, such as: billabong (river pool), gibber (stone), coolamon (bark dish), woomera (spear thrower), and wurley (shelter).

In addition, many hundreds of names of places in Australia come from Aboriginal languages. Some of these have descriptive meanings, while others have origins in the mythology and actions of the Ancestral Beings, and do not have direct translations (despite the often fanciful etymologies given in place name books in Australia). Some examples of descriptive names are:

Boggabri "having creeks" from *bagaaybaraay* (New South Wales)

Coonamble "full of feces" from *gunambil* (New South Wales)

Wonthaggi "fetch!" (Victoria)

Ali Curung "two dogs" from *alikerrenge* (Northern Territory)

Kata Tjuta "many heads" (also called The Olgas, Northern Territory)

Native species, such as the koala and kookaburra, are unique to Australia and New Guinea. European settlers, on first encountering these species, borrowed the Aboriginal names.

The Americas

The languages of the Sioux, Mayans, Incas, and Eskimos are just a few of the several hundred native tongues spoken before the Europeans' colonization of the Americas. Belonging to several families, they are complex and highly diverse, with histories that are still being disentangled. Today, although some indigenous languages such as Guaraní and Quechua still thrive in South and Central America, many others are on their way to extinction, and in the North most are already lost.

The United States welcomed immigrants from all parts of the world and, as a result, the country became a mixture of many different cultures and religions.

The native languages of the Americas, before the arrival of Columbus, were widespread and numerous. Over this vast territory there were, by any reckoning, dozens of language families, more varied than the Indo-European or the African Bantu, and hundreds, maybe thousands, of individual languages. Since the advent of the Europeans, the numbers of speakers of many of these have severely dwindled, with many formerly spoken over large areas now represented only by small isolated elderly groups. Some are no longer spoken at all.

Nevertheless, some languages have survived and retain an old and valuable literary tradition. The importance of these languages and cultures is now being acknowledged, and programs are currently being developed to support the use of native American languages in various settings, including movies such as *Dances with Wolves*, in which actual Lakhota Sioux is heard.

LANGUAGE GROUPS IN THE AMERICAS

A study of the original distribution and family relationships of these languages can help to establish whether similarities are due to chance, to prolonged contact, or to family relationships. The languages of the Americas will be divided into three separate groups: those of North America, of Mexico and Central America, and of South America. This grouping is arbitrary, for the native peoples themselves did not make the sort of political divisions that the European colonists subsequently imposed, but it does proceed from the languages with which linguists are most familiar (that is, the North American ones) and, perhaps not coincidentally, reflects the increasing vitality of the languages themselves as one goes from best to least known.

The languages of the Americas form a continuous chain from the Arctic Ocean in the North to Tierra del Fuego in the South, and from the Atlantic Ocean to the Pacific, with adjacent languages often, though not always, closely related. Several of the groups of North America also appear in Central America; in Mexico, for example, there are a number of Aztec-Tanoan languages, including Diegueño and Yaqui, and perhaps the best recorded earlier representative, Nahuatl, the language of Montezuma and the Aztec Empire. Hokan-Siouan languages, Penutian languages, and even a member of the Algonquian branch of Algic, a language called Kickapoo (made famous by Al Capp in the comic strip "L'il Abner") are also found in Mexico.

The large Mayan family is spread throughout Central America with numerous

Language Families of Central America

Aztec-Tanoan

Hokan-Siouan

Mayan

Oto-Manguean

Penutian

Totomac

The 1990 movie "Dances with Wolves" broke new ground by using the Lakhota language of the Sioux for at least a third of the dialog. Filmed on location in South Dakota, its positive portrayal of Sioux culture was a marked departure from traditional Westerns.

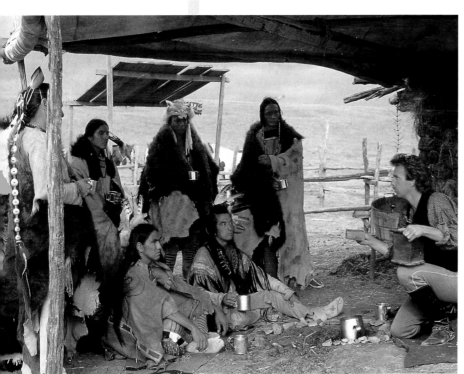

branches and many languages within each branch.

Oto-Manguean is found principally in Mexico, where it is represented by seven sub-families comprising around 150 different languages.

The Totonac family is small, with only two branches, Tepehua and Totonac, and less than a dozen different languages, yet their number of speakers is estimated at about 300,000, probably more than all the speakers of Native languages in North America. The Totonac languages tend to be spoken by people of all ages, who also speak Spanish, the national language of most of the countries of the region. On average there are several thousand speakers of each language and tens of thousands in each language family. In Mexico alone there are some 240 different languages belonging to all of the six major families listed in the table above, as well as the Algic Kickapoo found on the northeastern border.

The Mysterious Mayan Hieroglyphs

The Mayan hieroglyphs present one of the most fascinating puzzles of linguistic analysis since Jean-François Champollion, in the early nineteenth century, began the decipherment of Egyptian hieroglyphics with the aid of the Rosetta Stone. The Mayans had a highly developed system of writing based on hieroglyphics, which can be found on monuments all over the vast Mayan Empire. It

Mayan pyramid at Uxmal. Pyramids were built within formal geomatic layouts at the heart of Mayan ceremonial cities and held religious and astronomical significance.

LANGUAGE FAMILIES OF NORTH AMERICA

Eskimo-Aleut	Algic	Mosan	Na-Dene	Hokan-Siouan	Penutian	Aztec-Tanoan
Inuktitu	Cree	Nootka	Navajo	Lakhota	Tsimshian	Comanche

The large Algic family, including Algonquian and the Californian Ritwan languages Yurok and Wiyot, spreads across all ten Canadian provinces and over 20 U.S. states as well as to the northeastern corner of Mexico.

Algic
- Algonquian
  - Arapaho Blackfoot Cheyenne Cree E. Algonquian Ojibway Shawnee
- Ritwan
  - Wiyot Yurok

Mosan is a more contentious classification, first proposed by Sapir in the 1920s. Based on certain similarities, it groups together three distinct language families, Chemakuan, Salishan, and Wakashan. The name itself comes from the similar form of the word for "four" in the group which is typically *muu* or *mos* followed by the suffix *-an*.

Mosan
- Chemakuan
  - Chemakum Quileute
- Salish
  - Bella-Coola Coast Interior
- Wakashan
  - Northern Southern Nuuchahnulth

Na-Dene is a family which groups the Haida and Tlingit languages of the Pacific Northwest, together with another extremely widespread group, the Athabaskan languages, spoken from Alaska (Koyukon) to the American Southwest (Navajo and Apache), and from the West Coast (Hupa) to Hudson Bay (Chipewyan), over a thousand miles inland.

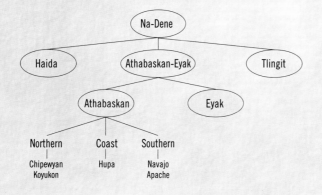

Na-Dene
- Haida
- Athabaskan-Eyak
  - Athabaskan
    - Northern
      - Chipewyan
      - Koyukon
    - Coast
      - Hupa
    - Southern
      - Navajo
      - Apache
  - Eyak
- Tlingit

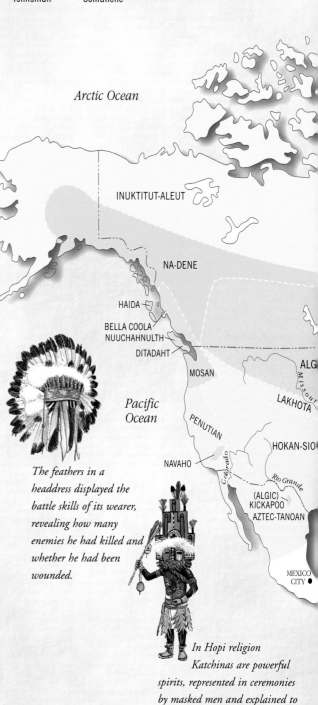

Arctic Ocean

INUKTITUT-ALEUT

NA-DENE

HAIDA

BELLA COOLA
NUUCHAHNULTH
DITADAHT

MOSAN

ALG

Pacific Ocean

LAKHOTA

PENUTIAN

HOKAN-SIO

NAVAHO

(ALGIC) KICKAPOO
AZTEC-TANOAN

MEXICO CITY ●

The feathers in a headdress displayed the battle skills of its wearer, revealing how many enemies he had killed and whether he had been wounded.

In Hopi religion Katchinas are powerful spirits, represented in ceremonies by masked men and explained to children through dolls.

The Hokan-Siouan family is represented by a number of languages which ranged west from New England over the Canadian and American plains down to Texas, California, and Mexico.

The Penutian family is composed of loosely-related sub-families located mainly in California and Oregon State, and also further south in Central America.

Finally, the Aztec-Tanoan family is found in Mexico, Central America, and over a large area of the western United States, in the form of languages such as Cahuilla, Cupeño, Diegueño, Kawaiisu, Luiseño, and Serrano (southern California), Comanche and Kiowa (Oklahoma), Paiute (Nevada/Oregon), Papago/Pima and Yaqui (Arizona), Tiwa (New Mexico), and Shoshone (California/Nevada/Idaho/Wyoming/Utah).

LANGUAGES OF NORTH AMERICA

The languages of North America, and of the Americas in general, can be subdivided in a number of different ways: by geographical region, political affiliation, or familial relationship. The latter method will be employed here, as it gives the best sense of the vast areas over which some languages or language families once ranged. As elsewhere in the world, political boundaries are rarely equated with linguistic ones.

So subdivided, native North American languages form six or seven super-families, leaving only a few isolated languages still defying classification. This scheme is based on the pioneering work of the American linguist Edward Sapir, some of which is still hotly debated by specialists.

Surviving examples of the Mayan writing system are typically carved on stone monuments. They recount tales of great heroes and battles.

is by far the most sophisticated writing system attested in the Pre-Columbian Americas and although linguists have some idea of how Mayan hieroglyphics worked, they are still not fully understood.

The decipherment of the Mayan script was delayed for many years by a common assumption among specialists that the symbols were merely pictographs, that is, pictures representing concepts without any phonetic value. This assumption was made despite early evidence from Spanish missionaries that the system was phonetically based. In fact, the Mayan writing system worked in many respects like Egyptian hieroglyphics. In the example above, there are some clearly picture-like or iconic aspects of the glyphs, but their

meanings are in no way transparent to someone unfamiliar with them. Glyphs could stand for their own meaning or could be used only for the sound value that their meaning carried, following the rebus principle (*see Part Three*); that is, a symbol may be used for its pronunciation alone, for example the use of ◉ to mean "I" or ☡ to mean "be." A specific example of this form of writing is shown below:

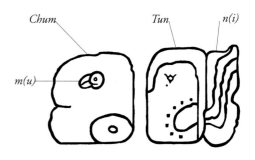

Chum tun "seating of the tun"
(tun is a time period in the Maya calendar)

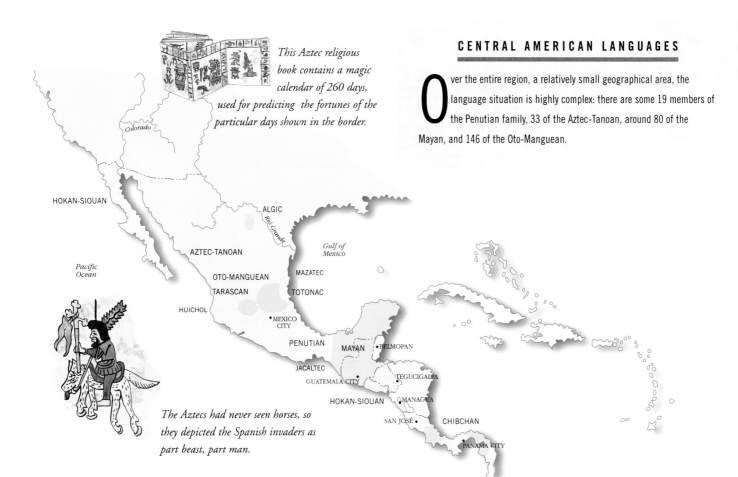

This Aztec religious book contains a magic calendar of 260 days, used for predicting the fortunes of the particular days shown in the border.

The Aztecs had never seen horses, so they depicted the Spanish invaders as part beast, part man.

CENTRAL AMERICAN LANGUAGES

Over the entire region, a relatively small geographical area, the language situation is highly complex: there are some 19 members of the Penutian family, 33 of the Aztec-Tanoan, around 80 of the Mayan, and 146 of the Oto-Manguean.

The principle seems to have involved taking the first part of one symbol, modifying it with another and then combining the modified symbol with others. The symbols of the product were not always left separate, but might be merged into a more compressed form:

It is estimated that there were at least 800 distinct hieroglyphs in the Mayan system with which, employing the rebus principle, any word of the spoken language could be represented.

Chum tun "seating of the tun"

LANGUAGES OF SOUTH AMERICA

Less is known about the languages of South America than about those of the remaining western hemisphere, yet there are many important languages in this region, including the Quechua of the Incas, which is spoken over a vast area including Argentina, Bolivia, Chile, Ecuador, and Peru. Guaraní, which along with Spanish is the official language of Paraguay, has 3 million speakers (almost as many as Norwegian).

In South America the native languages are more widely used than in either of the other two American regions and they have many speakers who may use only one of the local languages throughout their lives. Unfortunately, knowledge of the distribution and family membership of these languages is limited.

Languages within a particular family may have grown as diverse as English and French or, perhaps, as English and Russian. That said, a great number of individual languages clearly come from distinctly different origins.

NATIVE AMERICAN ORIGINS

Native American populations certainly came from Asia via the Bering Strait, which at various points in prehistory formed a land bridge, but we do not know when they first reached the New World. The archeological record shows clear traces of human inhabitation from 12,000 and perhaps as far back as 20,000 years ago. Johanna Nichols of the University of California has argued that the diversity of native American languages suggests a much earlier date, perhaps as long as 50,000 years ago.

The first recorded data on any native American language come from the time of Columbus, but they are inadequate, and fail to make important distinctions between sounds. For this and other reasons, most linguists would probably not employ data gathered

Language Families of South America

Araucanian

Chibchan

Macro-Ge

Paezan

Quechuan

Tucanoan

Carib

Witotoan

Arawakan

Jivaroan

Nambiquaran

Panoan

Yanomaman

Tacanan

Tupian

Zaparoan

European records of Native Americans, such as this 1844 depiction of the "Scalp Dance," frequently served to perpetuate misunderstandings about native culture. Linguistic data gathered before the twentieth century is also notoriously unreliable.

prior to the twentieth century in their analyses. Native peoples have inhabited the Americas for at least 20,000 years, but knowledge of their languages stems from work gathered only over the course of the last century. By contrast, written records of Indo-European languages date back approximately 3–4,000 years, and yet there is still much disagreement about proto-Indo-European, which would have preceded the writings by only a thousand years or so. If we consider how much English has changed over the past few hundred years, we cannot push realistic reconstructions of native American languages back more than a few thousand.

When the comparative method is extended

THE COMPARATIVE METHOD

The comparative method is used by linguists to determine relationships among languages. The following example is from the Cupan sub-family of Uto-Aztecan:

Cahuilla	Cupeño	Luiseño	
haal	hal	hal	"look for"
silʸi	silʸi	siili	"pour"
kiyul	qəyul	kiyuul	"fish"
qasilʸ	qəsilʸ	qaasil	"sagebrush"
puul	puul	puula	"doctor"
ʔawal	ʔəwal	ʔawaal	"dog"
mukilʸ	mukʔilʸ	muukil	"sore"

By comparing the forms in the three languages, we can conclude that there is far more than chance similarity among them. The correspondences between various sounds are often identical, always phonetically similar. On the principle of "majority wins," a Proto-Cupan language from which all three are descended can be reconstructed along the following lines:

Cahuilla	Cupeño	Luiseño	Proto-Cupan	
haal	hal	hal	*hal	"look for"
silʸi	silʸi	siili	*silʸi	"pour"
kiyul	qəyul	kiyuul	*kiyul	"fish"
qasilʸ	qəsilʸ	qaasil	*qasilʸ	"sagebrush"
puul	puul	puula	*puul	"doctor"
ʔawal	ʔəwal	ʔawaal	*ʔawal	"dog"
mukilʸ	mukʔilʸ	muukil	*mukilʸ	"sore"

to larger language groupings, the results become less reliable. One controversial proposal for family relationships among the native American languages comes from Professor Joseph H. Greenberg of Stanford University, who has gathered extensive data from various sources – mostly grammars of individual languages – to argue that all native American languages belong to three "super-families:" Eskimo-Aleut, Na-Dene, and Amerind. Each grouping would correspond to a wave of migration in the settlement of the Americas via the land bridge now covered by the Bering Straits. The Eskimo-Aleut and Na-Dene families, as shown above, are relatively well established and distinctive. The third family, Amerind, would include all the remaining languages of North, Central, and South America – a highly ambitious proposal which many specialists have found unconvincing. The most suggestive evidence for it involves the pronouns "I" and "you" which use *n-* and *m-* respectively in numerous languages of the Americas. This does not seem to be due to chance, since such forms are not common outside the Americas (m- is not "you" but "me" in many Eurasian languages), nor to borrowing, since pronouns are rarely borrowed from one language to another. Other items of vocabulary show less persuasive similarities, as in the case of the etymology for "wood" proposed by Greenberg:

Caddo	*nako*	"fire"
Pawnee	*laktit*	"fire"
Arikara	*nač*	"wood"
Kutenai	*łukʷ*	"wood"
Tillamook	*-alaq*	"wood"
Nuuchahnulth	*łoʔok*	"board"

Given l and n are similar consonants, as are k, kʷ and q, there is an initial resemblance between these words, as well as a plausible link between the meanings "wood," "fire," and "board." Since we know that the first three

(continued on page 138)

CARACAS

ARAWAKAN

CHIBCHAN
CARIB

GEORGETOWN
PARAMARIBO
BISSAU

BOGATA

PAEZAN
YANOMAMAN

QUECHU-
AYMARAN
QUITO

Hixkaryana

Amazon

Amazon

TUCANOAN

JIVAROAN

ZAPAROAN
WITOTOAN
MURA-PIRAHÃ

PANOAN

ARAWAKAN
TACANAN
NAMBIQUARAN
MACRO-GE

LIMA

Mamore

BRASILIA
São Francisco

QUECHU-
AYMARAN
LA PAZ

*Pacific
Ocean*

TUPI
GUARANI

ASUNCION
MACRO-GE

QUECHU-
AYMARAN
Paraná

As the Amazon is exploited formerly
isolated tribes begin to lose touch with
their traditional way of life.

Salado

SANTIAGO

MONTEVIDEO
BUENOS AIRES

ARAUCANIAN
Colorado

*South
Atlantic
Ocean*

A necklace of jaguar teeth was worn by warriors
and shamans in the Matto Grosso of Brazil as a
symbol of power. The jaguar is the giver of
hunting and fire.

The Chimu civilization
flourished between 1000-1470
in Peru.

LANGUAGES OF SOUTH AMERICA

Over the whole of South America, it is estimated that there are approximately 600 distinct languages, inevitably generating great communication difficulty and much multilingualism. The number of languages spoken in Brazil alone is estimated to be around 250, with 15 language families represented and another 35 or so languages as yet unclassified.

WORD ORDER

There are many aspects of the grammars of native American languages which help to distinguish them from one another; just a few instances will demonstrate their diversity, beginning with the ordering of words within sentences.

Greenlandic (Eskimo-Aleut)

Greenlandic is a dialect of the Inuit language spoken in Greenland. As can be seen from the example below, Greenlandic syntax is quite different from English, in fact, it is more similar to that of Japanese, a completely unrelated language, in which the main verb appears at the end of the sentence. Greenlandic, and Inuktitut more generally, does not make use of prepositions but, rather, marks the object with a suffix, much as in Classical Latin:

Subject	Object	Verb
tigianiaq	*iglu-mut*	*pisug-puq*
"fox"	"house-to"	"go" (past)

"The fox went to the house."

Object	Verb
tigianiaq	*tukuvaa*
fox	see-he

"He saw the fox"

Such grammatical choices divide the world's languages up into various groups and cut across territorial or familial boundaries.

Ditihaht (Mosan)

Ditihaht is a language spoken along the western coast of Vancouver Island on the West Coast of North America. In this language, unlike Greenlandic or English, the verb appears at the beginning of the sentence:

Verb	Subject	Object
tsasiiks	*be'itlqats*	*hupey'k*
"chase"	"boy"	"ball"

"The boy chases the ball."

This is certainly more rare than either the English or the Greenlandic pattern, but is still found in some fairly well known languages of the world, including Welsh and Irish Gaelic, which are both related to English.

Navajo (Na-Dene)

Navajo (also spelled Navaho) is a language spoken by over 100,000 people in the southwestern United States, particularly Arizona and New Mexico. It is a member of a family of languages which spreads from Northern Alaska to the Mexican-American border. In Navajo, the pattern is similar to Greenlandic, with the verb at the end of the sentence, but in Navajo prefixes, rather than suffixes, are used to mark grammatical relationships among words:

Subject	Object	Verb
diné	*ʔàškį́į́*	*yĭdĭhlę̀ę̀h*
"man"	"boy"	"begin to carry"

"The man begins to carry the boy"

In this example the verb is actually just *tę̀ę̀h*, and everything in the word before the root belongs to one or the other of the numerous grammatical markers used in Navajo. Thus:

yĭ - dĭ - hl -tę̀ę̀h
"him" (future) Classifier "carry"

"begins to carry him"

Or a more complex example:

ná - shi - zh - dĭ - ĭ - hl -tę̀ę̀h
"pick" "me" "he" "up" (imperfect) Classifier "carry"

"He picks me up"

There are at least ten distinct prefix positions for the verb and dozens of different prefixes.

Jacaltec (Mayan)

Jacaltec is a language spoken by some 20,000 speakers in the Central American country of Guatemala. Jacaltec, like Ditihaht, places the verb at the beginning of the sentence, but unlike Ditihaht, uses separate words to mark grammatical relations:

Verb	Subject	
xb'ey	*heb'*	*naj*
"went"	plural	"man"

"they went"

Verb	Subject	Object
x'il	*naj xuwan*	*ix malin*
"saw"	man "John"	woman "Mary"

"John saw Mary"

The words *naj* and *ix* are classifiers, serving only to mark the participants in the interaction, "John" as *naj* and "Mary" as *ix*.

Guaraní (Tupi)

The Guaraní language has approximately 3 million speakers in the South American country of Paraguay as well as another 50,000 in surrounding areas. Its word order is surprisingly similar to that of English, as demonstrated by the following sentence:

Subject-Verb	Object	
adzupi	*petei*	*ivirarakáme*
"I climb"	"one"	"tree"

"I climb a tree"

The verb precedes the object in this case, and the subject is marked, as it is in the English "I'll" for "I will," by attachment to the front of the verb.

Mohawk (Iroquoian)

Mohawk is a Iroquoian language spoken in the northeastern United States. Word order in Mohawk is actually quite free, as demonstrated by the following sentences, all of which mean:

ieksá:'a	*wahonwá:ienhte'*	*raksá:'a.*
"girl"	"hit"	"boy"

"The girl hit the boy"

raksá:'a	*wahonwá:ienhte'*	*ieksá:'a.*
"boy	hit	girl
wahonwá:ienhte'	*ieksá:'a*	*raksá:'a.*
hit	girl	boy
ieksá:'a	*raksá:'a*	*wahonwá:ienhte'.*
girl	boy	hit

All of these sentences are acceptable to Mohawk speakers and have basically the same meaning although there may be slight nuances which distinguish them. So how do Mohawk speakers know who is doing the hitting and who is being hit? This information is actually encoded on the verb; the presence of the infix *-honwa-* encodes the information that a female is doing something to a male. This type of agreement resembles that

Petroglyphs, such as the so-called "Newspaper rock" have been found in the "petrified forests" of Southwest America. These glyphs were probably carved on the rock some time before AD 1400 by peoples, possibly the Hopi and Zuni, who lived settled lives in the pueblos, or villages ,of the Southwest.

found in the Bantu languages of Africa (*see section 2.3*).

Hixkaryana (Carib)

Hixkaryana is a language spoken in the Amazonian rainforest of Brazil by approximately 350 people; it belongs to the Carib family of South American languages. The word order of Hixkaryana, in which the object precedes the verb, is very rare among the languages of the world. It may be interesting to note here that this is apparently the preferred word order in the Klingon language of Star Trek fame, chosen, perhaps, for the exotic "feel" of such a rare word order.

Object	Verb	Subject
kana	*yannimno*	*biryekomo*
"fish"	"he-caught-it"	"boy"

"The boy caught a fish"

As can be seen from this example, the subject comes at the end of the sentence, the object comes at the beginning, and the verb in the middle, just as if we had rotated an English sentence using the verb as axis. This rare pattern is unattested outside South America, and most languages which exhibit it are members of the Carib family.

languages all belong to the Caddoan family, the words here can be assumed to derive from a common ancestor. The remaining three are less clearly connected: Tillamook is a Salish language, not known to be related to Caddoan, while Kutenai is considered an isolate, without relatives. The last form, Nuuchahnulth *łoʔok* "board," in fact comes from a different source, which can be seen by comparing it with other Nuuchahnulth words:

łoʔok	"board"
łoʔał	"dish"
łołobïʔs	"halibut"
łoqak	"slanting flatwise"
łoʕa	"plate, tray"

What these items have in common is their flat shape, rather than the connection with wood. Hence the apparent relationship between Nuuchahnulth and Caddoan is probably due to chance – a factor which is notoriously difficult to calculate. This example shows some of the difficulties involved in the investigation of long-distance relationships in general; while the Amerind hypothesis would unify the languages of the Americas, such relationships among the native American languages must await further research.

WORD FORMATION

There is a great deal of variation among the languages of native America in the way in which words are built:

Mohawk (Iroquoian)

wa-hi-'sereht-óhare-'se

"he car-washed for me"or

("he washed the car for me").

This one-word sentence conveys all the information mentioned in the translation. This is not the only way that a Mohawk speaker may say this sentence, but it is one option which is not usually available to the speaker of English: although we can say either "I sat the baby last night" or "I baby-sat last night," this pattern, called incorporation, is extremely restricted in English, unlike in Mohawk.

Another aspect of word-structure that may appear odd to the English speaker is the possibility in several languages of building words from a single root combined with a fairly large number of suffixes, described by linguists as polysynthesis. This kind of extended word-building also occurs in English, for example in a word such as "antidisestablishmentarianism," but not usually to the extent that we find it in a language such as Nuuchahnulth. The following word, for instance, is nothing out of the ordinary for a Nuuchahnulth speaker, and words may contain up to six or eight suffixes without difficulty:

čuču·k̯ʷ aʕinmasitʔi

"those who had gone out to invite "

Again, not all words of Nuuchahnulth are this complex, but it is certainly not uncommon.

NOUNS AND VERBS IN MOSAN

One interesting aspect of the word structure of languages of the Mosan family is their tendency to employ roots which appear not to carry a distinction as to whether they are nouns or verbs, as if it did not matter. An early example of this from one of these languages is from Sapir, who states that the word ʔinkʷ-ił "fire in the house" in the Nuuchahnulth language is not as clearly a noun as its translation might suggest. He goes on to say that the root ʔinkʷ - "fire" is really as much a verbal entity as a nominal one; it may be glossed as "fire" or as "burn," according to the context:

'inkʷ-ił	=	"fire in the house"
		"burn in the house"
ts'ax	=	"a spear"
		"to spear"
yuxʷ	=	"lungs"
		"to float"
'ath	=	"night"
		"to become night"
'inma	=	"to suck milk"
		"breast"

TONE IN CHIQUIHUITLAN MAZATEC

Tones are represented in two fashions: first with the traditional numbering system following the word and then in a rough musical notation to represent the relative height of the pitch.

| *ča¹* | *ča²* | *ča³* | *ča⁴* |
| "I talk" | "difficult" | "his hand" | "he talks" |

These examples may be multiplied extensively with the same result; however it is important to note that while the category of the roots may be ambiguous, the final product is not, because context clarifies the meaning.

SOUND SYSTEMS

A further area of distinction among these languages involves the complexity and number of the sounds employed in speaking them. The number of sound distinctions made by the languages of the world may vary somewhere between 10 and 100, so it is not surprising to learn that the languages of the Americas also vary considerably in the number of distinctive sounds which they employ in constructing their words:

    Mura-Pirahã (8 consonants, 3 vowels)

    Huichol (13 consonants, 5 vowels)

    Nuuchahnulth (29 consonants, 5 vowels)

    Navajo (36 consonants, 8 vowels)

In addition to consonants and vowels which are combined in various ways to compose words, other factors must be taken into account in a full analysis of the sound system of these languages. One possible contributing factor is the presence of tone, a variation of the pitch at which a word is uttered.

TONE LANGUAGES

A number of languages of the Americas, including the Athabaskan members of the Na-Dene family as well as a number of languages in Central and South America, employ tone as a distinguishing characteristic. The Athabaskan system is typically quite simple, involving only a high and a low tone, but some of the systems in Central America are quite complex. In the Oto-Manguean

MAZATEC WHISTLED SPEECH

This interesting phenomenon, found in the Mazatec language, is fairly rare and yet is found in different parts of the world. It is quite common to encounter this phenomenon among languages of the same family as Mazatec, but it is also found outside the Americas, in the Canary Islands, France, Africa, Nepal, and elsewhere.

"Whistled speech" is more than just a prearranged set of conventions for communications, but rather a well articulated system for representing the Mazatec language by means of whistles made with the mouth. This method of communication is effectively used by speakers of the language over distances which would make normal speech difficult, if not impossible.

In Mazatec, a tone language, the individual tones of the words in a sentence are whistled at an agreed-upon key (the first person usually setting the key) and this mimics the pitch of the tones that would occur in the phrase.

Naturally, some ambiguity may occur, since only the tones are indicated in this fashion, but context and convention help to avoid misunderstanding in most cases. Below are two examples of this phenomenon taken from an early article by George M. Cowan, a specialist in the Mazatec language. Notice how the whistled tones match the tone numbers of the words.

| *ni³* | *ʔya²* | *khoa²* | *ʔai⁴* | *-nia³* | "I am coming from Huautla." |

| *ha⁴* | *vi²⁻⁴* | *ri³⁻⁴* | "Come here, friend!" |

The Americas

language Chiquihuitlan Mazatec, for example, there are four distinct tone levels.

As can be seen from these examples, changing only the tone will completely change the meaning of the word, just as in the varieties of Chinese and other tone languages found in different parts of the world. So a linguist investigating a language must be very sensitive to the possibility that a language may employ tone to make distinctions in the pronunciation of a word and make careful note of such distinctions.

WORDS WITH NO VOWELS?

In the Bella Coola language (Mosan) spoken in Central British Columbia, there are purported to be a number of words which contain no vowel at all. These words are perfectly acceptable forms in the language and stand alongside words which do contain vowels. This very rare phenomenon has been claimed to exist

linguists would describe as continuant, such as "m, x̟, ł." Continuant sounds are those that a speaker may "hold" for a period of time before letting go. So in English, when we want someone to be quiet, we will utter the single consonant command "Shhhh." We may hold or continue this sound for an extended period of time, often represented by the addition of further "h's" to the end of the word. Such sounds are not impossible for English speakers nor for the speaker of any language, but they are perhaps more productively used by speakers of Bella Coola than by speakers of any other language.

NATIVE AMERICAN WORD-MEANINGS

As can be seen from all of the cases above, there is a great deal of variation among these languages on all levels of the grammar. One other interesting aspect of language is the area of semantics or the meaning of words. The

BELLA COOLA VOWEL-LESS WORDS

płt	"thick"	*kxłc*	"I looked"
łmkmłp	"jack-pine tree"	*łk'tx̟'*	"make it big"

in other areas of the world, including North Africa where it is found among the Berber languages of Morocco and Algeria.

Note that the absence of vowels in these words does not make them impossible to pronounce, as might be the case given a different sequence of sounds, such as "pktgd." Each of the above words of Bella Coola contains at least one sound which

The origins of the totem pole are obscure, but they were most fully developed by the Haida. There are four different types: memorial poles, which were the equivalent of a family crest, mortuary poles to contain ashes, house-front poles and house-posts.

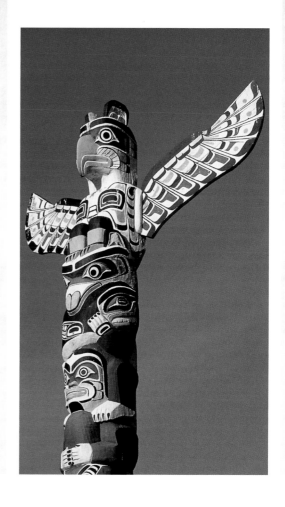

supposedly enormous treasure trove of words in the Eskimo language relating to "snow" is well-known, but there are other, less familiar examples. The Nuuchahnulth are a maritime people, living on the western coast of Vancouver Island in the Pacific Northwest. These people have probably always been seafarers and still make their living from the sea. The main staple of the Nuuchahnulth diet has always been salmon. The average Westerner probably sees little distinction among salmon, only possibly noticing that some salmon is more white while other salmon is more pink. In Nuuchaahnulth, the word for "salmon" is *se:min* (rather like "say mean"), a word borrowed from English.

Why should a maritime people who make their livelihood from fishing for salmon have no word of their own for this fish? For the Nuuchahnulth, "salmon" on its own can not be spoken of, it must always be referred to as "cohoe salmon" or "spring salmon" or "tyee salmon" or a number of other kinds. The age of the fish is also referred to, as in "young cohoe" or an "old spring salmon," because the particular life stage of the fish had a bearing on its availability, edibility, and palatability which could not be described by using just the word "salmon." Instead of one word, we encounter a large number of very different words relating to salmon and to salmon fishing, as befits a culture so heavily imbued with the importance of this staple.

As can be seen from this wide array of words to describe the fishing practices of the Nuuchahnulth, a culture will elaborate its vocabulary in particular ways which suit the culture at that time and place. English should not be considered deficient because its vocabulary lacks equivalents of all of these terms for "salmon," but this area of vocabulary is not particularly meaningful to the average English speaker. The Nuuchahnulth speaker has only a single word for "cow, " *mu·smus*, and that is borrowed from another

NUUCHAHNULTH SALMON TERMS

The words used by the Nuuchahnulth people of the west coast of Vancouver Island (Canada) in talking about "salmon" are listed below. These are all distinct, individual words with little or no apparent relationship to each other, unlike the English translations of the words, which employ combinations such as "sockeye salmon, spring salmon, young salmon, old salmon, salmon head, and so on."

Words for Types of Salmon

cuẃit	"cohoe salmon"
ča·p̓i	"humpbacked salmon"
hink̓u·ʔas	"dog-salmon"
hisit	"sockeye salmon" (when in the ocean or river)
hu·pin	"salmon trout"
kʷiḥnin	"old salmon"
ma·wił	"fresh-water salmon"
miʕa·t	"sockeye salmon" (when in the lake)
qiẃaḥ	"steelhead salmon"
saćup	"tyee salmon"
sa·cin	"young spring salmon"
sa·min	"salmon" (from English)
sina·waʔa	"cohoe salmon"(myth name)
su·ḥa·	"silver spring salmon"
ʕa·k	"dog-salmon" (Northern dialect)

Salmon-related Activities:

caka·št	"dried dog-salmon"
camuqʷa	"salmon roe boiling"
ća·čiqsim	"spear used for tyee salmon"
hu·qʷa·	"salmon going along with dorsal fin out of the water"
ḥuqstim	"salmon-drying pole"
kʷiła·	"salmon scraping bottom preparatory to spawning"
qʷa·ḥin	"fishing for tyee or dog salmon with a prong-spear at night"
λiḥata	"salmon jump as in spawning"
ʕaḥa·	"salmon go upstream"
yaḥa·k	"salmon weir"
pišin	"fishing" (from English)
pi·šme·n	"fisherman" (from English)

Words for Salmon Parts

cu·p̓i·	"fat back cut of salmon"
ćipuk	"salmon eggs"
ʕawin	"salmon head"

native American language, whereas English has numerous terms, including cow, bull, steer, calf, heifer, bullock, ox, not to mention the names for varieties of cattle, such as Holstein, Jersey, or Longhorn.

EUROPEAN LANGUAGES IN THE AMERICAS

After the arrival of the Europeans following Columbus, the linguistic situation in the Americas changed drastically, along with all other aspects of the cultures that were there before. Today, four major European languages are spoken across most of the continent; they more or less follow political boundaries. Spanish is the language of all of South and Central America with the exception of Brazil, where Portuguese is spoken. In most of North America English is the main language, with the exception of much of Eastern Canada, where French is spoken.

French was brought to Canada around 1500, and the province of Québec remains largely French-speaking. Its francophone identity is one of the incentives for autonomy, although Québec is known to linguists as a highly successful case of bilingual education. The other North American stronghold of French is in Louisiana, to which French-speakers came from both Canada and the Caribbean during the eighteenth century (Louisiana is named for King Louis XIV). Around New Orleans, the centre of Louisiana's French culture, some half a million people still speak a distinct variety of French.

A melting pot of cultures, the USA is also home to numerous minorities and immigrant communities. Most of these have adopted English within two to three generations, leaving traces of their ancestral languages only in their names and in local accents such as the Norwegian intonation in Minnesota.

The exceptions are languages whose use has been preserved for religious reasons, as with Yiddish in New York or Pennsylvania Dutch. Languages whose associated cultures and

community ties are especially strong, such as Italian and Chinese, are also used as everyday languages. Continuing immigration, especially from Eastern Europe and East Asia, rejuvenates the minority languages: Russian and Lithuanian communities have received a new wave of immigrants since the fall of the Iron Curtain, while Cantonese, the traditional language of America's Chinatowns, is brought to many cities anew by immigrants from Hong Kong.

Varieties of German are spoken by the Hutterite, Mennonite and Amish religious sects in the northeast. The most vigorous of these languages, with around 60,000 speakers, is Pennsylvania Dutch. This language is a dialect of central German which originated in the Palatinate region, and it is still used in certain sectarian schools. All these varieties of German appear to be in decline, however, with English gradually taking over all the non-religious functions of German.

Another language in decline is the Gaelic of Cape Breton, a fishing community in Nova Scotia. Since the 1930s Gaelic has been used less and less, and it is now used for purposes such as greetings, humor and secrecy.

In Central and South America, the colonial languages Spanish and Portuguese have not asserted themselves as definitively as English in the north. The European settlers mixed with native peoples, as in Colombia where 75 percent of the population is of mixed Hispanic/native descent. Spanish and Portuguese coexist alongside native languages, some of which are used for official purposes. Bolivia has three official languages: Spanish, Quechua and Aymara. In Peru, among some fifty indigenous languages, Quechua and Aymara are also used for broadcasting, and bilingual education programs have begun to develop. Such retention of indigenous languages alongside Spanish contrasts with the North American situation where only a few of the native languages seem likely to survive, on reservations.

Ethnic communities in America often create an area of a city or state that has a distinct flavor of their country of origin. The Californian town of Solvang (founded in 1911) displays many aspects of Danish culture – from architecture to food.

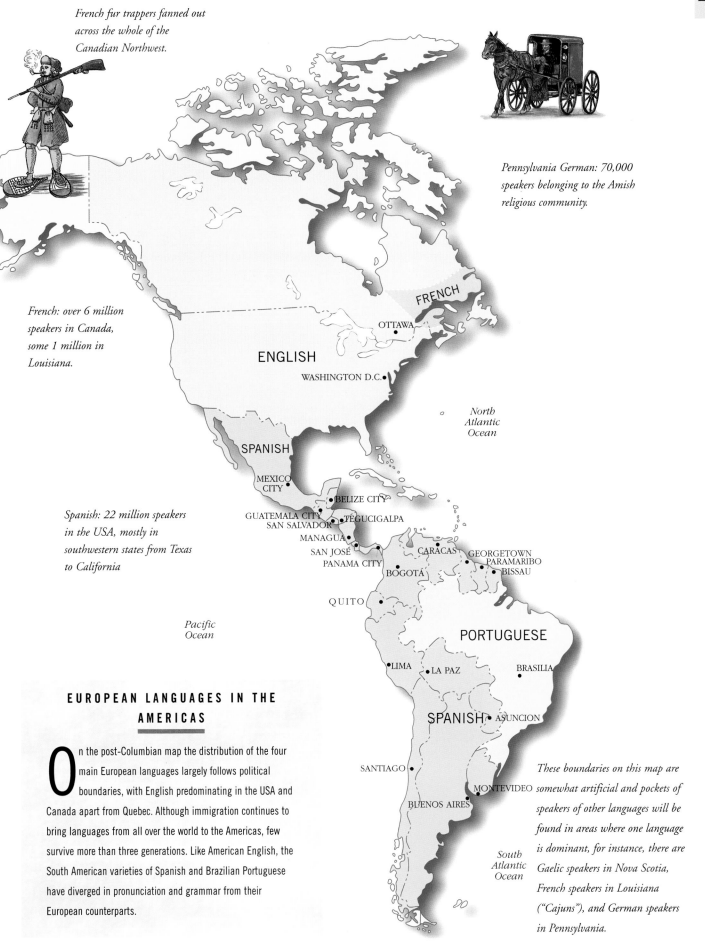

French fur trappers fanned out across the whole of the Canadian Northwest.

Pennsylvania German: 70,000 speakers belonging to the Amish religious community.

French: over 6 million speakers in Canada, some 1 million in Louisiana.

FRENCH

OTTAWA •

ENGLISH

WASHINGTON D.C. •

North Atlantic Ocean

SPANISH

MEXICO CITY •

Spanish: 22 million speakers in the USA, mostly in southwestern states from Texas to California

• BELIZE CITY
GUATEMALA CITY • • TEGUCIGALPA
SAN SALVADOR •
MANAGUA •
SAN JOSÉ • CARACAS
PANAMA CITY • GEORGETOWN • PARAMARIBO
BOGOTÁ • • BISSAU

QUITO •

Pacific Ocean

PORTUGUESE

• LIMA • LA PAZ • BRASILIA

EUROPEAN LANGUAGES IN THE AMERICAS

O
n the post-Columbian map the distribution of the four main European languages largely follows political boundaries, with English predominating in the USA and Canada apart from Quebec. Although immigration continues to bring languages from all over the world to the Americas, few survive more than three generations. Like American English, the South American varieties of Spanish and Brazilian Portuguese have diverged in pronunciation and grammar from their European counterparts.

SPANISH • ASUNCION

SANTIAGO •

MONTEVIDEO •
BUENOS AIRES •

South Atlantic Ocean

These boundaries on this map are somewhat artificial and pockets of speakers of other languages will be found in areas where one language is dominant, for instance, there are Gaelic speakers in Nova Scotia, French speakers in Louisiana ("Cajuns"), and German speakers in Pennsylvania.

Pidgins and Creoles

Pidgins and creoles arose in situations of contact between foreigners where communication was needed but no common language existed, situations created by international trade or by the more extreme upheavals of colonialism and slavery. Such languages typically evolved from a number of linguistic sources. Although some simplification is involved in this process, pidgins and creoles are not as crude as often thought, and can have their own distinctive structures. Once considered curiosities, they are now central to the study of linguistic development, and in the postcolonial era many have become the languages of independent nations.

The highlands of Papua New Guinea, where mountains rise to over 12,000 ft. The rugged, impassable terrain may account for the existence of many isolated tribal groups, each with their own language.

Nearly everyone has heard of "Pidgin English," but often the phrase is used very loosely to indicate various kinds of non-standard or imperfectly acquired English. Pidgin languages are best thought of as simplified forms which arise in situations where there is a temporary need to communicate among people who lack a common tongue. Usually words from one widely-used language become the basis of an improvised code.

For example, imagine you are a tourist in a foreign country where people are friendly and the markets are crammed with cheap and attractive food and artefacts. You want to buy and the market sellers want to sell, so how is this purpose achieved without a common language? In the beginning there would probably be a good deal of pantomime, such as pointing to objects, displaying money of various denominations, and indicating acceptance or rejection of an offer by whatever body language and facial gestures are available. If

A plantation worker in Barbados. Most Barbadians are descendants of African slaves brought to the island after the sixteenth century by the British to work on the sugar plantations.

you stayed longer you would probably learn some vocabulary, such as the names of particular fruits, words for "buy" and "sell," "yes" and "no," "come" and "go," personal pronouns, numerals, and so on. What would be more difficult would be to acquire the specifics of the language's grammar, its inflections, verb forms, noun cases, or peculiarities of syntax. Because of this, the pidgin languages which emerge in restricted trade settings often show a very simplified structure and minimal vocabulary. An example of this type of trade pidgin is Russenorsk which developed in the nineteenth century between Norwegian fishermen and Russian traders in their border region. This had about 300 words and very limited grammar.

Such trade pidgins have probably been used for millennia by people with limited contact, but a huge increase in their development started at the beginning of the eighteenth century, when some enormous population movements began. The major cause was the rise of the appalling slave trade and of the somewhat less brutal indentured labor schemes for the plantations of the tropics. People from a wide variety of linguistic backgrounds, usually African and Asian, were thrown together, and in the plantation environment it was often a European language

WHERE DID THE WORD PIDGIN COME FROM?

A number of possible origins of the word pidgin have been suggested. Peter Mühlhäusler, one of the leading experts on pidgin languages, has noted at least six different explanations which appear plausible, including words from Portuguese, Hebrew, and South American Indian languages as well as from English. He suggests that they may all have "conspired" to give the term currency. The most commonly suggested etymology is a Chinese rendering of the word "business," but the exact sound changes which would have produced this are hard to demonstrate. If the word did originate on the China Coast in the context of trade conducted in simplified English, a more likely origin might be the common expression "bei chin," which means "give money" or "pay" in Cantonese. The initial stop in "bei" is unvoiced, making it sound more like a "p" to English-speakers, and adding credence to this explanation.

Speakers of pidgin languages may have their own explanations for the origins of their speech. In Papua New Guinea, the language Tok Pisin can be translated as both "pidgin language" and "bird talk." This fits well with some traditional stories in the country which describe how language was first brought to human beings from birds.

Gauguin's "The Women of Tahiti" (1891). Paul Gauguin (1848–1903) was fascinated by the islands of the Pacific, and produced the major part of his work on the island of Tahiti. He was one of the many European travellers and artists who were drawn to the islands of the South Seas.

such as English, French, or Dutch which provided them with a common vocabulary.

MELANESIAN PIDGIN ENGLISH

Melanesian Pidgin English, which arose in the Pacific within the last two hundred years, is an example of a pidgin language based on English. European languages have actually been in the Pacific for considerably longer than this, as early explorers from Holland, Britain, France, Spain, and Portugal and other countries competed for national honor and wealth. One story tells of the famous Spanish explorer Mendaña, who arrived in the Southwest Pacific in the sixteenth century. He named the islands he surveyed the *Islas de Solomon* (Solomon Islands), in anticipation of the fabulous riches he hoped would be found there. Returning to Spain he announced his discovery and claimed the islands for the Crown. Unfortunately, the Spanish were unable to relocate their discovery, and Britain eventually became the colonizing power. The Pacific has long held a fascination for artists and writers, and romantic stories of a tropical paradise in the South Seas or of adventures amongst head-hunting tribes caught the imagination of Victorian Europe.

Much of the early communication between the Europeans and the indigenous peoples probably took place aboard ships or during brief on-shore trading encounters. Although a number of European languages were in use, it was English which became the basis of the most widespread pidgin. As communications improved in the nineteenth century, colonies, trading posts, government stations, and missions were established, and Melanesian Pidgin English became stable and widespread. In particular, the development of plantations growing cotton, copra, and sugar in Samoa,

The Solomons archipelago (below) consists of several hundred islands. The population of 326,000 people is spread over 1,000 miles, and over fifty languages are spoken, including the English-based Melanesian pidgin.

Fiji, Queensland, and elsewhere, with Melanesian laborers from the New Hebrides, the Solomon Islands, and New Guinea created an environment where the language thrived. In some cases indentured laborers were recruited for fixed periods under contract, but numerous accounts of "blackbirding" or kidnapping of laborers testify to much brutal abuse.

When the labor trade was abolished early

MELANESIAN PIDGIN - SISTER DIALECTS

A number of sister dialects of Melanesian Pidgin English are found in the southwestern Pacific. These dialects developed under the influence of words and grammatical structures from the languages of the region, and today the following are well established:

Tok Pisin is the variety currently spoken in Papua New Guinea. It was widely used by the colonial administration and missions in what was the territory of New Guinea, while a separate pidgin, Hiri Motu, was used in the territory of Papua. Since independence, Tok **Pisin** has been increasing in all areas of the country, including the Southern Region, formerly Papua.

Bislama is the name of the variety which emerged in the New Hebrides, now the independent state of Vanuatu.

Solomons Pijin developed in the Solomon Islands. Like other dialects of Melanesian Pidgin, it is becoming increasingly used as the first language of a new generation of urban children.

Broken is a variety of pidginized English related to Melanesian Pidgin which has developed in the islands of the Torres Strait between Queensland and Papua New Guinea. Its name, from "broken English," indicates the low status it has been ascribed. Other pidginized varieties of English in Australia include Kriol, spoken in Aboriginal communities across a wide area of northern Australia, and Queensland Plantation Pidgin, formerly spoken by indentured Melanesian laborers on the cane-fields of Queensland.

in the twentieth century, Pidgin English served little useful purpose in the largely monolingual communities of Samoa and Fiji and soon died out there. However, in the highly multilingual communities of the New Hebrides, Papua New Guinea, and the Solomon Islands, it became a useful *lingua franca* as these territories were opened up by

missionaries and colonizers. Returning laborers were an important factor in the spread of the language to their home areas and in its subsequent stabilization and development.

SANDALWOOD AND SEA SLUGS

Much of the early trade in the southwest Pacific was concerned with two naturally occurring commodities: sandalwood and sea slugs. Sandalwood trees, which are indigenous to the area, were in great demand for their fragrant wood which was used to construct boxes or to make into incense. "Sea slugs," or *trepang*, which strictly speaking are holothurians or sea cucumbers, were a seafood delicacy sought after in the Far East as much for their alleged medicinal properties as for their taste. Even today they are reputed to promote vitality and virility.

Early traders often spoke a simplified language using words from English, and sometimes known as "Sandalwood English." This nautical jargon was probably in widespread use throughout the vessels and ports of the Pacific in the early decades of the nineteenth century. Dr. T. Crowley, the leading expert on the languages of Vanuatu, traces the complex changes in the word for "sea slug" from the Portuguese *bicho de mar* meaning small sea creature, to the pseudo-French *bêche de mer*, used by English-speakers with semantic connotations of the English word "beach," eventually to the French reborrowing *biche la mar*. This became the most common name

The sandalwood is an evergreen tree, native to South Asia and Australia. Its wood, when burned, yields an aromatic oil.

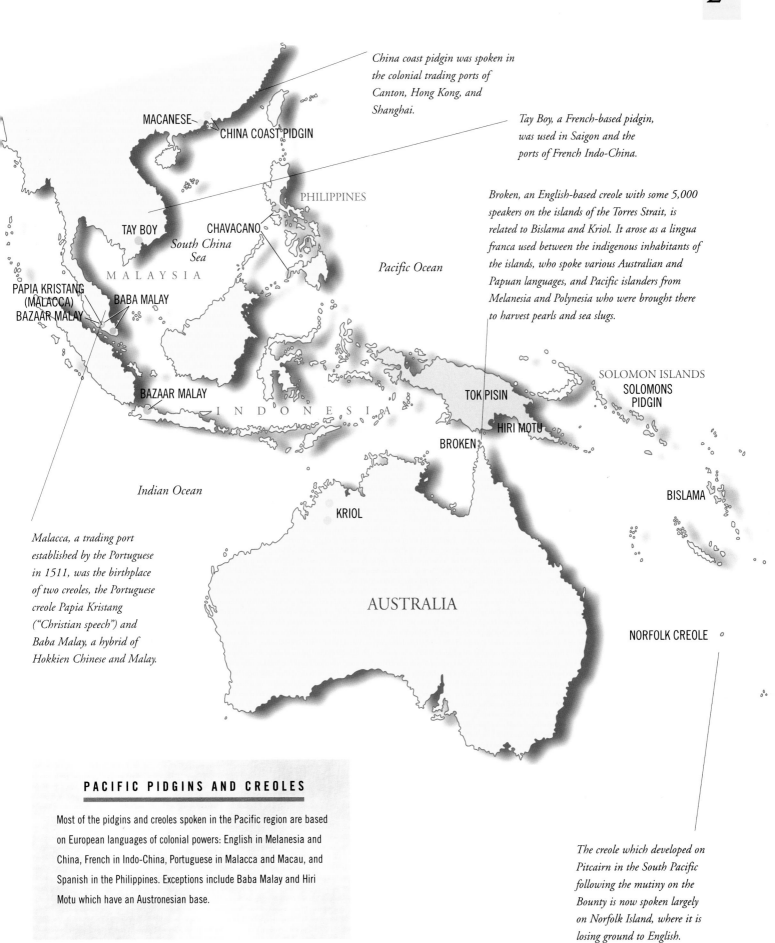

China coast pidgin was spoken in the colonial trading ports of Canton, Hong Kong, and Shanghai.

MACANESE

CHINA COAST PIDGIN

Tay Boy, a French-based pidgin, was used in Saigon and the ports of French Indo-China.

PHILIPPINES

TAY BOY

CHAVACANO

South China Sea

MALAYSIA

PAPIA KRISTANG (MALACCA)
BAZAAR MALAY

BABA MALAY

Pacific Ocean

Broken, an English-based creole with some 5,000 speakers on the islands of the Torres Strait, is related to Bislama and Kriol. It arose as a lingua franca used between the indigenous inhabitants of the islands, who spoke various Australian and Papuan languages, and Pacific islanders from Melanesia and Polynesia who were brought there to harvest pearls and sea slugs.

BAZAAR MALAY

INDONESIA

SOLOMON ISLANDS
SOLOMONS PIDGIN

TOK PISIN

HIRI MOTU

BROKEN

Indian Ocean

BISLAMA

KRIOL

Malacca, a trading port established by the Portuguese in 1511, was the birthplace of two creoles, the Portuguese creole Papia Kristang ("Christian speech") and Baba Malay, a hybrid of Hokkien Chinese and Malay.

AUSTRALIA

NORFOLK CREOLE

PACIFIC PIDGINS AND CREOLES

Most of the pidgins and creoles spoken in the Pacific region are based on European languages of colonial powers: English in Melanesia and China, French in Indo-China, Portuguese in Malacca and Macau, and Spanish in the Philippines. Exceptions include Baba Malay and Hiri Motu which have an Austronesian base.

The creole which developed on Pitcairn in the South Pacific following the mutiny on the Bounty is now spoken largely on Norfolk Island, where it is losing ground to English.

for the pidgin English of a wide area of the southwestern Pacific, and is now that of Vanuatu's national language, Bislama.

TOK PISIN AND BRITISH ROYALTY

Prince Philip, the Duke of Edinburgh and husband of the Queen of England, was evidently fascinated by Tok Pisin on his visits to New Guinea. Addressing the English-speaking Union in Canada in 1958, he referred to it as a "splendid language," although one suspects from his tone that he did not take the language very seriously. He reported that he was known in the language as *fella bilong Misis Kwin*. Unfortunately, this example was grammatically wrong. *Fella* is not actually used as a noun; the form *-pela* is a suffix attached to adjectives or plural pronouns (*bikpela* "big," *mipela* "we"). Prince Philip is sometimes described as *man bilong kwin*, but the damage has been done, and the phrase *fella bilong misis kwin* has erroneously taken its place as one of the many fanciful expressions now attributed to Tok Pisin.

Prince Charles, the Prince of Wales and heir to his mother's throne, did somewhat better when he opened Papua New Guinea's National Parliament during the independence celebrations in 1975. His address to the assembly included a speech in Tok Pisin, carefully read from a prepared script. Although it was apparent to listeners, for example from stress patterns, that he was not a speaker of the language, his use of it was generally appreciated. Tok Pisin is the language of the great majority of parliamentary debate in the country, and its status is growing in a variety of official contexts.

SIMPLIFYING SOUNDS IN TOK PISIN

English words adopted into Melanesian Pidgin have to fit the phonology of the "host" language. This may result in words which are

---

FALSE FRIENDS: FAMILIAR WORDS

WITH EXTRA MEANINGS

Many learners of Tok Pisin are fooled by *"faux amis"* or words which seem straightforward but have extra unexpected meanings. This can lead to much misunderstanding. The following are some examples of words which have an obvious or straightforward meaning plus an extra meaning. They illustrate how the semantic properties of similar words in the languages of the region may persist in the English-based pidgin.

Tok Pisin Term	Predictable Meaning	Additional Unexpected Meaning
gras	grass	hair, feather
karim	carry	give birth
nek	neck	voice
papa	father	owner
tambu	taboo	parents-in-law
bun	bone	strength
inap	enough	capable
lewa	liver	sweetheart
resis	race(s)	compete
laik	like	to be about to
planim	plant	bury
skru	screw	joint, knee
sindaun	sit down	way of life
sapim	sharpen	carve

Prince Charles addressed the New Guinea parliament in Tok Pisin when he visited the island in 1975.

quite distinct in English converging to become homophones (words which sound alike) in pidgin, as these Tok Pisin examples show:

English	Tok Pisin
shell	*sel*
sail	*sel*
cheese	*sis*
sister (informal)	*sis*
hard	*hat*
hot	*hat*

Potential ambiguity is avoided by added elements:

nail	*nil*
kneel	*nildaun*
ship	*sip*
sheep	*sipsip*
cut	*kat, katim*
cat	*pusi*

Pidgins are often characterized as "simple" languages. However, in expanded pidgins, as in creole languages, the grammar may be quite complex. Among pronouns, for example, there are a number of features not found in English which are important in Tok Pisin.

Firstly, while English has only one form, Tok Pisin has separate second person singular and plural pronouns: *yu* "you" (singular); *yupela* "you" (plural). Similarly, Tok Pisin makes an extra distinction between "inclusive" and "exclusive" first person plural pronouns, depending on whether the person spoken to is included or not: *yumi* "we" (including you); *mipela* "we" (excluding you). A third difference is the existence of forms indicating two or three people: *mitupela* "we" (two); *yumitripela* "we" (three).

Since these features are also found in other languages of the region, it is likely that they were adopted into Tok Pisin by speakers of those languages at the time Tok Pisin was being formed.

HOSTILITY TOWARDS PIDGIN LANGUAGES

Pidgin languages have often been subjected to ridicule, abuse, and even hostility. Pidgin English, for example, has been referred to as "broken English" or "bastardized English," and the general assumption has been that it is a poor attempt to speak English properly. Peter Mühlhäusler has catalogued some of the hostile comments directed towards Tok Pisin in Papua New Guinea early in the twentieth century. Comical circumlocutions were ascribed to the language as lexical items, such as "piano" rendered as *bokis i gat waitpela na blakpela tit misis i paitim na em i krai* ("box with black and white teeth the European woman hits and it cries") and "helicopter" as *miksmasta bilong Jisas Krais* ("Holy Mixmaster"). These

fanciful inventions no doubt served to hold the language in contempt, and by association, the thought processes of the people who spoke it.

A correspondent, Shelton-Smith, writing in the Rabaul Times in 1929, indicates the strength of feeling that could be generated by pidgin languages. He described Tok Pisin as a "tenseless, declensionless, and often obscene jargon that is the only general language of the islands." Another European refers to an "imbecile nursery talk which no German idealist could root out." Even an Australian

A weekly cartoon strip and a news item from the "Wantok Niuspepa." The first newspaper to be produced in Tok Pisin, its readership is increasing, particularly among younger readers.

government report to the League of Nations in 1922 states that Pidgin English "can hardly be dignified by the name of language, as its vocabulary is extremely limited and its construction and mode of expression are of the crudest." Even today, many people ridicule pidgin and creole languages as inferior, and educationalists and policy makers have been slow to accept them as the "real" languages of large communities.

TOK PISIN AS A NATIONAL LANGUAGE

The Papua New Guinea constitution does not bestow official status on any single language, instead recognizing three "national"

Primary school children are taught in English, although it may not be their home language. This policy is currently under review.

languages, English, Tok Pisin, and Hiri Motu. English is the major language of education, used in government schools as the medium of instruction from primary level. Hiri Motu was accorded "national" status as the language of the southern provinces of the mainland, formerly Papua, but its use is declining as the reach and importance of Tok Pisin expand.

Tok Pisin is the language used in the majority of speeches and reports in the National Parliament, and in a great deal of

verbal communication in government departments. Written communications, however, continue mainly in English, although Father Frank Mihalic, the author of the first dictionary of Tok Pisin, produced a translation of the constitution into Tok Pisin as a gift to the nation. There is a weekly Tok Pisin newspaper, known as *Wantok Niuspepa,* which is increasingly popular with the present generation. Most social interaction between people from different language backgrounds is now conducted in Tok Pisin, especially in urban areas and increasingly in rural communities.

With so many children now speaking Tok Pisin as their first language, the requirement that primary education be in English is coming under increasing scrutiny. Some experimental schools have been set up in the Sepik area in the northwest of the country where initial literacy is taught in Tok Pisin. While many linguists and educationalists applaud these efforts, much conservative opinion still regards Tok Pisin as an inferior version of English inadequate for "serious" education.

CREOLE: A NEW GENERATION

The name Pidgin is widely used to refer to Tok Pisin, but this is not always strictly accurate. Especially in urban areas, children are growing up speaking Tok Pisin as their first and only language, as a creole. When a pidgin language becomes nativized or creolized in this way, a number of changes typically take place. The speed of speech is greatly increased, which in turn leads to a reduction in the number of syllables and to the dropping of various sounds in the process of streamlining. New morphological and grammatical structures appear, and new words enter the vocabulary from a variety of sources.

The ways in which children "repair" the inherent deficiencies of a pidgin when it becomes their native language have been the subject of a great deal of debate. It has been suggested that language universals are brought into play, and that the resulting creole owes much of its development to the natural instinctive mechanisms of the brain. As noted in the following section, a specific "bioprogram" in the human brain has been suggested as the most likely source of such grammatical innovations.

In the case of creolized Tok Pisin, nativization has proceeded gradually over a number of generations, with innovations produced by children tending to be cancelled out by normative pressure from adults. However, in more extreme circumstances, creoles arise abruptly from the juxtaposition of a diverse mix of languages. In Hawaii, for example, workers were brought from China, Japan, and the Philippines to join native Hawaiians under the control of English-speaking Americans.

Derek Bickerton, whose work has contributed greatly to the recent interest in creoles, has shown how the variable structure of Hawaiian pidgin gave way to a systematic grammar as the language became the mother tongue of the population. The main difference between a pidgin and a creole is that a pidgin is a second or auxiliary language, while a creole is acquired by children as their first language.

Creoles are concentrated in those areas where slave or indentured labor was used: the Caribbean, the Indian Ocean, and Pacific islands where plantations were established. They are largely the products of European colonial expansion, and their vocabulary comes mostly from English, French, Spanish, or Portuguese. The European element is sometimes sufficient for a speaker of the standard language to understand: for example, *Mi did have a kozin im was a boxer, kom from Panama,* "I had a cousin from Panama who was a boxer" (Costa Rican Creole English), or *Van puasō dā bazar,* "They sell fish in the market" (Mauritian Creole French).

Creoles often resemble European languages spoken badly, and for a long time they were

regarded merely as degenerate forms, but while their European words are simplified, creoles do turn out to have their own grammar. For example, "did have," in Costa Rican Creole, is a form of the past tense found in many Caribbean creoles, taking the place of irregular forms such as "had," "was," "came." It is now accepted that far from being poor examples

of well-known languages, creoles provide a unique view of how languages develop the structure we recognize as grammar. While the origins of most languages are obscured by successive layers of history, the sources of creoles can be seen clearly. Creoles typically use a verb for "pass" to express comparisons, as in *One pig big pass all we pig come for we yard,* "A pig bigger than all our pigs came into our yard" (Kru English, Nigeria). The fact that such patterns reappear around the world suggests that the same set of concepts underlies all languages which arise in this way.

THE MYSTERY OF CREOLE ORIGINS

The origin of creoles has become one of the most disputed issues in modern linguistics. There are striking similarities between creoles

A farmer on the Indian Ocean island of Mauritius. The island was both a French and British colony, and the majority of the population are descendants of indentured laborers brought over from India in the nineteenth century. The French-based Isle de France creole is spoken in Mauritius.

GLOBAL DISTRIBUTION OF PIDGINS AND CREOLES

The distribution of pidgins and creoles reflects the colonial expansion of the European powers on whose languages they are based. Many trade routes passed through West Africa which was the main source of slaves in the seventeenth and eighteenth centuries, and the slaves' ancestral languages left their mark on many creoles.

English Based
1 Hawaiian Pidgin/Creole
2 Pitcairnese Creole English
3 Amerindian Pidgin English
4 Gullah
5 Belize Creole English
6 Caribbean Creole Engllish
7 Sranan
8 English Bush Negro
9 Trinidad and Tobago Creole
10 Guyanese Creole
11 Anglo-Romani
12 Sheldru (Shelta)
13 Inglés de Escalerilla
14 Gambian Krio (Aku)
15 Krio
16 (A) Merico (Settler English)
17 Kru English
18 West African Pidgin English
19 Cameroon Pidgin English
20 St Helena Creole
21 Madras Pidgin
22 China Coast Pidgin*
23 Japanese Pidgin*
24 Vietnam Pidgin*
25 Tok Pisin
26 Solomon Islands Pidgin
27 Bislama (Beach-la-Mar)
28 Kriol
29 Norfolkese
30 Maori Pidgin

French Based
31 Franco-Amerindian (Michif)
32 Souriquoien
33 Louisiana Creole French
34 Haitian French Creole
35 Antilles Creole
36 French Guyana Creole
37 Franco-Spanish Pidgin
38 North African Pidgin French
39 Sabir*
40 Petit-Nègre*
41 Réunionnais
42 Mauritian French Creole
43 Rodrigues Creole
44 Seychellois
45 Tay Boy*
46 New Caledonia Pidgin*

Spanish Based
47 Pachuco (Pochismo)
48 Papiamentu (Papiamento)
49 Pidgin Spanish
50 Spanish Creole
51 Trinidad and Tobago Creole
52 Cocoliche
53 Inglés de Escalerilla
54 Caviteño and Ermitaño
55 Zamboangueño

Portuguese Based
56 Nikari Karu Pidgin*
57 Portuguese Bush Negro*
58 Brazilian Creole Portuguese
59 Cape Verde Creole
60 Kryōl
61 Crioulo
62 Gulf of Guinea Portuguese
63 Sri Lanka Portuguese
64 Goanese
65 Indian Portuguese
66 Makista (Macanese)
67 Papia Kristang
68 Jakarta Portuguese*

Dutch Based
69 Virgin Islands Dutch Creole*
70 Berbice Dutch
71 Afrikaans Pidgin
72 Cape Dutch (Taal Dutch)

African Based
73 Fanagaló
74 Sango
75 Lingala
76 Kibiba

* extinct

The rituals of Voodoo were brought to Haiti by slaves from West Africa. Followers of voodoo believe that unseen spirit forces govern their lives; rituals involve dancing, drumming, chanting, and animal sacrifices.

Pacific Ocean

Atlantic Ocean

A sixteenth-century Spanish-Portuguese caravel. It was in vessels such as these that Iberian explorers made their epic journeys to South America and Southeast Asia.

Arctic Ocean

Pacific Ocean

Indian Ocean

Fifteenth-century French sailing boats. Failed attempts by the English and French to find a northwest passage nevertheless opened up northern America to European settlement.

The Chinese made extensive voyages in flat bottomed, square-rigged junks. Fifteenth-century Ming porcelain has been found as far afield as eastern Africa.

around the world: they have SVO word order, with a basic system of marking tense, mood, and aspect, and several characteristic syntactic patterns. These similarities have prompted a number of explanations. Formerly, the theory of monogenesis proposed that all creoles derive from a single maritime pidgin going back to the ancient Mediterranean *lingua franca*. Certain words of Portuguese origin, such as *savi* meaning "know" and *pickin* "child," do seem to be ubiquitous. A second theory attributes the similarities to a substrate – in the case of Caribbean creoles, the ancestral West African languages of the slaves – and many individual features have been traced in this way. A third, more controversial theory, Bickerton's bioprogram hypothesis, suggests that creoles develop in similar ways because they reflect children's innate ability to construct language. Scholars see elements of truth in each of these theories, so perhaps we should conclude that

creoles are true "mixed languages" with substrate, superstrate, and universal features.

ENGLISH-BASED CREOLES

The major English-based creoles are spoken in the Caribbean, West Africa, and the Pacific, with the best-known examples occurring on the Caribbean islands and along the coast of Central America from Belize to Panama. Many still flourish, and Jamaican, for example, has over 2 million speakers; with the renewed wide dissemination of English, Jamaicans today speak both the creole and standard English, in a continuum of styles from one extreme to the other. This variation can be found in the fiction of the Trinidadian novelist, Samuel Selvon. The following excerpt is taken from *A Brighter Sun:*

"Urmilla: Girl, I in big trouble. Big, big trouble. If you know what Tiger go and do! He go and invite two Americans he does work with to come for Indian food tonight!

THE *BOUNTY*: AN EXPERIMENT

IN CREOLIZATION

There is a unique experiment which some creole scholars would like to conduct: take speakers of half a dozen different languages, put them on a desert island with suitable provisions, and see what language their community develops. Although such an experiment has not been carried out and probably never will be, there are real cases where a comparable situation has arisen; one such resulted from the mutiny of 1789 aboard the *Bounty* in the South Pacific. Having cast off the captain and the remaining crew, the nine English-speaking sailors came to settle on the island of Pitcairn, with nineteen Tahitians. A mixed language developed, now spoken on Pitcairn and Norfolk islands. The fact that the history of the speakers and their languages are thoroughly known makes this close to an experimental situation: some of the words can even be traced to individual mutineers, such as donne ("don't") from the lone Scotsman. Like many Pacific creoles, Pitcairnese uses dual pronouns as in the phrase *dem tu* ("them two"), which is modelled on a Polynesian pattern.

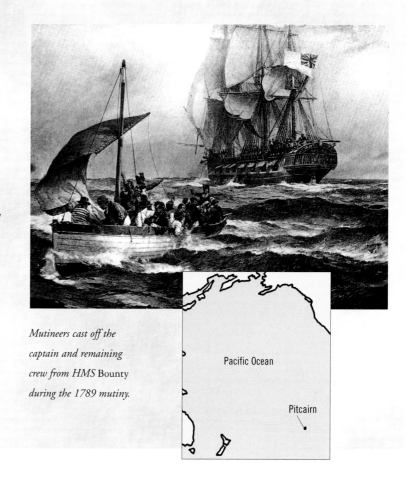

Mutineers cast off the captain and remaining crew from HMS Bounty *during the 1789 mutiny.*

Pacific Ocean

Pitcairn

Haitian has more speakers than any other creole – approaching six million. It originated with the predominantly French buccaneers who settled on Haiti in the seventeenth century and imported slaves to work on sugar plantations. Since 1987 it has been an official language alongside French. There are also large emigré communities speaking Haitian in Miami and New York City.

Berbice Dutch, spoken on the Berbice River in Guyana, is the last surviving Dutch creole of the Caribbean. Its close relative Skepi Dutch is practically extinct, as is the Negerhollands of the Dutch Virgin Islands

MEXICO

BAHAMIAN

CUBA

CAYMANIAN

DOMINICAN REPUBLIC

NEGERHOLLANDS (EXTINCT)

VIRGIN ISLANDS

HAITI

SAMANÁ

BELIZEAN
BAY ISLANDS CREOLE

JAMAICAN

HAITIAN

ST.BARTHÉLEMY

LEEWARD ISLANDS CREOLES

GUADELOUPE

ANTILLES CREOLE FRENCH

DOMINICA

HONDURAS

MARTINIQUE

MISKITO COAST CREOLE

PAPIAMENTU

ST.LUCIA

BARBADIAN

CURAÇAO

ST.VINCENT

NICARAGUA

COSTA RICAN CREOLE

PALENQUERO

GRENADA

WINDWARD ISLANDS CREOLE

TRINIDAD & TOBAGO CREOLE

PANAMA

TRINIDADIAN

COSTA RICA

VENEZUELA

GUYANESE
BERBICE DUTCH
SARAMACCAN

PANAMANIAN CREOLE

SRANAN

GUYANAIS

COLOMBIA

GUYANA

SURINAM

NOJUKA

FRENCH GUIANA

BRAZIL

Palenquero is spoken in the town of El Palenque, whose name means a fortified village, and the language is descended from that of the escaped slaves who built the fort as a refuge. The Spanish-based creole includes elements from African languages, as in ma bakita "the little cows" in which the Bantu plural form ma combines with a typical Spanish diminutive. It also has some Portuguese vocabulary which may derive from the West African islands through which the slaves passed.

CARIBBEAN CREOLES

The colonization of the Caribbean by European powers led to creoles based on English (green), French (pink), Spanish (lilac), and Dutch (blue). Most of those spoken on the mainland are dying out, but on the islands many flourish, notably Jamaican and Haitian.

Buccaneers were named after the boucan, a rack on which they smoked meat.

The creoles of Surinam derive from an English base with borrowings from Portuguese and Dutch. Although Dutch remains the official language, in post-colonial times Sranan has become a symbol of national identity and is much used in political discourse.

Rita: Is wat happen to him at all? He crack? He is a damn fool in truth. He bringing wite people to eat in dat hut? Tiger must be really going out of he head, yes. Gul, yuh making joke!

Urmilla: Man, Rita, I tell you is true! My head hot! I don't know what to do!"

Sranan, Saramaccan, and Ndjuka, the creoles of Surinam on the Caribbean coast of mainland South America, are especially interesting. They have been isolated from standard English since the seventeenth century, when the British colonies were ceded to the Dutch. As a result they gained much Dutch vocabulary and retained the very un-European creole grammar, featuring verb combinations known as serial verbs, as in Sranan *mi teki fisi seri,* meaning not "I take fish to sell," but "I sold the fish." Saramaccan and Ndjuka, spoken by the descendants of "maroons" or escaped slaves, have retained distinctively African features, including various distinctions of tone and complex consonants such as kp, mb, and nd (as in the name Ndjuka). Saramaccan also contains numerous Portuguese words whose origin is disputed.

FRENCH-BASED CREOLES

French creoles have developed in the Indian Ocean and in the Caribbean, where Haitian is the major example, with some 5 million speakers. Related varieties are spoken in the French Antilles, including Guadeloupe and Martinique, and in declining numbers in the American state of Louisiana.

In the Indian Ocean, the Seychelles, Réunion, and Mauritius were French colonies which produced spices, coffee, and later, cotton. A French-based creole known as Isle de France arose in Mauritius and the Seychelles, while that of Réunion is much closer to standard French and is described as a semi-creole.

A CARIBBEAN LULLABY

A lullaby recorded by Nicole Greaux shows some distinctive features of the creole of St. Barthélemy in the French Antilles.

Papa moin y pati en gué	My father has gone to war
Manman moin pati la montagne	My mother has gone to the mountain
Chèché ion ti po lapin	To get a little rabbit skin
Pou fai ion ti emmak pou moin	To make me a little hammock
Ti froué moin y pas vlé domi	My little brother doesn't want to sleep
Hay! Hay! Hay! Sa moin kalé fait?	Oh, oh, oh, what am I going to do?

Most of the vocabulary is recognizably French, but the grammar is quite different. The words appear in a different order (*papa moin* instead of *mon papa*) and *"moin"* functions, like many creole pronouns, as "I," "me," and "my." The future is expressed by a form *kalé* based on the French *aller* ("go").

Grenada (right) is the most southerly of the Windward Islands. Most Grenadians are descended from African slaves brought to the island to work on the sugar plantations, and an English-based Creole is spoken there.

Mauritian has about a million speakers, with a closely related creole spoken on the small island of Rodrigues.

SPANISH-BASED CREOLES

Spanish colonization left two creoles in the Caribbean. Palenquero, the language of a colony of runaway slaves near the coast of Colombia, was only recognized as a creole in the 1960s and is rapidly dying out. Papiamentu, spoken on the islands of Curaçao, Aruba, and Bonaire, is unusual in also containing Portuguese elements, reflected in the very name of the language and of the island Curaçao.

The creole Spanish of the Philippines, known as Chavacano, developed as a result of the construction of Spanish garrisons to protect the spice islands of the southern Philippines. It contains numerous elements of Tagalog and Cebuano vocabulary, and grammatical features such as reduplicated plural forms (*cosa-cosa* "things"), which are typical of the local Austronesian languages.

PORTUGUESE-BASED CREOLES

The Portuguese colonial expansion of the sixteenth century led to creoles in three main areas: West Africa, India and Sri Lanka, and Malaysia and Indonesia. In each case the local languages exerted an influence on the Portuguese base. The use of reduplication, typical of the local Austronesian languages, is found in the Malaysian creoles (for example, *gatu-gatu* "cats" in Papia Kristang). Sri Lankan creole Portuguese, under Sinhalese influence, even allows SOV word order as in: *e:w te:n dizey ta:l pesa:m-pe pe-kaza,* literally, "I have desire such person to marry."

The Portuguese colonies in the East Indies included Malacca and Macao. Here the Portuguese traders mixed with local populations, and creoles with largely Portuguese vocabulary resulted. The creole of Malacca in Malaysia, since it was spoken by a

MAURITIAN CREOLE

In Mauritius, speakers of Malagasy and Tamil as well as African languages contributed to the developing creole. Although much of the vocabulary is recognizably French, the grammar is not. Many nouns begin with a French definite article attached to them, as in *lagazet* "(a) newspaper," but Mauritian has developed a new article from the French demonstrative forms (*lagazet-la* "the newspaper").

The prefix *ti-* comes from French *petit,* but is used as a diminutive prefix in the manner of the Bantu languages (*en ti-lakaz* "a little house"). A reduplicated adjective after the noun has an attenuated meaning, as in *en rob ruz-ruz,* "a reddish dress"; this usage seems to derive from Malagasy (see Part Two, Chapter 4).

Most Mauritians work in the sugar industry. Mauritian creole includes Malagasy and Bantu elements, the legacy of slaves who worked the plantations until emancipation in 1835.

Catholic community, is known as Papia Kristang, "Christian Speech." In Macao, founded in 1555, Portuguese settlers and Malay women mixed with local Chinese, resulting in a Portuguese-based creole with Malay and Cantonese influences.

BERBICE: A DUTCH-BASED CREOLE

Berbice Dutch is the only surviving creole to derive from the Dutch colonies in the Caribbean; the Negerhollands creole of the Virgin Islands died with its last speaker in 1987. Now also dying out, it is spoken on the Berbice River in coastal Guyana. Its African substrate which clearly derives from Ijo, a Nigerian language spoken by the slaves, makes it especially interesting. For example, in the sentence *da di toko di kujara* ("That's the child's canoe"), the words *da* and *di* are Dutch, *toko* is from Ijo, and *kujara* is from Arawak, a local native American language.

SEMI-CREOLES

Languages with some creole features are known as semi-creoles. Some varieties of Afrikaans and Brazilian Portuguese, which have undergone grammatical change in the course of mixture,

ANTONYMS IN ZAMBOANGA

CHAVACANO

The vocabulary of Zamboanga's thriving creole is a mixture of Spanish and local Philippine languages. Curiously, adjectives with a positive meaning tend to be Spanish-derived, while their negative counterparts are of Philippine origin:

Spanish	Philippine
gránde "big"	*dyútay* "small"
buníto "pretty"	*ʔumálin* "ugly"
dulse "sweet"	*mapaʔit* "bitter"
sabróso "tasty"	*mataʔbang* "tasteless"
líso "smooth"	*makasap* "rough"

This distribution of vocabulary reflects the perception of Spanish terms as relatively formal or polite in the colonial context in which the creole arose.

are examples. African-American English, while moving progressively closer to mainstream American English, has some features which resemble the Caribbean creoles. It has even been suggested that Middle English underwent

Cajun cooking is based on French traditions, but has evolved around local ingredients and now has its own distinctive style.

BABA MALAY

While most of the creoles that have been studied are based on European languages, Baba Malay is especially interesting as it derives from Malay and Hokkien, a Chinese dialect. It has its origins in the fifteenth century when migrants from China's Fukien province began to settle in the trading port of Malacca, on the Malay peninsula. The Chinese married local women and the "Nyonya" culture developed, speaking a creole combining Hokkien elements with mostly Malay vocabulary. The pronouns illustrate how this mixture took shape:

"I"	*gua*	"we"	*gua orang, kita orang*
"you"	*lu*	"you"	*lu orang, lu samua*
"he/she"	*dia*	"they"	*dia orang*

The pronouns gua "I" and lu "you" are from Hokkien, while the third person dia "he/she" is Malay. The two forms for "we" use the Hokkien gua (excluding the person spoken to) and the Malay kita (including the person spoken to). This distinction is made in both Malay and Hokkien. All the plural pronouns add the Malay word orang "person" (as in orang-utan, the man-like ape), but use it in a way based on Hokkien forms such as lu nang "you people". The plural of "you" is lu orang "you people," or lu samua "you all." These two alternative forms may be compared to "you guys" and "y'all" respectively in US English.

Baba Malay is still spoken in Malacca and Singapore, but by dwindling numbers, threatened by Bahasa Malaysia and by Chinese. Perhaps the best known legacy of the Nyonya culture is the "Peranakan" cuisine, a blend of Chinese and Malay cooking popular in Singapore.

Outside restaurants on a Singapore street – the popular "Peranakan" cuisine reflects the mixing of Malay and Chinese cultures.

partial creolization under Norse and French influences. Although some of the simplification in word forms between Old and Middle English could be attributed to the mixture, English retained an essentially Germanic grammatical structure, making the idea of English as even a semi-creole rather far-fetched.

CREOLES TODAY

Creoles were largely the product of the colonial era, and the post-colonial period has sometimes raised their status and sometimes eclipsed them. Several creoles, such as Mauritian and Papiamentu, have become national languages, developing their own written forms. Others have come under renewed influence from standard European languages, leading to gradual decreolization, whereby the differences between creole and standard language become eroded. The Jamaican and Guyanese creoles, for example, have moved closer to standard English, while Macanese has given way to standard Portuguese. Many creoles of smaller communities such as Berbice Dutch and Palenquero are dying out, often leaving only cultural traditions such as "creole" cooking, as in the case of Louisiana's cajun French.

Part **3**/0

Writing Systems

Spoken language and written language are not to be confused: it is probable that this book will fall into the hands of people who through familiarity with its Latin script are able to give its letter symbols their approximate sound values, but who may not recognize what language they record. Almost everyone with certain basic cognitive abilities knows one language, but many are unable to read or write. Human language may have existed for one hundred millennia, but writing systems have developed in only the last five.

Sequoya, a Cherokee from North Carolina, created a phonetic writing system for his Iroquian tribe in 1821. In a very short time, most Cherokees had a high degree of literacy.

ALPHABETS

An alphabet is a phonetic writing system (unlike a logographic script) which consists of symbols representing individual consonant and vowel sounds (unlike a syllabic script). In this book, the term <u>alphabet</u> is reserved for phonetic writing systems which possess both consonant and vowel symbols. Phonetic writing systems, such as Phoenician, which have only consonant characters are identified as <u>consonantal scripts</u>.

The following pages examine writing around the globe — its origins, its spread, its diversification. "Writing" means the graphic representation or recording of language and excludes such things as prehistoric cave paintings, and the knotted string messages of the Yoruba. Our focus is on the attempts to record with symbols actual human speech, and the scope of our discussion includes most of the known writing systems, both ancient and modern.

MESOPOTAMIA

When the first humans began to write, they may have done so by building upon a system already in use for the recording of concepts, but not for the recording of speech. Professor

Small clay tokens from Choga Mish, Iran. They date from c. 8000 BC and are believed to have been used to record quantities of commodities such as grain.

D. Schmandt-Besserat (University of Texas) has argued that as early as c. 8000 BC, small clay tokens were in use at various sites in Mesopotamia for recording quantities of grain, and that the appearance of such tokens was occasioned by the advent of agriculture. These so-called plain tokens, normally smooth in finish, survive in various shapes – spherical, discoid, conical, cylindrical – but give no indication of the commodities which they quantified.

From a much later archeological period, tokens of a different sort emerge alongside plain tokens, apparently with the advent of the first cities on the Sumerian plain of southern Mesopotamia (in modern Iraq). Many of the earliest examples of these complex tokens have been recovered from the remains of the ancient Sumerian city of Uruk and are dated to approximately 3400 BC. Unlike all but a few plain tokens, these have a surface which had been marked with a stylus while the clay was still damp, and exhibit a great variety of shapes. In some cases their shape mimics that of the commodity which they recorded, resembling miniature tools and vessels. The early complex tokens at Uruk are found in and around the temple of the goddess Inanna, and Schmandt-Besserat has proposed that they were used to keep account of commodities entering as tax revenue.

Plain tokens were usually stored by the Sumerians in hollow, opaque clay envelopes; the tokens would be pressed into the envelope's moist surface and then sealed within. As a consequence, the persons responsible for cataloging and archiving tokens could readily determine the contents of any envelope. From the perspective of record-keeping, impressing a token into the surface of an envelope and then sealing it within is clearly redundant – the quantity is being recorded twice.

Such redundancy was eliminated in the second half of the fourth millennium BC when hollow envelopes containing plain tokens began to be replaced by small solid clay tablets whose surface was marked with impressions of plain tokens. Plain tokens were beginning to serve essentially as stamps.

Unlike plain tokens, it appears that complex tokens were usually stored by being threaded onto strings. These complex tokens also began to be reproduced in the surface of clay tablets, but rather than being impressed, complex tokens were inscribed free-hand into the surface with a stylus. With their etched surfaces, complex tokens perhaps produced a less acceptable facsimile when impressed.

The plain and complex tokens of ancient Mesopotamia may form the immediate precursor of humankind's earliest writing system, the pictographic script of the Sumerians. The earliest Sumerian writing occurs on clay tablets excavated from the remains of the city of Uruk and is dated to approximately 3400 BC, though a few scholars have proposed that tablets from Tell Brak in northern Mesopotamia are older. Tablets from Susa, written in an early form of the language called Elamite, are slightly later than the Uruk Sumerian tablets. Sumerian writing in its earliest form is pictographic in nature; that is, the symbols of the writing system resemble miniature pictures. However, the meaning-shape relationship of certain symbols is more transparent than that of others, perhaps suggesting some period of development and standardization of the symbols prior to the earliest attested examples.

Early Sumerian writing was nonphonetic. Unlike the Latin alphabetic writing system used for writing English and many of the other languages of the world, the symbols of the early Sumerian script do not reveal the individual phonetic components (consonants and vowels) from which Sumerian words are built; instead, each symbol represents a single word in its entirety. Compare the two "spellings" three and 3: both represent the same English word, but only the former is phonetically revealing. A reader of English who knows the phonetic values assigned to alphabetic characters and who has never before read this word, could, upon first encountering it in writing, determine its pronunciation with accuracy. The single symbol 3, however, gives no clue to its pronunciation. Conversely, in the

CUNEIFORM SIGNS

Sumerian Transliteration	Sumerian Meanings	Sumerian	Old Babylonian	Neo-Assyrian
DINGIR	god			
NAG	drink			
TÙR	animal pen			
DUB	tablet			
IZI	fire			
ANŠE	donkey			
GU₄	ox			
ŠÚR	angry			
GIŠIMMAR	date palm			
KUR	mountain			
MUŠ	serpent			
ŠÀ	heart			
GE₆	black			
KI	land			
KU₆	fish			

Mesopotamian cuneiform symbols at various stages in their development. At the left of each set is the early Sumerian pictogram (late fourth millennium BC); in the middle is the more stylized form typical of the Old Babylonian period (early third millennium BC); on the right is the classical Neo-Assyrian form (seventh century BC).

UKRAINE

Tartaria

Odessa

Dniepe

Don

Volga

Sea of Azov

KUBAN

Danube

Karanovo

BALKANS

Black Sea

Maikop

Caucasus

Istanbul

Troy

ANATOLIA

Hattusha

ARMENIA

Lake Sevan

Athens

Beycesultan

Araxes

Kanesh

Lake Van

Tushpa

Knossos

Carchemish

Lake Urmiah

CRETE

Aleppo

Ebla

Nineveh

Ugarit

Nimrud

Mediterranean Sea

Kition

Assur

Ganj Dareh

CYPRUS

MESOPOTAMIA

Byblos

Beirut

Damascus

Mari

Babylon

Tigris

ELAM

Jerico

Jerusalem

Euphrates

MOAB

Ur

Memphis

EDOM

Lake Fayoum

Sinai

Teima

el-Amarna

EGYPT

ARABIA

Thebes

DILMUN

Medina

Nile

Red Sea

HEJAZ

NUBIA

Mecca

Arabian Desert

Babylon is a Greek form
of the Akkadian Babilu
('Gate of the God').
Pieter Breughel the
Elder depicted the
famous Tower of Babel
in the 16th century.

proper context, the symbol 3 could represent several different phonetic realities: three or *trois* or *tres* and so forth. Writing systems which consist of characters that represent words in their entirety rather than their phonetic components are called logographic, and the symbols of such a system are called logograms.

The logographic (and pictographic) inscriptions of early Sumerian are often poorly understood. Toward the end of the fourth millennium BC, the logographic Sumerian script had begun to develop into a partially phonetic writing system. This transition occurred as Sumerian scribes began to exploit phonetic similarities between words. Every child who has solved a rebus puzzle is familiar with the principle involved. Consider a rebus such as the following: 👁 *want a* 🍐 *of* 📌 + 🗝 *shoes* (meaning "I want a pair of tacky shoes"). As English possesses a pair of homophones (words which sound alike but which have different meanings) "I" and "eye," a pictographic symbol for the latter (👁) can be used to represent "I." The same holds for "pair" and "pear" — the former can be written as 🍐. Furthermore, since the sequence of words "tack" and "key" is phonetically quite similar to the single two-syllable word "tacky", we can represent "tacky" as 📌 + 🗝.

Homophony is a property of all natural languages, including Sumerian. Because the Sumerian word meaning "arrow", *TI* (Sumerian logograms are usually transcribed in capital letters), is a homophone of the word meaning "life," the Sumerian logogram for "arrow" came to be used to represent the word "life." Further, the logographic symbol for "arrow" also began to be used to spell the syllable *-ti* (much as the pictograph 🗝 represents the second syllable of "tacky" in the rebus above). Once symbols representing syllables (syllabograms) were introduced into the writing system, it became partially phonetic; in other words symbols began to spell particular sequences of consonants and vowels.

Why were syllabic symbols ever introduced into Sumerian logography? If a writing system is capable of representing an entire word with a single character, what is the advantage of introducing symbols which can spell only individual syllables? Syllabograms were utilized in several ways by the Sumerian scribes. They distinguished, for example, between ambiguous logographic spellings. In some instances, a single logogram had acquired two or more word-values (a condition known as polyphony); for instance, the logogram transcribed as DU, meaning "leg," was also used for GIN, meaning "go." In order to distinguish DU from GIN, the latter was written with the aid of a syllabogram *-na* as GIN-*na*, with the *-n-* of *-na* representing the final consonant of the word and so providing a phonetic clue to the proper reading of the logogram. A syllabic symbol used in this

A cuneiform legal document from Syria. The tablet was sealed within a clay envelope, as such documents often were. At several places the scribe's finger prints can be seen frozen in the hardened clay envelope (as on the bulbous projection by the top right corner of the tablet).

For writing on their moist clay tablets, Sumerian scribes used a stylus of reed (or, far less commonly, bone or metal).

PERSIAN SYLLABARY

a	j	u	ka	ku	xa	ga	gu	ca	ja	ji	ta
tu	θa	ça	da	di	du	na	nu	pa	fa	ba	ma
mi	mu	ya	ra	ru	la	va	vi	sa	ša	za	ha

way is called a phonetic complement.

Another clue-providing feature of the Sumerian writing system is the determinative. While a phonetic complement offers overt phonetic information, a determinative provides semantic guidance. A determinative is a logographic symbol written either before or after another word symbol to reveal to what "class" the word belongs. For example, the Sumerian logogram GIŠ, meaning "wood," is written alongside logograms for objects made of wood; KI, "place," was written beside place names; MUŠEN, "bird," beside names of birds; DINGIR, "god," alongside names of deities, and so forth.

Like phonetic complements, determinatives could distinguish between ambiguous logograms. Both the name of the goddess *Nanše* and of the city *Sirara* were spelled with the same single logogram. When it was to be read as the divine name *Nanše*, it was preceded by the determinative DINGIR; when it was to be read as Sirara, it was followed by the determinative KI. At an early period, the determinative's position relative to its modified logogram was variable. Determinatives were merely text markers providing for the reader a key to the value of a logographic symbol, and as such would not have been read as words of the text; a Sumerian scribe would have read DINGIR NANŠE simply as *Nanše*.

Sumerian scribes used a stylus, or, as they called it, a "tablet-reed," to write on the wet clay tablets. The stylus of the earliest periods was probably sharply pointed at one end for drawing pictographic characters and blunt at the other for making circular impressions. Eventually the sharp end was modified to allow the scribe to write faster by simply impressing the tip of the stylus into the clay. The symbols produced in this way became progressively conventionalized and are distinguished by a characteristic wedge-shape; such characters are called cuneiform, after the Latin *cuneus*, meaning "wedge." With the waning of the Sumerian civilization early in

Stele bearing the Law Code of Hammurabi. The cuneiform inscription on this pillar preserves the lengthiest of the early Mesopotamian law codes, attributed to the eighteenth-century BC Babylonian ruler Hammurabi.

The Old Persian syllabary was inspired by the cuneiform script of Mesopotamia but is quite distinct from it. Some scholars believe that the Persian king Darius I (521–486 BC) commissioned the creation of the script. In contrast to the complex Mesopotamian script, the Persian system contains only 36 syllabic symbols and five logograms.

Logograms

xšāyaθiya (king)

dahyāuš (country)

būmiš (earth)

baga (god)

Auramazdā (Ahuramazda)

Numbers

	1
	2
	3
	10
	20
	40
	100

the second millennium BC, the Babylonians and the Assyrians came to prominence in Mesopotamia. Cultural heirs to the Sumerians, the Babylonians and Assyrians continued the practice of recording their language on clay, and on other materials such as stone, using cuneiform script.

The Assyro-Babylonian writing system is heterogeneous in nature, as the Sumerian system had come to be, utilizing logograms, syllabograms, and determinatives. Assyrian and Babylonian scribes extensively developed the syllabic symbols, the phonetic component of the script. While Sumerian logograms continued to be used, the phonetic reading of them naturally changed, as the Assyrians and Babylonians were speakers of various forms of East Semitic Akkadian, a language unrelated to and structurally quite unlike Sumerian. Sumerian logograms in Akkadian texts were often accompanied by a phonetic complement reproducing the final sounds of the Akkadian word represented. For example, the Sumerian word for "king" is *lugal*; in Akkadian the word is *šarrum*. When the logogram LUGAL occurs in Akkadian texts, it is frequently written as LUGAL-*um* or LUGAL-*rum*.

The Akkadian writing system possesses syllabic symbols which represent simple vowels (V symbols); consonant plus vowel sequences (CV symbols); vowel plus consonant sequences (VC symbols) and consonant plus vowel plus consonant sequences (CVC symbols). Variation occurs in the types of symbols used for spelling any given word. Just to take one example: *šarrum* ("king") could be written as *šar-rum* (with two CVC symbols), as *šar-ru-um* (CVC-CV-VC), as *ša-ar-rum* (CV-VC-CVC) or

The names of each of seven Egyptian monarchs, framed within a cartouche, appear on this limestone slab from the temple of Ramses II (c. 1279–1213 BC) at Abydos: (from left to right) Amenhotep II, Thutmose IV, Amenhotep III, Horemheb, Ramses I, Sety I, and Ramses II.

as *ša-ar-ru-um* (CV-VC-CV-VC).

The Babylonians in turn gave way to the Persians as the dominant power in Mesopotamia. Inscriptions written in a cuneiform script have survived from the Achaemenid dynasty of Persia (550-331 BC). Unlike the writing systems of the Sumerians, Babylonians, and Assyrians, which possessed hundreds of symbols (including determinative, logographic, and syllabic, and many characterized by polyphony and homophony), the Persian cuneiform script contains only 41 characters. As shown in the table (*on page 169*), the Persian system includes three V symbols, 33 CV symbols, five logograms, and a word-divider. Though a cuneiform script, Persian writing appears not to have been based directly upon any of the earlier known cuneiform systems; although inspired by them, it is of largely original design.

Perhaps the most famous monument bearing an inscription in the Persian syllabary is the massive Behistun Stone. Carved into living rock, it depicts the Persian king Darius (521–486 BC) with two of his attendants facing captured enemy kings. Around the figures are inscriptions written in three different languages, each using its own cuneiform script: Old Persian, Babylonian, and Elamite. This trilingual inscription was instrumental in the decipherment of these three languages. A principal figure in the decipherment of Old Persian and Babylonian was the nineteenth-century British scholar, Sir Henry Rawlinson.

EGYPT

Writing appears in the archeological record of ancient Egypt at about 3100 BC, slightly later than its earliest attestation in Mesopotamia. Although the Egyptian hieroglyphic script is clearly not a direct borrowing of the Sumerian script, it appears probable that the Egyptian writing system developed under Sumerian influence. Each of the character-types found in

EGYPT

Perhaps the most recognizable of all ancient writing systems is the monumental hieroglyphic script of the Egyptians, with its elegant and intricate symbols. The idea of writing was probably introduced into Egypt from Sumeria during a period of Mesopotamian cultural influence. The earliest examples of Egyptian writing, such as that on the Palette of Narmer (below left), are dated to the end of the fourth millennium BC. At this earliest known phase, however, the writing system already appears to be relatively sophisticated, suggesting an earlier period of development and use. During its long history of recorded use (from c.3100 BC to the present day liturgical use of Coptic), the Egyptian language was written with a variety of scripts: hieroglyphic, hieratic, demotic, and alphabetic Coptic.

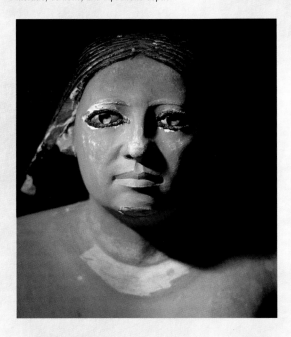

A limestone statue (left) of an Egyptian scribe of the Fifth Dynasty (c. 2498–2345 BC), from Saqqara in Lower Egypt (site of the earliest Egyptian pyramids). As in Mesopotamia, the scribes of Egypt occupied a position of prestige, if not wealth.

A contractual document (above) of the late sixth century BC, written on papyrus in the Egyptian demotic script. Descended from Egyptian heiratic, demotic is a highly cursive script which scribes were using by the seventh century BC.

The Rosetta Stone, a monument from Ptolemaic Egypt (dated to 196 BC), was crucial in the modern decipherment of Egyptian writing. It bears an inscription recorded with three scripts: Egyptian hieroglyphic, demotic, and the Greek alphabet (from top to bottom).

A slate palette (above) from Predynastic Egypt preserving early hieroglyphic writing. On the front, or obverse, of the palette (right), King Narmer (c.3100 BC) is depicted vanquishing one of his enemies; the king's name appears directly above his head.

SYMBOLS IN EGYPTIAN WRITING

L ike the Sumerian script, the Egyptian writing system is internally heterogeneous, employing various types of symbols: logograms, determinatives, and phonetic signs. Unlike the Mesopotamian system, however, the Eyptian phonetic component consists not of syllabic symbols but of characters which represent only consonants. This hallmark of Egyptian writing would be exploited in the next important step in the history of Near Eastern writing – the development of the Semitic consonantal script.

MONOCONSONANTAL SIGNS

Symbol	Transliteration
	3
	i
	y
	'
	w
	b
	p
	f
	m
	n
	r
	h
	ḥ
	ḫ
	ẖ
	s
	š
	ḳ
	k
	g
	t
	ṯ
	d
	ḏ

A monoconsonantal symbol (left) existed for each of the 24 consonantal sounds of the spoken language. These symbols could be used to spell a word one consonant at a time, but were more frequently employed in conjunction with other types of symbols.

A few of the c.100 hieroglyphic symbols which represent two consonants in sequence (top right). Multi-consonantal characters are used early in the history of Egyptian writing.

Symbols (right) representing three consonants in sequence also occurred in the phonetic component of the Egyptian writing system.

BICONSONANTAL SIGNS

Symbol	Transliteration
	ir
	pr
	mi
	mr
	ms
	ḥ3
	ḥr
	s3
	sw
	š3
	k3

TRICONSONANTAL SIGNS

Symbol	Transliteration
	'nḫ
	n'r
	nfr
	ḫpr
	ḫnt
	s3ḥ
	stp

the Sumerian system — logograms, phonetic symbols, and determinatives — also appears in Egyptian writing.

While phonetic characters occur in both the Mesopotamian and the Egyptian writing systems, the nature of the phonetic symbols in the two scripts is markedly different: the Sumerian and Assyro-Babylonian phonetic symbols are syllabic in value, representing a single vowel or a vowel plus consonant(s); Egyptian phonetic characters represent not vowels, but either one, two, or three consonants (*see page 172*). Altogether, the Egyptians used about one hundred biconsonantal characters and half as many triconsonantal signs. The twenty-six monoconsonantal symbols can be used to spell out entire words one consonant at a time, but are more commonly employed in conjunction with other types of symbols: Egyptian logograms, as well as biconsonantal and triconsonantal signs, are often accompanied by monoconsonantal symbols used as phonetic complements.

The curious inclusion of phonetic characters representing only consonants may be a reflection of the structure of Egyptian words. Egyptian, like the Semitic languages to which it is related, is characterized by a word-structure in which the consonantal component is quite stable. The Egyptian word root contains, most often, three consonants; while these consonants usually remain unchanged, the vowels associated with them will vary with the grammatical usage of the word. Some scholars believe that this conspicuous consonantal skeleton led the Egyptian scribes to develop phonetic characters from which specific vowel values were absent.

One of the notable elements of Egyptian orthography is the cartouche. By the time of the Fifth Dynasty of the Egyptian Old Kingdom (about 2400 BC), the ruler of Egypt, the Pharaoh, was using five names. Two of these names, designated the *praenomen* and

nomen by Egyptologists, were written within an ovoid outline called a cartouche, or, by the ancient Egyptians, a *shenu*. The outline was probably meant to represent the path of the sun and to suggest that the Pharaoh whose name appeared therein was ruler of all the lands lying within the sun's circuit.

The monumental hieroglyphic script, with its meticulous pictographic symbols, is probably the Egyptian script with which most readers are familiar; it is not, however, the only one. From an early period there also existed a cursive variant called hieratic, normally written with ink and a reed brush. An additional cursive script, demotic, having characters which are quite different from both the hieroglyphic and hieratic, had been introduced before the end of the seventh century BC. Demotic supplanted hieratic and remained in use until about the middle of the fifth century AD. The latest known hieroglyphic inscriptions are dated to the end of the fourth century AD.

In 1799, soldiers of Napoleon Bonaparte digging fortifications in the Nile delta, uncovered a large black basalt stele at the site of ancient Rosetta. The discovery was of crucial importance in the decipherment of Egyptian writing, for the Rosetta Stone bears an inscription commemorating the accession of Ptolemy V Epiphanes (205-180 BC) written in both Egyptian and Greek; furthermore, the Egyptian lines appear not only in hieroglyphic script but also in demotic. Ancient Greek was well known at the time of the discovery and so provided scholars with a key that unlocked the language and scripts of the Egyptians. The single most significant figure in the decipherment was the young French scholar Jean-François Champollion (1790-1832), who demonstrated the phonetic nature of much of Egyptian writing.

Semitic-speaking laborers, digging for turquoise and copper in the Egyptian mines of the Sinai-Peninsula, left behind inscriptions written in the script now called Proto-Sinaitic (c.1600–1500 BC). A consonantal writing system, the Proto-Sinaitic script was probably inspired by Egyptian phonetic spelling.

SYRIA-PALESTINE AND ARABIA

In 1904–1905, while digging at Serabit al-Khadim in the west of the Sinai Peninsula, the British archeologist Sir Flinders Petrie discovered several inscriptions written in a pictographic script previously unknown to modern scholars. Now called Proto-Sinaitic, the script records a Semitic language and is assigned a date of approximately 1600–1500 BC. These inscriptions, found by Petrie and

UGARITIC CONSONANTAL SCRIPT

'a	b	g	ḫ	d	h	w	z	ḥ	ṭ	y
k	s	l	m	ḏ	n	ẓ	s	ʿ	p	ṣ
q	r	ṯ	ġ	t	ʾi	ʾu	š		word divider	

With its roots in the Proto-Canaanite writing tradition, the Ugaritic script is a predominantly consonantal writing system, though it possesses three characters with syllabic values ('a, 'i and 'u). The Ugaritic script was obviously inspired by a cuneiform writing system, but some scholars contend that the Ugaritic symbol-shapes are derived from the Proto-Canaanite pictographic characters.

others, appear to be the handiwork of speakers of a Canaanite dialect of West Semitic who were mining the region's copper and turquoise deposits.

The Proto-Sinaitic script is a phonetic writing system which appears to have been inspired by the ancient Egyptian system of writing and derived from it in a quite deliberate fashion. Like the phonetic component of the Egyptian system, the Proto-Sinaitic script has symbols (probably at least 23) only for consonants. The British Egyptologist Sir Alan Gardiner proposed that these were derived from Egyptian characters on the acrophonic principle, according to which the Canaanite value assigned to an adopted pictographic

Egyptian symbol is the value of the first consonant in the Canaanite word for the object which the symbol resembles. For example, the Egyptian hieroglyphic symbol which looks like a cobra has the consonantal value transcribed as [dj] (similar to the consonant at the beginning and end of the English word "judge"). This symbol was adopted for use in the Proto-Sinaitic script but given the value [n]. According to Gardiner's acrophonic principle, this is because the Canaanite word for "snake" began with [n]: *naḥašu*. It is now known that the Proto-Sinaitic script is just one form of a consonantal writing system in use throughout Syria-Palestine and the Sinai which is called Proto-Canaanite. The script perhaps had its origin during the period of the Hyksos Dynasty of Lower (northern) Egypt (c. 1700–1550 BC), a time when Lower Egypt was ruled by an Asian people, among whom are attested Semitic names. The Proto-Canaanite script progressively lost its pictographic character, and by the eleventh century BC had evolved into the Linear Phoenician script.

From the remains of the ancient city of Ugarit (modern Ras Shamrah on the coast of

Sir Flinders Petrie (1853-1942) initiated the practice of excavating all objects from a site, not just those of artistic value. His careful fieldwork greatly extended knowledge of Ancient Egypt, as well as having a marked impact on archeological methods.

ETHIOPIC

a	u	ī	ā	ē	e	ō
ha	hū	hī	hā	hē	he	hō
la	lū	lī	lā	lē	le	lō
ḥa	ḥū	ḥī	ḥā	ḥē	ḥe	ḥō
ma	mū	mī	mā	mē	me	mō
ša	šū	šī	šā	šē	še	šō
ra	rū	rī	rā	rē	re	rō
sa	sū	sī	sā	sē	se	sō
qa	qū	qī	qā	qē	qe	qō
ba	bū	bī	bā	bē	be	bō
ta	tū	tī	tā	tē	te	tō
ḫa	ḫū	ḫī	ḫā	ḫē	ḫe	ḫō
na	nū	nī	nā	nē	ne	nō
'a	'ū	'ī	ā	'ē	'e	'ō
ka	kū	kī	kā	kē	ke	kō
wa	wū	wī	wā	wē	we	wō
'a	'ū	'ī	'ā	'ē	'e	'ō
za	zū	zī	zā	zē	ze	zō
ya	yū	yī	yā	yē	ye	yō
da	dū	dī	dā	dē	de	dō
ga	gū	gī	gā	gē	ge	gō
ṭa	ṭū	ṭī	ṭā	ṭē	ṭe	ṭō
p̣a	p̣ū	p̣ī	p̣ā	p̣ē	p̣e	p̣ō
ṣa	ṣū	ṣī	ṣā	ṣē	ṣe	ṣō
ḍa	ḍū	ḍī	ḍā	ḍē	ḍe	ḍō
fa	fū	fī	fā	fē	fe	fō
pa	pū	pī	pā	pē	pe	pō

The basic Ethiopic syllabary consists of 182 CV (consonant + vowel) characters. Each CV symbol represents a distinct combination of one of 26 consonants and one of seven vowels. Consonant + e syllabic symbols also serve to represent individual consonant sounds (without an ensuing vowel). The syllabary was originally a consonantal script derived from the South Arabian writing system.

Lebanon), which was a thriving center of international commerce in the second half of the first millennium BC, yet another phonetic script used for writing a West Semitic language has come to light. As in Proto-Canaanite, 27 of the Ugaritic characters are purely consonantal, but they are cuneiform, and thus appear quite unlike those of Proto-Canaanite. However, three of the symbols are syllabic, as in the cuneiform scripts of Mesopotamia: 'a, 'i, and 'u are characters representing the glottal stop [ʔ] plus each of three vowels. The character transcribed as ṡ was used only in the spelling of words from the Hurrian language of ancient Anatolia. In spite of the differences between the Ugaritic and Proto-Canaanite scripts, it is highly probable that the two scripts are historically linked.

The ancient Semitic language of South Arabia was written in a script which evolved from the Proto-Canaanite system, a development which perhaps had occurred by about 1300 BC. The earliest attested form of this script is found on documents dated as early as the eighth century BC. South Arabian was the writing system of the wealthy kingdoms of the southwest Arabian peninsula; the scripts of the kingdoms of Saba (Biblical Sheba) and Ma'in are dated to about the sixth century BC. South Arabian script, like its Proto-Canaanite ancestor, is one which has symbols only for consonants, and is striking in its elegant simplicity.

The South Arabian system was transported northward along the trade routes, and spawned consonantal scripts which were used to record pre-Arabic North Arabian languages. The Thamudic script is attested from about the sixth century BC, as is the Lihyanic, while the Safaitic script is known extensively from the first century BC.

The South Arabian script was exported not only to the north, but also into Africa. Here it evolved into the writing system used to record the Semitic language of Ethiopic. The earliest Ethiopic script, like its South Arabian ancestor, has symbols only for consonants. By the fifth century AD, however, this script has developed into a syllabary and its original consonantal symbols have acquired the CV value of *consonant* + the vowel *a*. Each of these is further modified in some way, often by the use of a diacritic, to produce CV symbols with the

PHOENICIAN	
Symbol	Transliteration
𐤀	'
𐤁	b
𐤂	g
𐤃	d
𐤄	h
𐤅	w
𐤆	z
𐤇	ḥ
𐤈	ṭ
𐤉	y
𐤊	k
𐤋	l
𐤌	m
𐤍	n
𐤎	s
𐤏	'
𐤐	p
𐤑	ṣ
𐤒	q
𐤓	r
𐤔	š
𐤕	t

vowel values *ū, ī, ā, ē, e, and ō*. This is only one of several examples from the history of the world's writing systems of a script which represents individual sounds developing into a syllabary. Unlike the South Arabian script, which is last attested in the sixth century AD, the Ethiopic syllabary has remained in use to the present day.

As was noted earlier, the Proto-Canaanite script evolved into the Linear Phoenician script by about the eleventh century BC. Several inscribed arrowheads found at 'El-Khadr, a village west of Bethlehem, are dated to 1100 BC and bear witness to the transitional phase. The Phoenician writing system contains 22 characters, representing consonant sounds only. The language of the Phoenicians is West Semitic, closely related to Hebrew. Plying the waves of the Mediterranean and beyond, the Phoenicians were the preeminent maritime culture of the Near East during the first millennium BC. Important Phoenician colonies appeared in Cyprus, Sicily, Sardinia, North Africa, and the western Mediterranean. The Phoenician script was thus introduced to new places and people, setting the stage for the next significant development in the history of writing. Beyond this, however, the Phoenician script would spawn further offspring in Palestine.

The Phoenician script was used in writing the earliest known Hebrew inscriptions, such as the tenth-century BC Gezer Calendar, the oldest known Hebrew document. Curiously,

The Phoenicians recorded their Northwest Semitic language with a consonantal script, the direct descendant of the Proto-Canaanite writing system. The earliest inscriptions which can be identified as distinctly Phoenician appear in the eleventh century BC.

SAMARITAN

Symbol	Transliteration
ᴎ	'
ᒑ	b
ᒑ	g
ᒑ	d
ᵌ	h
ᵡ	w
ᶚ	z
ᶓ	ḥ
ᶹ	ṭ
ᵯ	y
ᒺ	k
ᒷ	l
ᵘ	m
ᒯ	n
ᶘ	s
ᗞ	ʿ
ᒥ	f
ᶭ	ṣ
ᵡ	q
ᒑ	r
ᴡ	š
ᴎ	t

Following the sixth-century Babylonian Exile of the Jews, the Old Hebrew script gradually gave way to Aramaic. The old characters are, however, still used as a liturgical script by the Samaritans.

Modern Hebrew square characters have their origin in the Aramaic script. The characters kaph, mem, nun, pe and ṣade have variant forms which are used at the ends of words.

The tomb inscription of a woman named Mishta, daughter of David (c.AD 717). The Square Hebrew script is clearly quite close to the Modern Hebrew script illustrated right.

HEBREW

Old Hebrew	Modern Hebrew	Name	Transliteration
₭	א	aleph	'
૬	ב	beth	b
૧	ג	gimel	g
◁	ד	daleth	d
ㄱ	ה	he	h
Y	ו	waw	w
ㅍ	ז	zayin	z
Ħ	ח	heth	ḥ
⊘	ט	teth	ṭ
₴	י	yod	y
У	כ (ך)	kaph	k
৮	ל	lamed	l
ᵐ	מ (ם)	mem	m
৴	נ (ן)	nun	n
₮	ס	samekh	s
O	ע	ayin	ʿ
૰	פ (ף)	pe	p
ʮ	צ (ץ)	ṣade	ṣ
φ	ק	qoph	q
৭	ר	reš	r
W	ש	šin	š/s
×	ת	taw	t

the earliest extensively attested use of a distinct Hebrew script occurs on a tablet bearing an inscription, not in Hebrew, but in Moabite, a Canaanite Semitic language closely related to Hebrew; the Moabite Stone is dated to the ninth century BC. The Hebrew script was employed less and less after the Babylonian Exile of the sixth century BC, and eventually fell into disuse except among the sect of the Samaritans, who have continued to use it as a liturgical script until the present day.

The Arameans of Syria were writing their West Semitic language with the Phoenician script by approximately the eleventh century BC, and by about the eighth century BC, a distinctive Aramaic script had evolved. Owing to the status of Aramaic as a *lingua franca* and an official language of the Persian empire spoken in Anatolia, the Levant, Egypt and Mesopotamia, the Aramaic script enjoyed widespread use. With the ascendancy of Persia and the return to Palestine of the deported Jews of the Babylonian Exile, it was the Aramaic script which replaced the old Hebrew system. The modern Hebrew square print and its cursive variant are descended from the

Aramaic and were in use by the Roman period of Palestine history.

The Aramaic script, like its Phoenician parent, possessed only consonantal symbols. However, particular consonant letters came to be used for signalling the presence of long vowels: at the end of the word, *w (waw)* could represent *ū*, *y (yod)* could represent *ī*, and *h (he)* could represent *ē*, *ā* and even *ō*. These characters are the so-called *matres lectionis*, "the mothers of reading." By the ninth century BC, this aspect of Aramaic spelling had been adopted into the Hebrew writing system. Eventually, a variable use of the *matres lectionis* was extended to the interior of words.

In order to represent Hebrew vowels and so preserve the correct reading of the text of the Hebrew Bible, systems of vowel diacritics or vowel points were developed by the Jewish scholars known as the Massoretes. In about the eighth century AD, the Massoretes of the Babylonian school developed one such system, while two appeared at the hands of the Palestinian Massoretes. One of these latter systems, the Tiberian, eventually became standard. In modern Hebrew writing, vowel points are used in only a few contexts: for example, in the text of the Bible, in children's literature, and in poetry.

The Aramaic script was also utilized by an

Arab people called the Nabateans. In the second century BC, the Nabateans established a prosperous kingdom extending from Transjordan into the Sinai, with their capital at the city of Petra. Though speakers of the Semitic language of Arabic, the Nabateans wrote in Aramaic,

An early form of Arabic script called Kufic existed in addition to Nashki. As can be seen from this page of a manuscript of the Koran (c. ninth or tenth century), Kufic is a bold and thick script.

The modern Arabic script, with its delicately cursive consonantal symbols, is a descendant of the earlier Nashki script. All but six of the characters of the modern system have positional variants for use at the beginning, in the middle, and at the end of a word, as well as having independent forms.

ARABIC

Final	Medial	Initial	Independent	Transliteration
ﺎ			ا	ā
ﺐ	ﺒ	ﺑ	ب	b
ﺖ	ﺘ	ﺗ	ت	t
ﺚ	ﺜ	ﺛ	ث	θ
ﺞ	ﺠ	ﺟ	ج	ǰ
ﺢ	ﺤ	ﺣ	ح	ħ
ﺦ	ﺨ	ﺧ	خ	x
ﺪ			د	d
ﺬ			ذ	ð
ﺮ			ر	r
ﺰ			ز	z
ﺲ	ﺴ	ﺳ	س	s
ﺶ	ﺸ	ﺷ	ش	š
ﺺ	ﺼ	ﺻ	ص	ṣ
ﺾ	ﻀ	ﺿ	ض	ḍ
ﻂ	ﻄ	ﻃ	ط	ṭ
ﻆ	ﻈ	ﻇ	ظ	ẓ
ﻊ	ﻌ	ﻋ	ع	ʕ
ﻎ	ﻐ	ﻏ	غ	ɣ
ﻒ	ﻔ	ﻓ	ف	f
ﻖ	ﻘ	ﻗ	ق	q
ﻚ	ﻜ	ﻛ	ك	k
ﻞ	ﻠ	ﻟ	ل	l
ﻢ	ﻤ	ﻣ	م	m
ﻦ	ﻨ	ﻧ	ن	n
ﻪ	ﻬ	ﻫ	ه	h
ﻮ			و	w
ﻰ	ﻴ	ﻳ	ى	y

developing their own distinct variety of the script, which existed in both a monumental and a cursive form. There are also a few examples of it being used to record the Arabic language, and it was probably this Nabatean Aramaic script which later evolved into the Arabic writing system.

The earliest Arabic inscription in a distinctive, though perhaps transitional, Arabic script appears in about the fourth century AD. This is one of only a very few examples of Arabic script attested prior to the advent of Islam in the seventh century AD, when there is a marked increase in examples; it was in the middle of the seventh century that the Koran was compiled and published. Two principal varieties of Arabic script developed early in the Islamic period: Naskhi and Kufic. The former tends to be cursive and slanting, the latter beautifully thick. The modern Arabic script is a descendant of Naskhi. Vowels are marked by three vowel points and by the consonantal characters *alif, ya,* and *waw.*

Yet another writing system to evolve from the Aramaic is that of Syriac. The Syriac language was the dialect of Aramaic spoken in Edessa (now Urfa, Turkey) and its surrounding

areas. Owing to the city's position as a center of Christianity, the Bible was translated into Syriac, a large corpus of Christian Syriac writings appeared, and Syriac became widely used as a literary and liturgical language. The earliest known text in the Syriac script is dated to the first century AD. The Syriac system, being descended from Aramaic, is consonantal, but developed various means for marking vowels. The early, Nestorian system used diacritic vowel points together with the consonantal symbols *waw* and *yod,* while the Jacobite system of the eighth century used small subscript and superscript Greek vowel letters. The Syriac use of vowel points is likely to be the source of the Arabic and Hebrew practice of so representing vowel sounds.

There is another possible descendant of the Phoenician script; in the North African Phoenician colony of Carthage, established in the late ninth century BC, a dialect of Phoenician developed known as Punic. In antiquity, the Libyan peoples of North Africa used a writing system which has survived in the form of the modern script called Tifinagh used by some Berber-speakers. Perhaps, at least in part, the ancestor of Tifinagh developed from the Punic system.

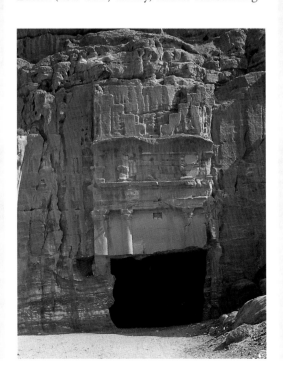

Petra, in modern Jordan, the "rose red city, half as old as time", was capital of the wealthy Nabatean kingdom (second century BC to 106 AD). The Nabateans spoke an early form of Arabic but wrote in the Aramaic language, using their own Nabatean variety of the Aramaic consonantal script.

SYRIAC

Estrangelā	Nestorian	Jacobite	Transliteration
			'
			b
			g
			d
			h
			w
			z
			ḥ
			ṭ
			y
			k
			l
			m
			n
			s
			'
			p
			ṣ
			q
			r
			š
			t

Three varieties of the consonantal Syriac script are illustrated here. The earliest of these is Estrangela (first century AD). The later Nestorian and Jacobite scripts were used by the eastern and western Syriac churches respectively.

Writing Systems

TIFINAGH

Name	Symbol	Translit.
Tar'erit	•	'
leb	⊡ ⊕	b
let	+	t
led	⊓ ∧ ⊔	d
lej	⊐⊏	j
lez	#	z
lez'	ⵅ ⵅ	z'
ler	◻ ◯	r
les	⊡ ⊙	s
leg	ⵗ ⵗ	g
leg'	ⵝ	g'
lef	ⵂ ⵊⵐ	f
lel	‖	l
lem	⊐	m
len	ⵏ	n
lek	ⵗ	k
lak'	ⵗⵗ	q
ler'	ⵗ	ɣ
lech	ⵛ	š
lah	ⵗ	h
ladh	ⵉ	d,t
lakh	::	x
laou	:	w
léy	ⵉⵉ	y
lebt	ⵟ	bt
lezt	ⵟ	zt
lert	⊞	rt
lest	ⵟ	st
legt	ⵟ	gt
leg't	ⵗⵅ	g't
lelt	ⵙ	lt
lemt	ⵟ	mt
lent	ⵝ	nt
lecht	ⵟ	št
lenk	ⵗ	nk

Tifinagh, descended from a Libyan script of antiquity, is a writing system used by the Tuareg, a pastoralist people of North Africa, for recording their dialect of Berber.

ANATOLIA

During the second millennium BC, several Indo-European languages were being spoken and written in Anatolia. Of these, the best known is Hittite, with texts dating to perhaps the seventeenth century BC. The scribes of the Hittite empire kept their records utilizing Babylonian cuneiform. The Hittites introduced an additional complication into the already complex Babylonian system of Sumerian logograms, syllabic symbols, and determinatives by retaining certain Akkadian phonetic spellings, so-called akkadograms. The cuneiform documents excavated at Bogazköy, site of the ancient Hittite capital, also preserve texts written in the Indo-European languages Palaic and Luvian, and the non-Indo-European Hattic.

The Luvian language of Anatolia was also recorded using a highly pictographic writing system called Hieroglyphic Luvian (formerly erroneously labeled Hieroglyphic Hittite), attested from approximately 1500 BC to 700 BC. Like the cuneiform script of Anatolia, the Hieroglyphic Luvian system contains logograms, syllabograms, and determinatives; it also existed in a cursive form.

BRONZE AGE AEGEAN

Between 2000 BC and 1450 BC, the Minoan civilization flourished on the Aegean island of Crete. Within their brilliantly colored palace complexes decorated with marvelous frescoes of dolphins and acrobats, Minoan scribes used a variety of scripts. Throughout much of their history the Minoans used a pictographic script classified, by the British archaeologist

The Phaistos Disk has long been an object of fascination for orthographic sleuths, but it has foiled all attempts at convincing decipherment. The hieroglyphic script appearing on this document is known from no other source.

Sir Arthur Evans, as Cretan Hieroglyphic. Some scholars have conjectured that this still-undeciphered script may possibly be linked to Hieroglyphic Luvian.

A second pictographic script from Minoan Crete, dated to approximately 1700 BC, appears only on a single double-sided document, a clay disk recovered from the ruins of the palace at Phaistos. Each of the 45 symbols appearing on the Phaistos Disk was produced by impressing a stamp into the moist clay medium. The script of the disk probably has the distinction of being the world's most frequently deciphered writing system. It seems likely that the script is syllabic in nature, though none of the decipherments so far proposed carries conviction.

From about the middle of the eighteenth century BC, yet another writing system was employed by the Minoans, the much more stylized, linear script called Linear A. Though the exact nature of the process is unclear, Linear A almost certainly evolved out of Cretan

THE WRITING OF BRONZE AGE GREECE

The Minoan civilization of Bronze Age Crete has left evidence of three different writing systems: Cretan Hieroglyphic, the Phaistos Disk script and Linear A. At the same time that the Minoans flourished in Crete, mainland Greece was home to the Mycenaeans, whose era is remembered in Homer's *Iliad* and *Odyssey*. From the Minoans, the Mycenaean Greeks acquired a writing system, now called Linear B. Most of the surviving Linear A and Linear B inscriptions are found on clay tablets. The scripts' symbols, which are curvilinear, are not easily incised in wet clay, however, perhaps suggesting the scripts were designed for and most often written on some other, perishable medium.

LINEAR A

Sym.	Translit.	Sym.	Translit.	Sym.	Translit.	Sym.	Translit.	Sym.	Translit
(glyph)	AB(01)	(glyph)	AB(22)	(glyph)	AB(41)	(glyph)	AB(66)	(glyph)	AB(120)
(glyph)	AB(02)	(glyph)	AB(22')	(glyph)	AB(44)	(glyph)	AB(67)	(glyph)	A(120b)
(glyph)	AB(03)	(glyph)	AB(22ᵐ)	(glyph)	AB(45)	(glyph)	AB(69)	(glyph)	AB(122)
(glyph)	AB(04)	(glyph)	AB(23)	(glyph)	AB(46)	(glyph)	AB(70)	(glyph)	AB(123)
(glyph)	AB(05)	(glyph)	AB(23ᵐ)	(glyph)	AB(47)	(glyph)	AB(73)	(glyph)	AB(131a)
(glyph)	AB(06)	(glyph)	AB(24)	(glyph)	AB(49)	(glyph)	AB(74)	(glyph)	AB(131b)
(glyph)	AB(07)	(glyph)	AB(26)	(glyph)	AB(50)	(glyph)	AB(76)	(glyph)	A(131c)
(glyph)	AB(08)	(glyph)	AB(27)	(glyph)	AB(51)	(glyph)	AB(77)	(glyph)	AB(164)
(glyph)	AB(09)	(glyph)	AB(28)	(glyph)	AB(53)	(glyph)	AB(78)	(glyph)	AB(171)
(glyph)	AB(10)	(glyph)	A(28b)	(glyph)	AB(54)	(glyph)	AB(79)	(glyph)	AB(180)
(glyph)	AB(11)	(glyph)	AB(29)	(glyph)	AB(55)	(glyph)	AB(80)	(glyph)	AB(188)
(glyph)	AB(13)	(glyph)	AB(30)	(glyph)	AB(56)	(glyph)	AB(81)	(glyph)	AB(191)
(glyph)	AB(16)	(glyph)	AB(31)	(glyph)	AB(57)	(glyph)	AB(82)	(glyph)	A(301)
(glyph)	AB(17)	(glyph)	AB(34)	(glyph)	AB(58)	(glyph)	AB(85)	(glyph)	A(302)
(glyph)	AB(20)	(glyph)	AB(37)	(glyph)	AB(59)	(glyph)	AB(86)	(glyph)	A(303)
(glyph)	AB(21)	(glyph)	AB(38)	(glyph)	AB(60)	(glyph)	AB(87)	(glyph)	A(304)
(glyph)	AB(21')	(glyph)	AB(39)	(glyph)	AB(61)	(glyph)	A(100/102)	(glyph)	A(305)
(glyph)	AB(21ᵐ)	(glyph)	AB(40)	(glyph)	AB(65)	(glyph)	AB(118)	(glyph)	A(306)

Linear A is the name given by the British archeologist, Sir Arthur Evans, to this Bronze Age Minoan script, descended from the Cretan Hieroglyphic writing system. The symbols illustrated here are known to have syllabic value, though the script is still being deciphered.

LINEAR B

Symbol	Translit.	Symbol	Translit.	Symbol	Translit.	Symbol	Translit.	Symbol	Translit.
(glyph)	a	(glyph)	e	(glyph)	i	(glyph)	ɑ	(glyph)	o
(glyph)	pa	(glyph)	pe	(glyph)	pi	(glyph)	pu	(glyph)	po
(glyph)	ta	(glyph)	te	(glyph)	ti	(glyph)	tu	(glyph)	to
(glyph)	da	(glyph)	de	(glyph)	di	(glyph)	du	(glyph)	do
(glyph)	ka	(glyph)	ke	(glyph)	ki	(glyph)	ku	(glyph)	ko
(glyph)	kwa	(glyph)	kwe	(glyph)	kwi	(glyph)	kwo		
(glyph)	sa	(glyph)	se	(glyph)	si	(glyph)	su	(glyph)	so
(glyph)	za	(glyph)	ze			(glyph)	zo		
(glyph)	ma	(glyph)	me	(glyph)	mi	(glyph)	mu	(glyph)	mo
(glyph)	na	(glyph)	ne	(glyph)	ni	(glyph)	nu	(glyph)	no
(glyph)	wa	(glyph)	we	(glyph)	wi	(glyph)	wo		
(glyph)	ya	(glyph)	ye			(glyph)	yu	(glyph)	yo
(glyph)	ra	(glyph)	re	(glyph)	ri	(glyph)	ru	(glyph)	ro
(glyph)	a₂	(glyph)	a₃	(glyph)	au				
(glyph)	pa₃	(glyph)	pu₂	(glyph)	pte				
(glyph)	ta₂	(glyph)	two						
(glyph)	dwe	(glyph)	dwo						
(glyph)	swa	(glyph)	swi						
(glyph)	nwa								
(glyph)	ra₂	(glyph)	ra₃	(glyph)	ro₂				

LINEAR B
The Unidentified Signs

(glyphs of unidentified signs)

The descendant of Linear A script, Linear B, has been deciphered. In 1952 Michael Ventris, a British architect who in boyhood had encountered an aged Sir Arthur Evans and his Linear B tablets, succeeded in deciphering the script and discovered that the language behind this syllabic writing system is an early dialect of Greek. Only a few signs (left) are still unknown.

This clay tablet, bearing an inscription in Linear B, was recovered from the remains of the Mycenaean palace at Pylos, home of the Homeric hero Nestor.

subfamily – a language such as Luvian.

During the mid-fifteenth century BC, the Minoans were superseded in Crete by the Mycenaeans, a Greek people whose culture first appears in the archeological record of the Greek mainland at about 1600 BC. In AD 1877, the Spanish consul in Crete reported finding an inscribed clay tablet at the site of the ruined Mycenaean palace at Knossos. Since that time, many such clay documents have been unearthed at Knossos and other Mycenaean palace sites both on Crete and on the Greek mainland. These documents remained unreadable until 1952, when a young British architect named Michael Ventris deciphered their script. This, the earliest known writing system of the Greeks, is Linear B, so named by Sir Arthur Evans long before its decipherment.

The Linear B script, descended from Minoan Linear A, is a syllabic system. Logograms also occur but are usually used only in conjunction with numerals to specify a quantity of some commodity – olive oil, grain, chariots, swords, and so on – which is often also spelled out using syllabic symbols; most of the Linear B tablets are palace business records.

Linear B syllabograms, with only a few exceptions, are of the V and CV type; thus the spelling of two or more consonants in sequence and of consonants occurring at the end of a word is problematic. Linear B scribes responded to this problem by developing a spelling strategy which involves, in some cases, simply not writing the consonant and, in other cases, writing a vowel which does not actually occur in the spoken form of the word being written. Thus Greek *sperma* ("seed") is spelled *pe-ma*, while *tektones* ("carpenters") is spelled *te-ke-to-ne*. As a rule, the script does not distinguish voiced, voiceless, and voiceless aspirated consonants which are produced at a single point in the vocal tract; and so, for example, the phonetic CV sequences [ba], [pa], and [pʰa] are all written as the same syllabic symbol. Also not distinguished are the liquid

Hieroglyphic, which continued to be used alongside Linear A. Both syllabograms and logograms occur within the symbol inventory of Linear A, the decipherment of which is ongoing. Various attempts have been made to match it with known languages of antiquity; the one which seems perhaps to hold some promise is that which sees behind the script an Indo-European language of the Anatolian consonants [l] and [r]. Exceptionally, however, [d] is distinguished from [t] and [t^h].

The use of the Linear B script disappears from the archeological record at about 1200 BC as the Mycenaean civilization comes to an end, victim of a great conflagration which swept across the Aegean and eastern Mediterranean at the close of the Bronze Age.

CYPRUS

With the collapse of the Mycenaean civilization, large numbers of Greeks left their homeland for other regions, including the island of Cyprus. The earlier Cypriot writing dates to about 1500 BC, and is attested in a set of scripts called Cypro-Minoan. As the name implies, these evolved from a Minoan system, probably Linear A. Traditionally, three separate Cypro-Minoan scripts, designated simply as Cypro-Minoan I, II, and III have been identified, the last found at Ugarit rather than on Cyprus. All remain undeciphered, though it has been conjectured that each writes a different language. Recently, however, some authorities have begun to question this three-way division.

The Mycenaean Greek settlers of Cyprus adapted one of the Cypro-Minoan scripts for their own use by at least the mid-eleventh century BC, thus creating the second (known) Greek writing system, the Cypriot syllabary. This syllabic script consists, much in the manner of the earlier Mycenaean system, of only V and CV symbols, plus a very few CCV symbols. The strategy of Linear B scribes for spelling sequences of consonants was employed by the Cypriot Greek scribes, though with one fundamental and significant modification: those very consonants occurring in sequence which had not been spelled within the Linear B system are now represented in the Cypriot syllabary by using a CV symbol whose vowel component matches the first vowel preceding the consonant sequence. *Artemidi* ("for Artemis"), for example, is written *a-ra-te-mi-ti.* Voiced, voiceless, and voiceless aspirated

CYPRIOT									
Symbol	Translit.	Symbol	Translit.	Symbol	Translit.	Symbol	Translit.	Symbol	Translit.
⋇	a	⋇	e	✗	i	⩒	o	Υ	u
‡	pa	⌇	pe	⩔	pi	⌇	po	⩲	pu
⊢	ta	⩔	te	↑	ti	F	to	兀	tu
⤊	ka	⩔	ke	Ϋ	ki	∩	ko	⋇	ku
V	sa	⊔	se	⌂	si	⩔	so	⋇	su
						⑅	zo		
⋇	ma	⋇	me	⋎	mi	Φ	mo	⋇	mu
T̄	na	⋈	ne	⋇	ni	⫫	no	⋗	nu
⋉	wa	I	we	⋊	wi	⌃	wo		
⍴	ya					⋌	yo		
Ω	ra	⋔	re	⋑	ri	8	ro	⋊	ru
Υ	la	8	le	⪦	li	+	lo	⍥	lu
⋈	ksa	Ǵ	kse						

consonants which are produced at a single point in the vocal tract are not distinguished from one another, including dentals, as can be seen by the example cited above. In contrast to the Linear B practice, [l] and [r] are distinguished in the Cypriot system. Also, special mechanisms are devised for spelling both word-final consonants and the first consonant occurring in word-initial consonant sequences.

GREECE

The Greek alphabet is yet a third Greek writing system. Though much earlier dates have been proposed, the most widely accepted for the first appearance of the Greek alphabet is the eighth century BC.

As with the two earlier Greek scripts, the alphabet was based upon a writing system already used by a people with whom the Greeks came into contact, in this instance the Phoenicians. Various places have been suggested for the Greek adaptation of the Phoenician consonantal script, including

The syllabic Cypriot script was probably devised by émigrés from Mycenaean Greece. A comparison of this Greek script with Linear B reveals similarities between the two; these correspondences were utilized by Michael Ventris in his decipherment of Linear B.

Cyprus, Crete, Rhodes, and the Syrian coastal town of Al Mina. Wherever this adaptation occurred, it must have been carried out within a bilingual Phoenician-Greek context. In the view of the author, the evidence points overwhelmingly to Cyprus, on which there had been a significant Phoenician presence since the middle of the ninth century BC. Certain peculiarities of the Greek alphabet suggest that the Greeks who adapted the Phoenician writing system were accustomed to spelling their language with the Cypriot syllabary. For

The first writing system to contain symbols for individual consonant sounds (as in Proto-Canaanite) and for individual vowel sounds (as in the various Near Eastern and Greek syllabaries) was the Greek alphabet. There were many local varieties of the Greek alphabet, such as the four illustrated here.

GREEK

Euboea	Ionia	Athens	Corinth	Modern Capitals	Modern Lower Case	Transliteration	Name
AA	AA	AA	AA	A	α	a	alpha
B	B	B	⊔⊓	B	β	b	beta
<C	Γ	Λ	C<	Γ	γ	g	gamma
DD	Δ	Δ	Δ	Δ	δ	d	delta
ЯE	ЯE	ЯE	B	E	ε	e	epsilon
F	—	F	F	F	F	w	digamma
I	I	I	I	Z	ζ	zd	zeta
—	ВH	—	—	H	η	ē	eta
ВH	—	ВH	ВH	—		h	
⊗⊕⊙	⊗⊕⊙	⊗⊕⊙	⊗⊕⊙	Θ	θ	th	theta
I	I	I	₹	I	ι	i	iota
K	K	K	K	K	κ	k	kappa
ι	ᴧΛ	ᴠ	ᴧΛ	Λ	λ	l	lambda
ᴧᴧM	ᴧM	ᴧM	ᴧM	M	μ	m	mu
ᴧN	ᴧN	ᴧN	ᴧN	N	ν	n	nu
X	⊞	(X⟨)	⊞	Ξ	ξ	ks	xi
O	O	O	O	O	o	o	omicron
ΓΓ	Γ	Γ	Γ	Π	π	p	pi
M(?)	—	—	M	M	—	s	san
9	9	9	9	,Q	,ϙ	k	qoppa
P	PD	PR	PR	P	ρ	r	rho
⟨	₹	⟨	—	Σ	σς	s	sigma
T	T	T	T	T	τ	t	tau
ᴦYV	VY	ᴦYV	ᴦYV	Y	υ	u	upsilon
Фⴲ	Ф	Фⴲ	Фⴲ	Φ	φ	ph	phi
ᴪᴠ	X	X	X	X	χ	kh	chi
(Ф⟨)	ᴪᴠ	(Ф⟨)	ᴪ ᴠ	Ψ	ψ	ps	psi
—	⋂Ω	—	—	Ω	ω	ō	omega

This Greek cantharus, from about 540BC, has a double head representing a Greek woman and an African woman.

LOCAL GREEK ALPHABETS

The local, or *epichoric*, alphabets of the ancient Greeks can be divided into four different types according to the manner in which they represent certain consonant sounds. In 1887 the German scholar Kirchhoff published a study of the Greek alphabets in which he included a map showing the distribution of the alphabet types. The four types were color-coded as green, red, blue, and light blue; the practice of identifying the alphabets in this way has persisted.

A warrior strides across the black background of this Greek red-figure vase.

Drawings of heads decorate this example of 4th century BC Greek pottery.

This funerary amphora, dating from around 800BC, depicts the prothesis (laying out) and lamentation over the dead.

The head of a satyr is depicted on a 4th century BC painted rhyton.

185

| ETRUSCAN | | |
Archaic Etruscan	Neo-Etruscan	Transliteration
A	A	a
)	)	k
∃	∃	e
ꟻ	ꟻ	v
I	⅋⅋	ts
⊟	⊟Ø	h
⊗O	☉O	th
I	I	i
K		k
↓	↓	l
W	M	m
Ч	Π	n
ſ	ſ	p
M	M	ś
Q		k
٩	)	r
₹	₹	s
T	↑↑	t
Y	V	u
X		s
Φ	Φ	ph
Y	Ψ	kh
⧂	8	f

The Etruscans, a non-Indo-European people from Italy, acquired a variety of the red alphabet type from the Greeks who settled in the area of Pithkoussae and Cumae in southern Italy (modern Naples). The approximate values of individual symbols are known, but much remains a mystery.

example, the Greek alphabet contains a symbol with the value [k] + [s] (the progenitor of the x symbol used in spelling English); with both a symbol for [k] and one for [s], the alphabet has no need at all for such a double consonant character. Within the Cypriot syllabary, however, *ksV* syllabic characters are needed as a consequence of the peculiar strategy used for spelling consonant sequences. Provision was made in the new alphabetic script for a [k] + [s] character because the adapters were already familiar and writing with a system in which [k] + [s] symbols occurred.

The Greek alphabet was unlike any earlier writing system. As with the Phoenician and Aramaic scripts and their descendants, it is a phonetic script, representing individual sounds; but unlike these, the Greek script employs not only consonant symbols but vowel symbols as well. *Matres lectionis* were used at the end of words in the Aramaic script prior to the advent of the Greek alphabet, but their use is sporadic and limited. Moreover, the *matres lectionis* are consonant symbols which are at times employed to signal the presence of vowel sounds; they are not distinct vowel characters. Owing to phonetic differences between the Greek and Phoenician languages, the Greek adapters of the Phoenician script had at their disposal more consonant symbols than were required for spelling Greek. To these extra consonant characters, the Greeks assigned vowel values, and so was born the first alphabet.

Many local varieties of the Greek alphabet developed as the script spread across the Greek-speaking world. These local alphabets have traditionally been classified into three

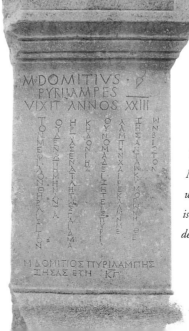

This funerary inscription on the gravestone of M. Domitius Pyrilampes from Dion, Greece is written in both Latin and Greek. The main text is in Greek, while the name and age of the deceased appears horizontally in Latin at the top.

This romanticized nineteenth-century engraving depicts the artist's conception of the "women's quarters" in the ancient Italian city of Pompeii (completely buried in AD 79 by a volcanic eruption of Vesuvius). Among the activities in which the women are engaged are reading and writing. Actual portraits survive from Pompeii which represent women holding writing implements.

major groups and named after the colors used to encode their distribution on the map which appeared in A. Kirchhoff's 1887 *Studien zur Geschichte des Griechischen Alphabets* (*see map*). The green alphabets were used on Crete and certain neighboring islands, and were characterized by the absence of so-called supplemental characters, consonantal symbols appended to the end of the adapted Phoenician script; a vowel symbol for ō, called *omega*, would also sometimes be added. The red

the island of Pithekoussae in the bay of Naples. These letters comprise a verse inscription on the so-called Cup of Nestor, dated to approximately 725 BC.

ITALY

In the seventh century BC, a non-Indo-European people called the Etruscans lived in western central Italy. The southern reaches of Etruscan settlement neighbored upon the Euboean Greeks colonies of Pithekoussae and

Cumae. From the Greeks of southern Italy, the Etruscans learned to write. As the sounds of the Etruscan language differed from those of Greek, the Etruscans introduced certain changes into the red Greek alphabet which they acquired. Etruscan lacked voiced stops (sounds such as [b], [d], and [g]), and although the earliest Etruscan alphabets retained the Greek letters for such consonants, eventually the Greek symbols B and Δ, representing [b]

The Tomb of the Leopards, Tarquinia. An Etruscan chamber tomb dating from c. 550-520 BC. Some of the tombs of Tarquinia preserve painted Etruscan inscriptions.

alphabets, such as those of Euboea and Laconia, have the supplemental characters Φ and Ψ, with the respective values [pʰ] and [kʰ]. The blue alphabets are of two subtypes: dark blue, used in Corinth and Rhodes, with supplementals Φ, X, and Ψ, representing [pʰ], [kʰ], and [pˢ] respectively; light blue from Attica, with only Φ and X, taking the same values as in the dark blue subtypes.

Much of Sicily and the south of Italy was colonized by the Greeks. One of the oldest known examples of Greek alphabetic writing comes from the ruins of the Greek colony on

and [d], were dropped. The Greek letter Γ, for [g], was, however, retained to represent the voiceless stop [k] when it occurred before the vowels *e* and *i*. The Etruscans used the Greek K to spell [k] before the vowel *a*, and the Greek symbol Ϙ (called *qoppa*) to spell [k] before *u*; the Greeks had used *qoppa* for representing a *k*-sound produced a bit further back in the oral cavity than [k].

The longest single Etruscan document yet discovered was found not in Italy but in Egypt. A Croatian travelling in Egypt in the

Rome not only gave its version of the alphabet to Italy, Europe, and much of the world but is the source of the elegantly sublime lapidary letter-style, as used on this monument from Grado, Italy.

nineteenth century acquired for the Zagreb National Museum a mummy which was entombed in linen bandages with an inscription of about 1,200 words detailing a sacred Etruscan calendar. Why and how such a document came to wrap an Egyptian mummy is unknown.

Also coming to light in the nineteenth century was a stele on the island of Lemnos in the Aegean. The Lemnian Stone, dated to the sixth century BC, bears an inscription in a script which is quite similar to the Etruscan alphabet. This inscription is not yet understood, though it has been conjectured that it writes a language similar to Etruscan.

The Etruscan alphabet was introduced to the region of Latium and its Latin-speaking inhabitants in the seventh century BC. Again, because of consonant and vowel differences between their own Indo-European language and Etruscan, the Latin-speaking users of the Etruscan script made certain modifications.

While early Latin writers continued the Etruscan practice of using three different characters to represent the voiceless stop [k], the third letter of the adapted Etruscan script, C (which was Greek γ in origin) was eventually generalized for spelling Latin [k] in all contexts. A modified form of this C, designed G, was used for spelling the Latin voiced stop [g], and placed seventh in the Latin alphabet, replacing an unneeded Etruscan character, the Greek *zeta* in origin. Latin Q, from Etruscan (and earlier Greek) *qoppa*, came to represent the voiceless labiovelar stop [k^w]. The early form of the Etruscan alphabet acquired in Latium retained

OSCAN		UMBRIAN	
Symbol	Translit.	Symbol	Translit.
�писать a	a	ꝷ a	a
B	b	B	b
ꭾ	g	ꝗ	ř
Я	d	Ⴝ	e
Ⴈ	e	Ⴈ	v
Ⴐ	v	⚹	ts
Ⴈ	ts	⊘	h
Ⴀ	h	Ⅰ	i
Ⅰ	i	Ⴉ	k
Ⴉ	k	Ⴈ	l
Ⴈ	l	ꟽ(Λ)	m
ꟽ	m	Ⴈ	n
Ⴈ	n	Ⴈ	p
⨅	p	Ⴈ	r
ꟼ	r	Ⴉ	s
Ⴉ	s	ⴕ(Ⴘ)	t
Ⴕ	t	Ⴘ	u
Ⴘ	u	8	f
8	f	ꝺ	ç
Ⴈ(Ⴈⴉ)	í		
Ꝟ	ú		

Oscan and Umbrian were two of the several Italic (Indo-European) languages of ancient Italy. Each used an alphabet derived from the Etruscan script. Within the last three centuries BC, these languages and their alphabets fell victim to the spread of Latin and its script throughout Italy.

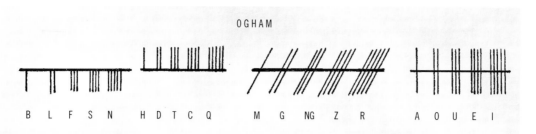

OGHAM

B L F S N   H D T C Q   M G NG Z R   A O U E I

One of the more unusual alphabetic scripts of early Europe is Ogham, the writing system of the Celts of Britain and Ireland.

the Greek symbols for [b] and [d], but the Etruscan letters which continued the Greek symbols for the voiceless aspirated stops [p^h], [t^h], and [k^h] (Φ, θ, and Ψ in the red alphabet of the Euboean colonies) were not required for spelling Latin and so were deleted. The letters Y and Z were appended in the first century BC in order to spell more accurately the many Greek loan words entering the Roman language.

Latin was only one of several Indo-European languages of the Italic subfamily spoken in Italy when the Latin alphabet appeared. Oscan and Umbrian, for example, both developed their own Etruscan-based alphabets. With Rome's highly effective colonization of the Italian peninsula, these languages and their scripts were supplanted by Latin and its alphabet. The preeminent status of the Latin alphabet would in time be extended considerably beyond Italy.

EUROPE

The Celts of the European continent were writing with both the Greek and Latin alphabets by the first two centuries BC. In Britain and Ireland a rather unusual script was in use among the Celts by the second century AD; this is the alphabetic script called Ogham, perhaps named after Oghma, the divine Celtic strong man. The Ogham inscriptions are seen principally, though not exclusively, on boundary or grave stones. The 20 characters of the script consist of short lines of one to five strokes, touching or crossing a horizontal or vertical reference line at right angles or diagonally. Vowel characters sometimes consist of one to five dots, rather than lines. The origin of the script is uncertain. Some scholars have speculated that Ogham is based upon a secret finger-language of the Druidic priests, citing a medieval Irish manuscript in which such a finger-code is described. It has also been proposed that the script developed under the influence of the Latin or Greek alphabets and the Germanic runes.

St. Luke is portrayed penning his Gospel in this illumination from an eleventh-century Biblical manuscript produced at the monastery of Echternach (Luxembourg). The Gospel writer holds a quill and a penknife, tools of the Medieval scribe.

This illuminated page from the Luttrell Psalter (c. AD 1340) is written in the script known as gothic or black letter. The style of illumination is that of the East Anglian school.

The runic script of the Germanic peoples first appears in the archeological record in the third century AD (though a date of the second century AD has been proposed for certain recent finds). The runic symbols, with their characteristic vertical and diagonal lines, are arranged in an alphabetic order which scholars call a *futhark*, after the value of the first six characters (f, u, th, a, r, and k). The earliest *futharks* consist of 24 symbols, and it was perhaps the Latin alphabet which provided the inspiration for their development. By the fifth century AD, a *futhark* (or more accurately *futhork*) of 31 symbols, had evolved for writing Anglo-Saxon.

During the fourth century AD, the Visigothic bishop Wulfila who translated the Bible into Gothic did not simply appropriate a runic script, but designed his own alphabet for the translation. The symbols of his Gothic writing system were based upon Greek and Latin alphabetic characters with the exception of *u* and *o*, which appear to be of runic origin.

The non-Latin scripts of much of Europe gave way as the Latin alphabet advanced. Roman armies had already transported their system across the European continent and Britain, but it was the spread of Christianity and the concomitant status of the Latin language and writing which would in the end be the undoing of runes and oghams. In the Christian monasteries of Europe, many distinct styles of Latin script evolved — Irish, Anglo-Saxon, Carolingian, Gothic (not to be confused with Wulfila's script), Italic, and Roman. Medieval monks not only filled pages of books with sacred words written in these styles, but transformed them into magnificent works of art, producing lavish illuminated manuscripts.

Runes were the alphabetic symbols used by the various Germanic people of Europe, known from at least the third century AD. The runic system, or futhork, of the Anglo-Saxons contains 31 characters. Runes were commonly inscribed on wood, metal, and stone.

ANGLO-SAXON RUNES

f	u	th	o	r	c	g	w	h	n	i	y	ï	p	x	s

t	b	e	m	l	ng	æ	d	a	æ	ü	ea	ğ	k	k

GOTHIC

a	b	g	d	e	u	z	h	θ	i	ī	k	l

m	n	y	u	p	r	s	t	w	f	ch	hw	o

The Gothic alphabet, not to be confused with the gothic script of the Roman alphabet, was invented for the purpose of translating the Bible into the East Germanic language of Gothic.

LYCIAN

Symbol	Transliteration
ᚠ	a
↑	e
B b	b
ᛘ	β
Υ	g
Δ	d
E	i
F	w
I	z
Χ	ϑ
Ϊ	y
K	k
✳	q
Λ	l
Μ	m
Ν	n
Χ	ṁ
I	ñ
O	u
Γ	p
P	r
Ϸ	s
Τ	t
Ͳ	τ
ᛉ ᛉ	ā
ᛉ ᛉ	ɪe
✝	h
Ͷ Υ Ϋ	x

In southwest Asia Minor, speakers of Lycian (an Indo-European language) were writing with their own script, derived from a Greek alphabet of the red type, by the fifth century BC.

COPTIC

Name	Symbol	Transliteration	Name	Symbol	Transliteration
Alfa	Ⲁ ⲁ	a	Ro	Ⲣ ⲣ	r
Vida	Ⲃ ⲃ	v [b]	Sīma	Ⲥ ⲥ	s
Gamma	Ⲅ ⲅ	g	Dau	Ⲧ ⲧ	t
Dalda	Ⲇ ⲇ	d	He	Ⲩ ⲩ	y, u
Ei	Ⲉ ⲉ	ĕ	Phi	Ⲫ ⲫ	ph
Sīta	Ⲍ ⲍ	z	Chi	Ⲭ ⲭ	kh
Hîda	Ⲏ ⲏ	i, é	Epsi	Ⲯ ⲯ	ps
Tīda	Ⲑ ⲑ	th	O	Ⲱ ⲱ	ō
Jōda	Ⲓ ⲓ	i	Shāi	Ϣ ϣ	š
Kappa	Ⲕ ⲕ	k	Fāi	Ϥ ϥ	f
Lōla	Ⲗ ⲗ	l	Chāi	Ϧ ϧ	ḫ
Mi	Ⲙ ⲙ	m	Hori	Ϩ ϩ	h
Ni	Ⲛ ⲛ	n	Džandža	Ϫ ϫ	j
Exi	Ⲝ ⲝ	ks	Schima	Ϭ ϭ	č
O	Ⲟ ⲟ	ŏ	Di	Ϯ ϯ	ti
Bi	Ⲡ ⲡ	p			

The demotic script of Egyptian was supplanted by a new writing system based on the Greek alphabet, Coptic (the Bohairic version is shown here). The ancient writing system of the Egyptians would not, however, disappear without a trace – the last seven characters of this Coptic alphabet were furnished by demotic.

OLD CHURCH SLAVONIC

Symbol		Transliteration	Symbol		Transliteration
Ⰰ	ⰰ	a	Ⱈ	ⱈ	ch
Ⰱ	ⰱ	b	Ⱉ	ⱉ	o
Ⰲ	ⰲ	v	Ⱌ	ⱌ	ts
Ⰳ	ⰳ	g	Ⱍ	ⱍ	č
Ⰴ	ⰴ	d	Ⱎ	ⱎ	š
Ⰵ	ⰵ	e	Ⱋ	ⱋ	št
Ⰶ	ⰶ	ž	Ⱏ	ⱏ	ŭ
Ⰷ	ⰷ	dz	Ⱐ	ⱐ	y
Ⰸ	ⰸ	z	Ⱐ	ⱐ	ĭ
Ⰻ	ⰻ	i	Ⱑ	ⱑ	ě
Ⰹ	ⰹ	i	Ⱓ	ⱓ	ju
Ⰽ	ⰽ	k	Ⱔ	ⱔ	ja
Ⰾ	ⰾ	l	Ⰵ	ⰵ	je
Ⰿ	ⰿ	m	Ⱔ	ⱔ	ę
Ⱀ	ⱀ	n	Ⱘ	ⱘ	ǫ
Ⱁ	ⱁ	o	Ⱗ	ⱗ	ję
Ⱂ	ⱂ	p	Ⱙ	ⱙ	jǫ
Ⱃ	ⱃ	r	Ⰷ	ⰷ	ks
Ⱄ	ⱄ	s	Ⱚ	ⱚ	ps
Ⱅ	ⱅ	t	Ⱎ	ⱎ	θ
Ⱆ	ⱆ	u	Ⱛ	ⱛ	ü
Ⱇ	ⱇ	f			

Old church Slavonic, or Old Bulgarian, is the south Slavic language into which the Bible was translated by the ninth-century Greek missionaries St. Cyril and St. Methodius. The Cyrillic alphabet script which was devised for recording this language bears the name of one of the Greek brothers.

Then, with the ensuing age of global European exploration and colonization, the Latin script was spread around the world.

The Etruscan writing system was by no means the only offspring of the Greek alphabet. In Asia Minor, the Phrygians had adopted the Greek system in the eighth century BC, and distinct Lydian and Lycian alphabets, based upon the Greek, were in use in the fifth and fourth centuries BC. The Greek script had also been adapted for the alphabetic spelling of the Egyptian language by as early as the first century AD, the standard form of this Coptic alphabet being built from 24 Greek characters plus seven symbols from demotic, which Coptic supplanted.

In the ninth century AD, a group of Greek missionaries led by St. Cyril and St. Methodius went to spread their faith among the Slavs of southern Europe. The Slavs were converted to Christianity, and Cyril and Methodius prepared a translation of the Bible in the language now called Old Church Slavonic. Two alphabetic scripts were used by the early Slavic Christians, Cyrillic and Glagolitic. Early Slavic tradition credits St. Cyril with the development of a Slavic alphabet, and Cyrillic bears his name. The tradition is ambiguous, however, and there is disagreement among scholars as to which of the scripts was the creation of Cyril. With its 43 characters, the Cyrillic script was clearly based upon the Greek alphabet, but with many supplementary symbols added.

The early Cyrillic script evolved into the alphabets of many of the modern Slavic languages, such as Russian, Ukrainian, Bulgarian, and Serbian, while in those Slavic areas in which the leading sect of Christianity is the Roman Catholic Church, such as Czechoslovakia, Poland, and Croatia, the Latin alphabet is used. Before the dissolution of the former Soviet Union, when the influence of Russian language and culture was widespread, the Russian variety of Cyrillic was adapted for writing many non-Slavic, and even non-Indo-

RUSSIAN		
Capitals	Lower Case	Transliteration
А	а	a
Б	б	b
В	в	v
Г	г	g
Д	д	d
Е	е	e
Ё	ё	ë
Ж	ж	ž
З	з	z
И	и	i
Й	й	j
К	к	k
Л	л	l
М	м	m
Н	н	n
О	о	o
П	п	p
Р	р	r
С	с	s
Т	т	t
У	у	u
Ф	ф	f
Х	х	x
Ц	ц	c
Ч	ч	č
Ш	ш	š
Щ	щ	šč
	ъ	"
	ы	y
	ь	'
З	з	e
Ю	ю	ju
Я	я	ja

The form of the Cyrillic script which is now used for recording Russian is a descendant of the Old Church Slavonic writing system. Russian Cyrillic has been or is still used for spelling various non-Slavic languages which were drawn into the realm of Soviet influence.

193

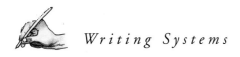

The origin of the Armenian alphabet is traditionally assigned to the early fifth century AD and its inventor is identified as St. Mesrop, who is said to have been assisted by St. Sahak.

ARMENIAN

Symbol		Transliteration
Ա	ա	a
Բ	բ	b
Գ	գ	g
Դ	դ	d
Ե	ե	e
Զ	զ	z
Է	է	ē
Ը	ը	ə
Թ	թ	t'
Ժ	ժ	ž
Ի	ի	i
Լ	լ	l
Խ	խ	ch
Ծ	ծ	ts
Կ	կ	k
Հ	հ	h
Ձ	ձ	j
Ղ	ղ	ł
Ճ	ճ	č
Մ	մ	m
Յ	յ	y
Ն	ն	n
Շ	շ	š
Ո	ն	o
Չ	չ	č'
Պ	պ	p
Ջ	ջ	ǰ
Ռ	ռ	ṙ
Ս	ս	s
Վ	վ	v
Տ	տ	t
Ր	ր	r
Ց	ց	ts'
Ւ	ւ	w
Փ	փ	p'
Ք	ք	k'

GEORGIAN

Symbol	Transliteration
ა	a
ბ	b
გ	g
დ	d
ე	e
ვ	v
ზ	z
თ	t
ი	i
კ	ķ
ლ	l
მ	m
ნ	n
ო	o
პ	p̣
ჟ	ž
რ	r
ს	s
ტ	ţ
უ	u
ფ	p
ქ	k
ღ	γ
ყ	q
შ	š
ჩ	č
ც	ts
ძ	dz
წ	ţs
ჭ	č̣
ხ	x
ჯ	j
ჰ	h

St. Mesrop is also credited with designing the Georgian writing system. An alternative tradition attributes this version of the script called Mkhedruli to the Georgian king, P'arnavaz.

European languages, including Kurdish, Chechen (Caucasian), Chuvash, Mongolian, and Yuit (an Eskimo language).

The characters of the Glagolitic script are not so easily matched with those of a preexisting writing system. Many scholars believe Glagolitic to have been developed prior to Cyrillic and contend that, as with Cyrillic, the Greek alphabet provided the model. The Georgian, Albanian, and various Semitic scripts are among other writing systems which have been conjectured to have exerted influence in the development of this Slavic alphabet. Glagolitic has survived in modern times only as the liturgical script of a very few Roman Catholic Slavs in southern Europe.

Two other alphabets used to record languages of Europe are attributed to a saint: St. Mesrop is traditionally identified as the inventor of both the Armenian and Georgian scripts. He is said to have begun designing a writing system for the Armenian Christians in 406 AD. The source of this script is uncertain, with the Aramaic and Iranian Pahlavi systems proposed as candidates, and the presence of vowel characters suggesting a Greek derivation.

If St. Mesrop did invent the Georgian alphabet, he was perhaps responsible only for Khutsuri, the ecclesiastical script. Some scholars detect similarities between Khutsuri and Armenian script, though the former preserves an Aramaic letter-order not found in the latter, which clearly suggests that Aramaic, or Syriac, played some role. Again, vowel characters also betray a Greek template. The Georgian script commonly used today developed from the earlier Mkhedruli system, the so-called script of warriors. The chronology of its development relative to Khutsuri is another matter of disagreement.

INDIA

The earliest writing of India was left by the people of the Indus Valley civilization (2500–1750 BC); their script is poorly understood, though recent advances have been claimed. From the third century BC, however, Indic writing of a quite different sort is well attested. There were two writing systems in use by this period: Kharoshthi and Brahmī. The Kharoshthi, or Bactrian, is believed to have developed from the Aramaic consonantal script of the Persian Empire. The origin of Brahmī is probably the same, though on this point there is less agreement; it is undoubtedly of Semitic origin however. Both of these scripts were used for recording the edicts of the Maurya prince Ashoka between approximately 257 and 235 BC. The Kharoshthi system remained in use until about the fifth century AD. Brahmī appears to be the parent of all of the many modern scripts of India, recording both Indo-Aryan and Dravidian languages. Roughly following this linguistic bifurcation, the writing systems of India are divided into a North and a South branch. Among the North Indian group are the scripts of Devanagari, Bengali, Gujarati, Gurmukhi, and Oriya. The unusual, distinctive appearance of the characters of the Oriya script, reminiscent of so many melted light bulbs, is said to be a consequence of the material on which the script was written during an early period. The long slender palm leaves used were easily split by horizontal strokes, so rounded characters were more generally favored.

The South Indian group of writing systems includes those of Tamil, Kannada, Telugu, and Malayalam. On the island nation of Sri Lanka, the Sinhalese script appears to have developed under the influence of both North and South Indian groups.

From 2500-1750 BC the Indus Valley was the focus of a flourishing civilization. Its people were literate but their writing system is now poorly understood.

A women's cooperative in Sri Lanka producing a newspaper. Sinhalese script appears to have been influenced by both North and South Indian writing systems.

DEVANAGARI

Vowel Symbols

अ	आ	इ	ई	उ	ऊ	ऋ	ॠ	ऌ	ए	ऐ	ओ	औ
a	ā	i	ī	u	ū	ṛ	ṝ	ḷ	e	ai	o	au

Consonant + Vowel Symbols

क	ख	ग	घ	ङ			ह	:
ka	kha	ga	gha	nga			ha	ḥ

च	छ	ज	झ	ञ	य		ःश
ca	cha	ja	jha	ña	ya		śa

ट	ठ	ड	ढ	ण	र	ळ	ष
ṭa	ṭha	ḍa	ḍha	ṇa	ra	ḷa	ṣa

त	थ	द	ध	न	ल		स
ta	tha	da	dha	na	la		sa

प	फ	ब	भ	म	व
pa	pha	ba	bha	ma	Va

Sample Vowel Diacritics

का	की	कु
kā	kī	ku

Sanskrit, one of the earliest recorded Indo-European languages, is written with the syllabic script called Devanagari (meaning "script of the city of the gods"). Each of the basic consonant + vowel symbols has the value of consonant + a. The vowel value of basic CV symbols can be modifed by the addition of a diacritic stroke.

ORIYA

Vowel Symbols

ଅ	ଆ	ଇ	ଈ	ଉ	ଊ	ଋ	ୠ
a	ā	i	ī	u	ū	ru	rū

ଌ	ଏ	ଐ	ଓ	ଔ	ଂ	ଃ
lu	ē	ai	ō	au	aṅ	a'

Consonant + Vowel Symbols

କ	ଖ	ଗ	ଘ	ଙ
ka	kha	ga	gha	nga

ଚ	ଛ	ଜ	ଝ	ଞ
ca	cha	ja	jha	ña

ଟ	ଠ	ଡ	ଢ	ଣ
ṭa	ṭha	ḍa	ḍha	ṇa

ତ	ଥ	ଦ	ଧ	ନ
ta	tha	da	dha	na

ପ	ଫ	ବ	ଭ	ମ
pa	pha	ba	bha	ma

ଯ	ର	ଲ	ଳ	ୱ
(ja)	ra	la	ḷa	wa

ଶ	ଷ	ସ	ହ	କ୍ଷ
śa	ṣa	sa	ha	khya

Oriya is an Indo-Aryan language of eastern India, closely related to Bengali. The symbols of this script have a conspicuously curved dome, a feature which is attributed to the early practice of writing Oriya on palm leaves which were easily split by horizontal scoring.

While the syllabic writing system of Kannada shares common roots with the Devanagari and Oriya scripts, the language of Kannada, spoken in southwestern India belongs to the Dravidian family.

KANNADA

Vowel Symbols

ಅ	ಆ	ಇ	ಈ	ಉ	ಊ	ಋ
a	ā	i	ī	u	ū	ru

ಎ	ಏ	ಐ	ಒ	ಓ	ಔ
e	ē	ai	o	ō	au

Consonant + Vowel Symbols

ಕ	ಖ	ಗ	ಘ	ಙ
ka	kha	ga	gha	nga

ಚ	ಛ	ಜ	ಝ	ಞ
ca	cha	ja	jha	ña

ಟ	ಠ	ಡ	ಢ	ಣ
ṭa	ṭha	ḍa	ḍha	ṇa

ತ	ಥ	ದ	ಧ	ನ
ta	tha	da	dha	na

ಪ	ಫ	ಬ	ಭ	ಮ
pa	pha	ba	bha	ma

ಯ	ರ	ಲ	ವ
ya	ra	la	va

ಶ	ಷ	ಸ	ಹ	ಳ
śa	ṣa	sa	ha	la

SINHALESE

Vowel Symbols

a	ā	æ	ǣ	i	ī	u	ū

ri	e	ē	ai	o	ō	au

Consonant + Vowel Symbols

ka	kha	ga	gha	nga
ca	cha	ja	jha	ña
ṭa	ṭha	ḍa	ḍha	ṇa
ta	tha	da	dha	na
pa	pha	ba	bha	ma
ya	ra	la	va	
śa	ṣa	sa	ha	la

Sinhalese is the Indo-Aryan language of the island of Sri Lanka. A script was probably introduced into Sri Lanka from northern India by the third century BC but was subsequently influenced by south Indian writing.

TIBETAN

Consonant + Vowel Symbols

ka	kha	ga	nga
ca	cha	ja	ña
ṭa	ṭha	ḍa	ṇa
ta	tha	da	na
pa	pha	ba	ma
tsa	tsha	dsa	
ya	ra	la	wa
śa	sa	ṣa	ža za
ha	'a	a	

Sample Ligatured Symbols

	kra
	lca
	nra
	sba
	rtsva
	bya
	hra

Vowel Diacritics

ki		ku		ke		ko	

Kharoshthi, Brahmī and its offspring are syllabic writing systems. Devanagari is the script of Sanskrit, the ancient and sacred language of India, and is also used for various modern languages such as Hindi. Its fundamental characters are of two types, V and CV. The value of CV characters alone is always consonant + *a*. In order to mark a CV symbol as representing some vowel other than a, a diacritic is added, as illustrated by the characters for kā, ki, ku in the table (*left*). To represent a sequence of two or more consonants, ligatures are used, that is, composite symbols created by actually combining various CV characters into a single form, usually with modification of the appearance of some of the characters being combined. In this way, symbols become available of the type CCV (such as *kra* and *dya*), CCCV and so on –even CCCCCV as in *rtsnya*. A consonant occurring at the end of a word is written using the appropriate consonant + *a* symbol, accompanied by a sublinear diacritic called a *virama* which indicates that the *a* of the CV symbol is not to be read. Some scholars have suggested that Devanagari and other Indian scripts are not truly syllabic because

The Tibetan script is of Indic origin and, like Indic scripts, has basic symbols representing consonant + vowel sequences. The Tibetan system, however, has only a single vowel character, a. Other individual vowels are indicated by the use of diacritics with the a symbol.

197

CAMBODIAN

Vowel Symbols

আ						
ā	i	ī	u	ū	ri	rī

lī	e	ai	o	ao	au

Consonont + Vowel Symbols

ka	kha	ko	kho	ngo
ca	cha	co	cho	ño
da	tha	do	tho	na
ta	tha	to	tho	no
ba	pha	po	pho	mo
yo	ro	lo	wo	
sa	ha	la		

Vowel Diacritics

Symbol	Transliteration 1st Series	2nd Series
	ā	ie
	e	i
	ei	ī
	e	i
	ei	ī
	o	u
	ou	ū
	ue	ue
	ae	ē
	ie	ie
	ie	ie
	ei	i
	ae	ē
	ai	ī
	ao	ō
	au	iu

CV represents the position of a syllabic symbol relative to the diacritic.

Cambodian, or Khmer, belongs to the Austro-Asiatic family of languages. The Cambodian writing system developed from a Brahmī script. Like other writing systems derived from Brahmī, the Cambodian system is a syllabary with basic consonant + vowel symbols. However, in the case of the Cambodian script, the vowel value of the basic CV symbols shows variation: some symbols have an a vowel (as in Devanagari, Sinhalese, Tibetan, and so forth), but others have an o vowel. The former symbols are said to belong to the "first series," the latter to the "second series." To indicate that a consonant + vowel symbol has a vowel value other than a or o, diacritic strokes are used in conjunction with the symbol.

The writing system of Lao descends from Indic Brahmī. The vowel of of the basic consonant + vowel symbols of Lao is o and the script has no indepedent vowel symbols. To write individual vowels, diacritics are used in conjunction with the symbol 'o.

LAO

Consonants + Vowel Symbols

ko	kho	kho	ngo	cho	so	so
nyo	do	to	tho	tho	no	bo
po	pho	fo	pho	fo	mo	yo
ro	lo	wo	ho	'o	ho	

they possess a means for adjusting both the consonant and vowel values of the basic CV symbols. The value of the fundamental symbols of these scripts (including those symbols which are compounded to produce ligatures) is, however, plainly syllabic; they are better seen as syllabaries which operate more economically than those with distinct symbols for all expressed combinations of consonants and vowels.

CENTRAL AND EAST ASIA

The writing systems of India, like their Semitic predecessor, were exported far from home. Tibetan script, which had its origin in the seventh century AD, is based upon an early North Indian writing system. The spelling practices are similar to those described above for Devanagari, one difference being that Tibetan has only a single V character, which represents *a*. Several symbols were added for sounds not occurring in Indic, and superfluous ones were omitted. While Tibetan spelling has remained quite conservative, the sounds of Tibetan have changed considerably since the script's inception; consequently, its spelling no longer closely fits its pronunciation.

Also descended from Indian scripts are the writing systems of Cambodian (Khmer), Lao, Thai, and Burmese. In both the Thai and Burmese systems, means have been devised for representing tones; Tibetan is also a tone language, but its tones are not marked in Tibetan script. The modern writing system of the Javanese is descended from the early Kavi script of Java, known from at least the eighth century AD, itself developed from an Indic script. The Javanese script, in turn, is the likely source of the Batak system of Sumatra and the Buginese of Celebes.

CHINA

Linear etchings occur on Chinese pots dated to the fifth millennium BC. There is no indication, however, that such marks are symbols of a

THAI

Consonants

Mid		High		Low		
ก ko	ข kho	ฃ kho	ค kho	ฅ kho	ฆ kho	ง ngo
จ co	ฉ cho		ช cho	ซ so	ฌ cho	ญ yo
ฎ do	ฏ to	ฐ tho		ฑ tho		ฒ tho	ณ no
ด do	ต to	ถ tho		ท tho		ธ tho	น no
บ bo	ป po	ผ pho	ฝ fo	พ pho	ฟ fo	ภ pho	ม mo

Low
ย yo	ร ro	ล lo	ว wo

High
ศ so	ษ so	ส so

High	Low	Mid	Low
ห ho	ฬ lo	อ 'o	ฮ ho

Vowel Diacritics

CV a	CV a	CV ā	CV i
CV ī	CV u	CV ū	CV u	CV ū
CV e	CV ē	CV e	CV e	CV ē
CV o	CV ō	CV o	CV am
CV ai	CV ai	CV au

Thai script was probably based upon that of Cambodian, and so is ultimately also of Brahmī origin. As with the script of Lao, the basic consonant + vowel symbols have an o vowel value, and there are no independent vowel symbols (to write a single vowel, as in Lao, vowel diacritics are used together with the symbol 'o), Thai is a tone language and the variant forms of the basic consonant + vowel symbols are used to distinguish mid, high, and low tone classes. CV represents the position of a syllabic symbol relative to the diacritic.

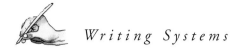

JAVANESE

Consonant + Vowel Symbols

Aksara Jawa	Aksara Pasangan	Transliteration
		ha
		na
		ča
		ra
		ka
		da
		ta
		sa
		wa
		la
		pa
		da
		ja
		ya
		ña
		ma
		ga
		ba
		ta
		nga

The Javanese syllabic script, with its roots in Indic writing, consists of basic consonant + a-vowel symbols. These are the characters listed beneath the heading Aksara Jawa. The corresponding Aksara Pasangan characters are used in conjunction with the basic CV symbols to spell consonant sequences.

The Batak script of Sumatra is believed to have developed from the early Kavi writing system. The script has vowel and consonant + a symbols. The vowel value of the basic CV characters can be adjusted with vowel "diacritics."

BATAK

Vowel Symbols

Symbol	Transliteration
	a
	i
	u

Consonant + Vowel Symbols

Symbol	Transliteration	Symbol	Transliteration
	ha		ga
	ma		dya
	na		da
	ra		nga
	ta		ba
	sa		wa
	pa		ya
	la		ña

Vowel Diacritics

Symbol	Transliteration
	i
	u
	o
	e

The writing system of the Buginese language of Celebes is probably likewise descended from Kavi. The CV symbol qa is also used for writing the vowel a at the beginning of a word. Vowel diacritics are used in conjunction with this symbol for writing other word-initial vowels and for changing the vowel value of the basic syllabic symbols.

BUGINESE

Syllabic Symbols

ka	ga	nga	ngka
pa	ba	ma	mpa
ta	da	na	nra
ca	ja	ña	ñca
ya	ra	la	wa
ha	qa	sa	

script. The advent of Chinese writing can be dated to the early second millennium BC, and it appears to have developed independently, without influence from a Near Eastern or Indus Valley system.

The earliest known form of Chinese writing occurs on oracle-bones which have survived from the Shang dynasty of the mid to late second millennium BC. These are usually tortoise shells or bovine scapulas bearing carved inscriptions which were sometimes then painted. The oracle bones were heated until they cracked, and the cracks then used to determine the divination.

The fundamental principles of the Chinese

writing system are already displayed in these the earliest of Chinese documents. Chinese writing, like the early Sumerian script, is logographic and pictographic. Homophonous logographic characters (symbols for words which sound alike but have different meanings) were derived by application of the rebus principle. As homophonous words are particularly common in the Chinese language, this rebus technique enjoyed extensive use. In early Chinese writing, rebus spelling was not systematic, resulting in various spellings of a single word, but in time such homophonous spellings were regularized. However, even in the writing of the Shang dynasty, a means had already been developed for making certain homophonous spellings less ambiguous; as in both Mesopotamia and Egypt, a semantic tag was used to mark the meaning of a logographic character. Unlike the determinatives of both Mesopotamian and Egyptian the semantic tags of the early Chinese scribes were actually integrated into the character with which they were used, producing a compound character or *hsieh-sheng*. Such compound logograms thus consist of a phonetic component and a semantic component; this became a highly productive method of character formation, with 90 percent of modern Chinese characters being of this type. Another method of producing compound characters, also in use during the Shang dynasty, involved simply the writing together of individual logograms (that is, the combining of semantic components); these are called *hui yi* characters. For example, the symbols for "sun" and "moon" were compounded to produce the character meaning "bright."

The Chinese script was adapted by Japanese-speakers for writing their own language. Japanese tradition preserves accounts of Korean scholars introducing Chinese script to the island of Japan in the third or fifth century AD. The earliest Japanese writing now known is dated to the eighth century. In the earliest materials, the writing consists solely of

Chinese logographic symbols, though perhaps they were read as Japanese words. Owing to significant grammatical differences between the two languages (such as the occurrence in Japanese of many suffixes and grammatical particles), some Chinese logograms came to be used phonetically to represent individual

The earliest known form of Chinese writing has been found on oracle-bones from the Shang dynasty.

Chinese characters began as pictograms, gradually becoming logograms as they became more stylised and lost their pictorial element. Four stages of this development are shown here. Whereas the oracle-bone symbols for "fish" and "moon" are easily recognized, few if any of the modern forms are so transparent that their meaning can be guessed without knowledge of the language.

EVOLUTION OF CHINESE WRITING

Modern Pronunciation/ Meaning	Oracle-bone form (Shang Dynasty)	Greater Seal (W. Chou)	Lesser Seal (E. Chou-Han)	Modern Form (3rd cent. AD on)
Objects				
jen / man				
nü / woman				
erh / ear				
yü / fish				
jih / sun				
yueh / moon				
yü / rain				
ting / cauldron				
ching / well				
Relationships				
shang / above				
hsia / below				

A typical Chinese character combines a radical, indicating some aspect of the word's meaning, with a phonetic clue to the pronunciation of the word. Thus the character for "hear" incorporates the "ear" as a radical, the rest of the character serving as a phonetic cue. Hand-written characters may be written in more or less cursive fashion, reaching an extreme in calligraphy where impressionistic distortions of the printed forms are appreciated as art.

CHINESE SCRIPT

Eight full-form printed characters

中 海 茶 飯
zhōng　hǎi　chá　fàn
middle　sea　tea　food

錢 龍 聞 識
qián　lóng　wén　shí
money　dragon　hear　know

The same characters in standard written form

中 海 茶 飯
zhōng　hǎi　chá　fàn

錢 龍 聞 識
qián　lóng　wén　shí

Japanese syllables — a process similar to the one displayed in the development of Sumerian writing.

By the ninth century, two Japanese syllabaries had developed: *kata-kana* was devised for use alongside Chinese characters (the name means "side-kana"); *hira-gana*, with a more cursive appearance, could be used without accompanying Chinese symbols. In modern Japanese writing, these two syllabic scripts continue to be employed, as do Chinese logograms, called *kanji*. Kanji are normally used for writing nouns, verbs, and adjectives, *hira-gana* for spelling suffixes and grammatical particles, and *kata-kana* for loan words and emphasis. Japanese writing is commonly cited as the most complex of all current systems.

Japanese is sometimes also written in the Latin alphabet with the system called *romaji*. *Romaji* is used, for example, for writing acronyms and in public areas for the assistance of tourists. In the nineteenth and twentieth centuries, there have been unsuccessful

JAPANESE

Hiragana

あ	か	さ	た	な	は	ま	や	ら	わ	ん
a	ka	sa	ta	na	ha	ma	ya	ra	wa	n
い	き	し	ち	に	ひ	み		り		
i	ki	shi	chi	ni	hi	mi		ri		
う	く	す	つ	ぬ	ふ	む		る		
u	ku	su	tsu	nu	fu	mu		ru		
え	け	せ	て	ね	へ	め	ゆ	れ		
e	ke	se	te	ne	he	me	yu	re		
お	こ	そ	と	の	ほ	も	よ	ろ	を	
o	ko	so	to	no	ho	mo	yo	ro	wo	

Katakana

ア	カ	サ	タ	ナ	ハ	マ	ヤ	ラ	ワ	ン
a	ka	sa	ta	na	ha	ma	ya	ra	wa	n
イ	キ	シ	チ	ニ	ヒ	ミ		リ		
i	ki	shi	chi	ni	hi	mi		ri		
ウ	ク	ス	ツ	ヌ	フ	ム		ル		
u	ku	su	tsu	nu	fu	mu		ru		
エ	ケ	セ	テ	ネ	ヘ	メ	ユ	レ		
e	ke	se	te	ne	he	me	yu	re		
オ	コ	ソ	ト	ノ	ホ	モ	ヨ	ロ	ヲ	
o	ko	so	to	no	ho	mo	yo	ro	wo	

The Hiragana and Katakana syllabaries of Japanese consist of vowel and consonant + vowel characters, as well as a symbol for the single nasal consonant n. Voiced consonants are written by using a diacritic in conjunction with the symbol for the corresponding voiceless consonant (+ vowel). Palatalized consonants are represented by using the symbols ya, yu and yo in conjunction with the appropriate CV symbol.

attempts to institute *romaji* as the regular form of Japanese writing.

According to Korean tradition, the Chinese writing system was brought to Korea in the third century AD. As with Japanese, the writing of Korean with the Chinese script is problematic, given the appreciable grammatical differences between the two languages; nevertheless, Korean was written in this way for hundreds of years. This situation was remedied from the early fifteenth century with the creation of the Korean alphabet, *Han'gul*, traditionally credited to the Korean king Sejong. *Han'gul* consists of 40 characters and has been claimed the most phonetically efficient of the world's writing systems. Chinese characters are still used in South Korean script to spell Chinese loan words.

The Mongolian writing system, which is written in left-to-right vertical columns, appears to have developed in the fourteenth century AD. It was derived from the Uighur script, the system of the Turkic people of that name, which in turn has its roots in Aramaic. Still earlier, by the seventh century AD, an early Turkic language of central Asia was being written in Turkic runic script, the origin of which is uncertain.

THE NEW WORLD

Various scripts developed among the native peoples of the New World. In Mesoamerica, the Maya people independently developed a system which is strikingly reminiscent of the scripts of ancient Mesopotamia, Egypt, and China, and is attested to about AD 300 .

The Mayan script is still in the process of being deciphered, although important gains have been made in recent years. It is now clear that it uses more than a single type of character. Many of the Mayan symbols, or glyphs, are logographic. As in other systems, a single logogram came to be used to represent homophonous words by application of the rebus principle. Syllabic symbols also make up part of the glyph inventory. These phonetic symbols are used to spell individual words and affixes (prefixes and suffixes) syllabically, and are also conjoined with logograms as phonetic complements, just as syllabic symbols are in Mesopotamia and Egypt. In addition, glyphs are similarly used as determinatives, semantic tags which clarify ambiguous readings.

Among later writing systems used by native peoples of North America, one of the most important is the Cherokee syllabary, appearing in the 1820s. The inventor of this script, a Cherokee by the name of Sequoya, had encountered English writing and decided to devise a logographic script for the spelling of his own language. This enterprise was jettisoned, however, in favor of a syllabic script. The resulting writing system consisted of 85 syllabic symbols, many of which are based on Latin letters, but with entirely different values.

Another syllabic script devised for spelling a native American language is the Cree syllabary. In this case, however, the designer of the script was not native American, but an English missionary named James Evans. By 1833 Biblical texts were translated using this script into the Algonquian language of Cree. The script consists fundamentally of 12 sets of characters, the syllabic symbols which compose each set varying from one another by spatial orientation. Somewhat different forms are used in final position (at the end of a word).

DIRECTION OF WRITING

It is usually the case that at any given time a writing system will be characterized by a particular direction of writing, though

The Japanese writing system is probably the most complex script presently in use. The address on this Tokyo street sign is written using four different types of symbols – kanji, syllabic kana, alphabetic romaji, and Arabic numerals.

MONGOLIAN			
Initial symbol	Medial symbol	Final symbol	Translit.
			a
			e
			i
			o
			u
			ö
			ü
			n
			q
			g
			k
			g
			p
			b
			m
			l
			r
			t
			d
			y
			j
			č
			s
			š
			w

KOREAN			
Symbol	Translit.	Symbol	Translit.
	i		k
	e		n
	æ		t
	ü		l
	ö		m
	ŭ		p
	ə		s
	a		ng
	u		č
	o		čh
	ya		kh
	yæ		th
	yə		ph
	ye		h
	yo		k'
	yu		t'
	wa		p'
	wæ		s'
	wə		c'
	we		
	ŭi		

A little more than 150 years after Ramkhamhaeng is said to have devised the Thai script, yet another East Asian king developed a system for recording his language. The Korean king Sejong is credited with designing what has been called the world's most perfect writing system. The Han'gul script is fundamentally alphabetic, but consonant and vowel characters are typically written together as a syllabic unit.

Not all of the scripts of East Asia are derived from Chinese and Indic writing systems. The Mongolian script traces its roots to the Syriac form of Aramaic. Symbols take different forms, depending upon whether they occur at the beginning of a word, in the middle, or at the end.

variability does occur, and within the history of a script the direction of writing may change. Early Sumerian writing shows a somewhat random distribution of symbols, with, however, a general right-to-left progression across the tablet. By the beginning of the second millennium BC the direction of writing had shifted and Sumerian scribes were writing in horizontal lines running left-to-right. In addition, the orientation of

Sumerian symbols had rotated 90 degrees counter-clockwise. Later Mesopotamian cuneiform scripts maintained the left-to-right direction.

The overall direction of Egyptian hieroglyphic writing was commonly right-to-left, though the reverse order did also occur. Writing may proceed in vertical columns from top to bottom, with columns progressing to the left (and less commonly to the right), or in horizontal rows.

205

Egyptian Demotic script is written from right-to-left in horizontal rows.

The Proto-Canaanite script, which had its roots in the Egyptian system, used a variety of directions: vertical, horizontal, right-to-left, left-to-right, and boustrophedon. The latter term (meaning "as the ox turns," referring to plowing) describes written lines which alternate in direction — for example, right-to-left, left-to-right, right-to-left, and so on. Boustrophedon direction occurs among other scripts as well, such as Hieroglyphic Luvian, the Cypriot syllabary, and the Greek alphabet. The offspring of Proto-Canaanite, Phoenician and Aramaic, and many of the scripts descended from them, are written horizontally from right-to-left.

Greek scripts display a variety of directions. The Mycenaean Linear B is left-to-right. The Greek Cypriot syllabary scripts are mostly right-to-left, with some left-to-right, and others boustrophedon. Early Greek alphabetic writing also shows all three patterns, but left-to-right predominates and continues in its descendants: Etruscan, Latin, Coptic, Cyrillic, and so forth.

Writing in vertical columns is not unique to Egyptian and Proto-Canaanite. Chinese is written in columns from top-to-bottom, with columns proceeding right-to-left. Mongolian writing is also from top-to-bottom, but with the columns left-to-right. The Batak script is vertical but from bottom-to-top with columns proceeding left-to-right.

This table displays consonant + vowel symbols of the Mayan script.

CHEROKEE

Syllabary

a	e	i	o	u	v
ga	ge	gi	go	gu	gv
ka					
ha	he	hi	ho	hu	hv
la	le	li	lo	lu	lv
ma	me	mi	mo	mu	
na	ne	ni	no	nu	nv
hna					
nah					
qua	que	qui	quo	quu	quv
sa	se	si	so	su	sv
s					
da	de	di	do	du	dv
ta	te	ti			
tla	tle	tli	tlo	tlu	tlv
dla					
tsa	tse	tsi	tso	tsu	tsv
wa	we	wi	wo	wu	wv
ya	ye	yi	yo	yu	yv

CREE

Vowel Symbols

ē	i	o	a

Consonant + Vowel Symbols — **Final Consonant Symbols**

pē	pi	po	pa	p
tē	ti	to	ta	t
čē	či	čo	ča	č
kē	ki	ko	ka	k
mē	mi	mo	ma	m
nē	ni	no	na	n
lē	li	lo	la	l
sē	si	so	sa	s
yē	yi	yo	ya	y
rē	ri	ro	ra	r
vē	vi	vo	va	v
zē	zi	zo	za	z
fē	fi	fo	fa	f

In 1821 Sequoya, a Cherokee from North Carolina, created a phonetic writing system for his Iroquoian language. The system is primarily a syllabary, though symbols with consonantal value also occur. Within a few years after its invention, a high level of literacy had been achieved within the Cherokee community.

In the early nineteenth century James Eliot designed a script for writing a Cree dialect of western Canada. This was adapted for other native languages of North America, including Choctaw, Chippewa, and Slave. Fundamentally a syllabary, the script is also able to spell single consonants at the end of a word.

ARCTIC OCEAN

LATIN

LATIN

LATIN

LATIN

LATIN

NORTH
ATLANTIC
OCEAN

LATIN

SOUTH
ATLANTIC
OCEAN

THE SCRIPTS OF NEWSPAPERS ACROSS THE GLOBE

This map illustrates the principal writing systems which are used in the major newspapers of the world's political regions. The extensive spread of that writing system which was once the script of Rome is quite remarkable.

RUSSIAN

RUSSIAN

ARCTIC OCEAN

LATIN

RUSSIAN

N

GEORGIAN

RUSSIAN

LATIN

EEK

GREEK
HEBREW

ARMENIAN

ARABIC

BIC

MONGOLIAN

ARABIC

KOREAN

JAPANESE

CHINESE

URDU

TIBETAN

GUMUKHI

BURMESE

GUJARATI

DEVANAGARI

ORIYA

BENGALI

LAO

THAI

LATIN

PACIFIC OCEAN

TELUGU

CAMBODIAN

AMHARIC

TAMIL

ARABIC

SINHALESE

ARABIC

MALDIVIAN

LATIN

INDIAN OCEAN

LATIN

LATIN

LATIN

LATIN

Epilogue:
Language Loss
and Revival

The diversity of the world's languages is at least as threatened as that of its plant and animal species. The passing of traditional ways of life and the economic lure of major languages is driving local tongues towards extinction. But today dying languages are at least being recorded for posterity, and much work is underway to reverse their decline; the revival of Hebrew offers an inspiring success story.

Red Thundercloud, who died in January 1996, was the last speaker of the Sioux language, Catawba. He recorded examples of the language for the Simithsonian Museum.

I n the last years of the twentieth century it has become commonplace to hear of the extinction of yet another language. When the last speaker of Catawba, Red Thundercloud, died in January 1996, the world heard, and the London *Times* took note, because he had consciously made himself the last representative of this particular Siouxan language, recording hunting songs and hymns for posterity at the Smithsonian Museum. He became something of a celebrity, like Ishi, the last speaker of Yahi, who had lived in hiding in northern California after the destruction of his tribe. Edward Sapir, the leading specialist in native American languages of the time, elicited aspects of his language and myths, but contact with American society led to Ishi's death from tuberculosis. More often the last speakers die in obscurity, and the languages with them.

The loss of languages parallels the extinction of animal and plant species in many respects. In many parts of the world, such as the Amazon region, destruction and industrial exploitation of the natural habitat lead to a breakdown of the communities in which minority languages survive. Just as we do not know what natural medicines lie within vanishing rainforests, we do not know what wisdom is recorded in the grammar and vocabulary, poetry and stories of dying languages, many of which have vanished without being studied in depth. At the current rate of extinction, it has been estimated that the twenty-first century will see as many as 90 percent of the world's languages become extinct or moribund (the estimate for plant and animal species is 50 percent). The environmental problem is now widely seen as urgent, and the loss of language diversity is increasingly seen in the same light.

HOW AND WHY LANGUAGES DIE

Languages have always been eclipsed and extinguished, but recent centuries have seen an acceleration of the process. Between 1490 and 1990 around half the world's languages died out. Allowing for the problems involved in distinguishing languages from dialects, a maximum of 10–15,000 languages would have been spoken at the point of greatest linguistic diversity.

There are several ways in which languages become extinct; the native Tasmanians were hunted and removed from their habitat, while some native American tribes suffered a similar fate as the West was settled. More often, tribes have succumbed to disease and western plagues – alcoholism is endemic in some North American Indian populations and cocaine addiction is now spreading in Amazonian villages. As tribal groups disappear or are wiped out, their languages naturally disappear with them.

The main cause of extinction, however, is less dramatic and perhaps more insidious. Language shift occurs where speakers adopt the language of the majority, of prestige, or of wealth. Hispanic and other immigrants to the USA exemplify this process, which takes place over only three generations. The first generation is monolingual and learns little of the dominant language. The second generation becomes bilingual, learning the ancestral language from their parents and the dominant language from the surrounding community. The third generation learns only the dominant language both at home and in the community. It may be that in some such cases loss is inevitable, but languages at least deserve a dignified death. In some Asian American families children cannot communicate with their grandparents, because they know only English and their grandparents only Chinese, Korean, or Vietnamese. Amy Tan's novel, *The Joy Luck Club,* turns on the clash of generations and failure of understanding between Chinese mothers and their Chinese-American daughters. Equally sad is the case of grown-up

Some two million native peoples once occupied the vast area of the Amazonian rainforest; today only about 50,000 survive. With the disappearance of traditional communities, languages, folklore, and an unrivalled knowledge of the potential of the rainforest are also irretrievably lost.

MINORITY LANGUAGES IN EUROPE

I n an increasing federal Europe, a new awareness of local languages and cultures has fueled campaigns to promote the use of minority languages, and even to revive extinct ones, for use alongside national languages.

third generation children who blame their parents for not transmitting their ancestral language to them: if they begin re-learning such languages in adulthood, they will at best become second-language speakers.

In the later stages of shift we find "semi-speakers," who may understand the language well but do not speak it, or speak it in a way which mixes it with the dominant language,

❶ *Scots Gaelic: 88,000 speakers, mainly on Hebridean islands.*

❷ *Manx: extinct in 1974, retrieved in the 1980s.*

❸ *Irish: declining use in western counties. Known by 700,000, but used regularly by 120,000.*

❹ *Welsh: widely taught in bilingual schools. 575,000 speakers.*

❺ *Cornish: extinct in 19th century, revived in 20th century and taught in a few schools.*

❻ *Breton: nearly a million speakers but in daily use by only 500,000.*

❼ *Occitan: descended from the Provençal of medieval poets. Spoken in rural communities in southern France.*

❽ *Gascon: a distinctive variety of Occitan with 250,000 speakers.*

❾ *Catalan: 10 million speakers in eastern Spain and the Balearic islands. Now used in several universities.*

❿ *Galician: between Spanish and Portuguese. Now used in broadcast media, higher education, and in literature.*

⓫ *Basque: growing recognition, including university devoted to Basque studies, with teaching in Basque.*

⓬ *Romantsch: Fourth language of Switzerland.*

⓭ *Ladin: 35,000 speakers in four mountain valleys.*

⓮ *Friulan: 60,000 speakers, under strong Italian influence.*

⓯ *Istro-Rumanian: 147,000 speakers, mainly on Istrian peninsula in former Yugoslavia.*

⓰ *Arumanian: related to Romanian, spoken in northern Greece. Estimated 50,000 speakers.*

⓱ *Macedonian: Slavic language related to Bulgarian. Spoken in south of former Yugoslavia and northern Greece. Upper and Lower*

⓲ *Sorbian: isolated Slavic languages surrounded by German-speaking territory, with 67,000 speakers in 1987.*

⓳ *Frisian: 20,000 speakers on islands off German coast; 700,000 speakers in Friesland, Netherlands. Losing ground to Dutch, despite bilingual education.*

⓴ *Faroese: relative of Icelandic, with 47,000 speakers.*

㉑ *Letzebuergisch: German dialect of Luxembourg; 335,000 speakers.*

⓴ *not shown*

and which the older generation finds imperfect. As one of the last speakers of the Australian language Dyirbal commented: "That Phyllis, she don't talk Guwal right. She mixes up the English. She got it wrong." Many children of Cantonese parents raised in Canada speak Cantonese without the tones. Their vocabulary is replaced by words from the dominant language, and their grammar becomes simplified. As the vocabulary becomes impoverished, the meanings of words become generalized. Hungarian, for example, like many languages, distinguishes between old people (*öreg*) and old things (*régi*), but to shifting semi-speakers both are "*öreg*" – a simplification which reflects English usage.

REVERSING LANGUAGE SHIFT

When a language ceases to be transmitted to children, it is considered moribund and on the way to extinction unless intervention can stop the decline in its use. This process can be reversed; in Wales, bilingual schooling means that many children speak Welsh more fluently than their parents. Perceptions of the language's worth have shifted, and the decline has been reversed. In Brittany, on the other hand, no such policy supports Breton, whose status and rate of transmission to children are low. Welsh is now the only Celtic language whose future seems secure.

The will to reverse a language's shift is inevitably associated with the assertion of the distinct cultural identity of its speakers. Sometimes this involves the desire for greater political status or autonomy, as in the cases of Basque and Catalan in Spain, so that there are likely to be political aspects to the question. Some fear that the preservation of distinct identities will lead to discord. Others argue that speakers of a minority language would do

better to shift to a major one; while this may be true in short-term material terms, the abandonment of a language on these grounds may be cause for regret in the longer term. These concerns can be countered by promoting bilingualism, which serves as a bridge to the dominant language and culture without abandoning the minority language.

Preservation of minority languages is linked to traditional lifestyles, and often to the preservation of the environment as well. According to a recent study, the Menomini of Minnesota, by using traditional methods to harvest mixed forests, practice the only truly sustainable timber industry in the U.S.A. Such cases suggest an intimate connection between biological and linguistic diversity.

LANGUAGE REVIVAL

Just as plants and animal species can be preserved and recreated by preserving their DNA, the sounds, grammar, and vocabulary of languages can be stored on tape and disk for posterity and even for later resuscitation. Although there is room for question as to whether the recreated language would be the same following a break in its transmission to children, it can be done if the will is there.

The most successful case of revival has been that of Hebrew, driven by the reuniting of the Jewish people in Israel after World War I. The original language of much of the Old Testament, for centuries Hebrew was not spoken on a daily basis, but was kept alive by scholars and through use in worship. From the nineteenth century Hebrew began to be spoken again in Palestine, in a movement led by Eliezer Ben-Yehuda (1858–1922), whose son became the first native speaker of Modern Hebrew. With the foundation of the state of Israel in 1948, Hebrew was taught in Israeli schools, and immigrants to Israel have since shifted to Hebrew, often at the expense of other languages of Jewish culture such as the Germanic Yiddish and the Romance Ladino.

Like the Chinese, Korean immigrants to the USA have formed close-knit communities where their language, food and other aspects of their culture can be preserved. Thriving Koreatowns have developed in cities such as New York and Los Angeles.

Hebrew demonstrates that revival of a dead or moribund language is feasible. Recent efforts have sought to revive the moribund Occitan and Gascon in France, and even the extinct Manx and Cornish in Britain. These modest movements may suggest that in Europe, the tide is beginning to turn from centralization to regionalism.

The potential for revival is one motivation for studying endangered languages. Another is the light that each language may throw on the human language faculty. It is ironic that in linguistics the detailed study of a single language currently enjoys less prestige than theoretical pursuits and the study of language as a faculty: this focus may allow languages to disappear unnoticed, thereby making it impossible to answer questions about certain types of language. Languages with the object-subject-verb word order, for example, exist only in the ecologically threatened Amazon region. Much of the crucial documentation work has been done by missionaries engaged in Bible translation, coordinated by the Summer Institute of Linguistics.

Language extinction also has an impact on the the study of the prehistory of languages and cultures. The question of whether the Tasmanian languages were related to the Papuan, Australian, or any other languages has become controversial, but we may never know the answer because the Tasmanian language and culture were wiped out within a few decades of the British conquest. As the indigenous languages of Taiwan die out, the history and affiliations of the Austronesian family may also be buried with them. As Samuel Johnson wrote: "I am always sorry when any language is lost, for language is the pedigree of nations."

LANGUAGE DIVERSITY IN THE MEDIA

The communications media have sometimes been blamed for the spread of major languages at the expense of local ones, and television is

REVIVAL PROBLEMS

Recent attempts to revive the Cornish language have confronted the problem of which variety to adopt. There are three options:

- **Unified Cornish:** Based on the medieval literature from the Middle Cornish period (1200–1500), most of which is in verse, this language was developed in the 1930s. This is rather like reconstructing Elizabethan English from the poetic language of a Shakespearean play. The language is felt to be unsystematic and dauntingly complex.
- **Modern Cornish:** Based on the most recent surviving documents from the eighteenth century. This variety shows some of the characteristic simplification of a dying language.
- **Common Cornish:** A recent compromise between the medieval and modern varieties.

Some enthusiasts are raising their children bilingually in English and a chosen variety of Cornish, which may result in convergence on a new standard. By the mid-1990s around 2,000 people could speak some Cornish. As for Welsh, widespread knowledge of Cornish may depend on its adoption in schools.

Cornwall, in the extreme southwest of England, is a rugged and remote area which for many centuries preserved a celtic language and identity which was quite separate from the rest of England.

especially guilty as minority language programming is rarely commercially viable. However, this need not be the case with all technological media. Regular radio programs in Ladin and Romantsch help to keep these languages in use for more than merely domestic purposes. The Internet already hosts communications in such minority languages as Galician, Occitan, and Gascon, and even the aboriginal languages of Australia. Global communications media, which have been instrumental in spreading English and other dominant languages, may yet play a vital part in the preservation of endangered languages. Multimedia technology, able to store speech, song, and images in any desired combination, is far better suited to the task than the traditional book. If the twenty-first century sees a continued decline in linguistic diversity, the blame will not fall entirely on technology or on the media.

Glossary of terms

Acrophony The use of a pictogram or hieroglyph of an object phonetically to represent the initial syllable or sound of the word that denotes the object.

Affixes One or more sounds or syllables added to a word to modify its signification; a general term including prefixes, infixes and suffixes.

Alphabet A phonetic writing system which consists of symbols (letters) representing individual consonant and vowel sounds (from the first two Greek letters *alpha, beta*).

Alveolar A sound formed by the tongue touching or near the alveolar ridge, just above and behind the upper front teeth.

Agglutination The formation of words by adding separate constituents, each with a distinct meaning.

Antonyms Words of opposite meaning.

Aspirate A consonant in which breath is released.

Augmentative suffix A suffix indicating bigness.

Bilabials Consonants formed by the use of both lips (English *p, b, m*).

Bilingual Able to use two languages.

Cartouche An oval or oblong figure used in Egyptian script for the name of a monarch.

Case One of the inflectional forms of a noun, pronoun, or adjective that indicate its gramatical relation to other words, as that of subject, object, attribute, and so on. For example, the six cases in Latin are: nominative (for subject), vocative (for address), accusative (for object), genitive (for possession), dative (for donation or attribution), and ablative (for external causation or removal). Other languages have more cases, especially locatives (denoting spatial relations). *See also* **Ergative** *below.*

Continuant sounds Sounds which a speaker may prolong, like English *shhhh.*

Creoles New languages formed by children exposed to a pidgin or mixture of languages.

Cuneiform Writing system (e.g. Sumerian) using wedge-shaped characters.

Demotic A simplified form of the hieratic writing used by the ancient Egyptians (literally, *of the common people*).

Dentals Consonants formed with the tip of the tongue against the front teeth (English *t, d, s, z*).

Determinatives Elements attached to words to distinguish meanings.

Diacritic A mark placed over, under, or through a letter to denote a modification of its sound value.

Diphthong A speech sound changing continuously from one vowel to another in the same syllable.

Dialects, dialectology Geographical variations within a language, and the study of them.

Diminutive suffix A suffix indicating smallness.

Discontinuous root A word root whose consonants do not occur next to one another (for example in Arabic)

Ejective A consonant produced by expulsion of air under pressure with the glottal passage closed.

Ergative A case system involving special forms for the subjects of transitive verbs.

Fricative A speech sound characterized by a frictional rustling of the emitted breath (English *f, z, th*).

Fusional language A language in which the affixes are merged with roots and may express more than one meaning.

Glottal stop A speech sound produced by closure of the glottis (the space between the vocal chords).

Glyph A carved figure or mark.

Gutturals Sounds formed in the throat.

Hieratic Writing in a simplified form of ancient Egyptian hieroglyphics used by priests.

Hieroglyphs, hieroglyphics A system of writing using mainly pictorial characters.

Homonym A word having the same pronunciation as another, but differing from it in origin, meaning, or spelling.

Homophones, homophony Words which sound alike but have different meanings.

Honorific A form of address conferring honor or respect.

Ideogram, ideograph A picture or symbol used in a writing system to represent a thing or an idea, but not the word or sound for it .

Incorporation A process whereby a word (usually a verb) forms a compound with its object and modifiers but retains its original function in the sentence.

Infix One or more sounds or syllables combined in the body of a word to modify its signification.

Inflections The changes of form which words undergo to mark distinctions of case, gender, number, tense, person, mood, voice.

Isoglosses Lines on a map which represent the dialectal divides between the domain of one word, form or pronunciation from that of another.

Isolates Languages for which no relationship with any other language can be demonstrated.

Isolating language A language wherein grammatical concepts are expressed by separate words which do not divide into smaller units.

Labials Consonants formed by the lips (English *b, p, m*)

Labiodental A sound formed with the lips, or one lip, and the teeth (English *f, v*).

Labionasal A sound made by the joint use of the lips and the nasal passage (English *m*).

Labiovelar A sound formed with the lips rounded, narrowed or closed, and with the back of the tongue touching or near the velum (the soft palate).

Language family A set of languages which can be shown to derive from a common ancestor.

Language phylum A larger grouping encompassing several language families which are distantly related.

Language shift When speakers of one language adopt another.

Language typology The study of language types.

Language universals Statements which hold true for all languages.

Lateral velar affricate A rare sound produced at the back of the mouth (like *g*) but with the side of the tongue (like *l*).

Lingua franca A hybrid or simplified language used for commerce between peoples with different native languages.

Loan words Foreign words adapted and added to the vocabulary of a "borrowing" language.

Logograms, logographs Symbols used by a logographic system.

Logographic script Writing systems consisting of characters which represent words in their entirety rather than as their phonetic components.

Matres lectionis or "the mothers of reading" The consonantal characters of ancient Aramaic script.

Mixed languages Languages derived from two or more ancestors.

Morphemes The individually meaningful constituents of words.

Morphology The study of the structure of words and their components.

Modifier A word or word group which modifies another (for example English *this* and *that*).

Multilingual Able to use more than two languages.

Nominal prefix A prefix added to a noun.

Orthography A writing system, usually standardized.

Palatal A sound formed with the tongue near or touching the hard palate, in the roof of the mouth (English *y* as in "yield").

Pharyngeal A sound formed in the pharynx (the part of the alimentary canal between the mouth and the esophagus), as found in Arabic.

Phoneme The smallest unit of speech that in any given language distinguishes one word from another (English *p* in *pin* and *b* in *bin*).

Phonetic, phonetics Of or pertaining to the voice, the science of speech sounds.

Phonetic complement A syllabic symbol which provides a phonetic clue to the correct reading of a logogram.

Phylum A group of languages related more remotely than those of a family or stock.

Pictogram, pictograph A picture or hieroglyph used in a writing system to represent a thing or an idea.

Pidgins Simplified or hybrid forms of a language, used for restricted purposes such as trade between speakers of different languages.

Polyphones, polyphony Single logograms that have acquired two or more word-values.

Polysynthetic language A language in which, by incorporation, whole sentences can be expressed by a single compound word.

Predicate The word or words in a sentence or clause which express what is said of the subject.

Prefix One or more sounds or syllables added to the beginning of a word to modify its meaning or to indicate a grammatical change (e.g. *un-* in *unbreakable*).

Pronominal Pronoun-like.

Rebus A mode of expressing words and phrases by pictures of objects whose names resemble those words, or the syllables of which they are composed; hence a puzzle made up of such representations.

Reduplication The doubling of a word or syllable.

Retroflex A speech sound produced by raising and bending back the tip of the tongue under the hard palate, as in a rolled *r*.

Semantics The science of language meanings.

Stock A language family.

Substrate An underlying language structure, such as the influence of a language A on a language B when speakers of A adopt B.

Suffix One or more sounds or syllables added to the end of a word to modify its meaning or to indicate a grammatical category (e.g. *-s* in *trips*).

Syllabic script A writing system in which words are broken down and recorded syllabically by means of a set of symbols (the syllabary), each of which denotes a spoken syllable.

Syllable One or more speech sounds constituting an uninterrupted unit of utterance and forming either a whole word (man) or a division of a word (*A-mer-i-ca*); also, one or more letters representing a spoken syllable.

Syllabogram A symbol representing a syllable.

Synonyms Different words with the same meaning.

Tone languages Languages which use pitch to distinguish words. Lexical tone is used to distinguish words' meanings, grammatical tone is used to distinguish their grammatical functions.

Vowel harmony A rule that a word can contain only a certain type of vowel.

Bibliography

Introduction

Comrie, B. (ed.), *The World's Major Languages,* Routledge, London, and Oxford University Press, New York, 1987

Grimes, B. F. (ed.), *Ethnologue* (12th ed.), Summer Institute of Linguistics, Dallas, 1990

Hawkins, J. A. and Gell-Mann, M. (eds.), *The Evolution of Human Languages* (Santa Fe Institute Studies in the Sciences of Complexity XI), Redwood City, Addison-Wesley, California, 1989

Lieberman, P., *The Biology and Evolution of Language*, Harvard University Press, Cambridge, Mass., 1984

Robins, R. H. and E. M. Uhlenbeck (eds.), *Endangered Languages*, Berg, Oxford/New York, 1991

Stringer, C. and Gamble C., *In Search of the Neanderthals*, Thames and Hudson, New York, 1993

Chapter 1 Development and Spread of Languages

Asher, R. E. and Moseley, L., *Atlas of the World's Languages*, Routledge, 1994

Dtv-Atlas zur Deutschen Sprache, München, Deutscher Taschenbuch Verlag, 1978

Comrie, B., *Language Universals and Linguistic Typology*, Blackwell (Oxford, 2nd edition 1989)

Jeffers, R. J. and Lehiste, I., *Principles and Methods in Historical Linguistics,* (MIT Press, Cambridge, 1979)

2.1 Europe and Eurasia

Ball, M. (ed.), *The Celtic Languages*, Routledge, London, 1994

Collinder, B., *An Introduction to the Uralic Languages,* Berkeley, California, 1965

Comrie, B., *Languages of the Soviet Union*, Cambridge University Press, 1981

Harris, M. and Vincent N.(eds.), *The Romance Languages*, Routledge, London, 1988

Miller, R. A., *Nihongo: In Defence of Japanese*, Athlone Press, London, 1986

Shibatani, M., *The Languages of Japan*, Cambridge University Press, 1990

Sohn, Ho-Min, *Korean*, Cambridge University Press, 1993

2.2 South and Southeast Asia

De Francis, J., *The Chinese Language: Fact and Fantasy*, Honolulu: University of Hawaii Press, Honolulu, 1984

Ramsey, S. R., *Languages of China*, Princeton University Press, 1987

2.3 Africa and the Middle East

Arnott, D. W., *The Noun and Verbal System of Fula*, Clarendon Press, Oxford, 1970

Bauer, L., *Introducing Linguistic Morphology*, Edinburgh University Press, 1988

Bleek, W. H., *Comparative Grammar of the Bantu Languages*, Juta, Cape Town, 1869

Doke, C. M., *A Comparative Study in Shona Phonetics*, University of the Witwatersrand Press, Johannesburg, 1931

Encyclopedia Britannica. Nigeria

Fortune, G., *A Grammar of Shona: Notes from the Department of African Language*s: University of Rhodesia, 1969–94

Gary, J. O. and Gamal-Eldini S., *Cairene Egyptian Colloquial Arabic*, Lingua Descriptive Studies, Vol 6. North-Holland, Amsterdam, 1982

Guthrie, M., *Comparative Bantu* (4 vols), Gregg International Publishers, Farnborough, 1969–90

Hannon, *Shona Dictionary*, Salisbury, Rhodesia

Khalafallah, A. A., *A Descriptive Grammar of Saei:di Egyptian Colloquial Arabic*, Mouton, The Hague, 1969

McEvedy, C., *The Penguin Atlas of African history*, Viking-Penguin, London, 1980

McKie, R., *Genes Rock the Fossil Record*, Geographical Magazine, November 1992

Nancarrow, O. T., *A Grammar of Ndebele: Notes from the Department of African Languages*: University of Rhodesia 1969–74

Oxford Encyclopedia of Linguistics: African Languages (Oxford University Press)

Ruhlen, M., *A Guide to the World's Languages, Vol 1*, Stanford, California, 1991

Ruhlen, M., *The Origin of Language*, Wiley, New York, 1994

Spencer, A., *Morphological Theory*, Blackwell, Oxford, 1991

The Gospel in Many Tongues, British and Foreign Bible Society, London, 1965

2.4 Pacific

Bellwood, P., *Man's Conquest of the Pacific: The Prehistory of Southeast Asia and Oceania,* Oxford University Press, New York, 1979

Bellwood, P., *Prehistory of the Indo-Malaysian Archipelago*, Academic Press, Orlando, Fla., 1985

Bellwood, P., *The Polynesians: Prehistory of an Island People*, Thames and Hudson, London, 1987

Benedict, P., *Austro-Thai Language and Culture, With a Glossary of Roots*, HRAF Press, New Haven, 1975

Clark, R., "Austronesian Languages" in B. Comrie, (ed.) *The World's Major Languages*, Croom Helm, London, 1987

Dahl, O.C., *Malgache et Maanjaan*, Egede-Instituttet, Oslo, 1951

Duranti, A., *From Grammar to Politics: Linguistic Anthropology in a Western Samoan Village*, University of California Press, Berkeley, 1994

Dutton, T. and Tryon, D.T. (eds.), *Language Contact and Change in the Austronesian World,* Mouton de Gruyter, Berlin, 1994

Foley, W. A., *The Papuan Languages of New Guinea*, Cambridge University Press, Cambridge, 1986

Ochs, E., *Culture and Language Development: Language Acquisition and Language Socialization in a Samoan Village*, Cambridge University Press, Cambridge–New York, 1988

Pawley, A., 1974, "Austronesian Languages" in *The New Encyclopedia Britannica, Macropaedia (Vol. 2)*,15th ed. Encyclopedia Britannica Inc. Chicago

Wurm, S. A. and Shiro Hattori, *Language Atlas of the Pacific area*, Canberra: Australian Academy of the Humanities, Canberra, 1981–84

2.5 Australia

Lonely Planet Australian Phrasebook. Lonely Planet Publications, 1994.

Horton, D. (ed.), *The Encyclopaedia of Aboriginal Australia*, Australian Institute of Aboriginal and Torres Strait Islander Studies, 1993

Thieberger, N. and McGregor, W. (eds.), *Macquarie Aboriginal Words, The*

Macquarie Library, (Sydney), 1994
For additional information on Australian Aboriginal languages contact the Australian Institute of Aboriginal and Torres Strait Islander Studies, GPO Box 553, Canberra, ACT 2601, Australia. The Aboriginal Studies Electronic Data Archive is available on the World Wide Web at: http://coombs.anu.edu.au/SpecialProj/A SEDA (or contact them by electronic mail at aseda@aiatsis.gov.au).

2.6 The Americas
Grimes B.F. (ed.), *Ethnologue Index*, 12th ed. Summer Institute of Linguistics, Dallas, Tex., 1992
Coe, M. D., *Breaking the Maya Code*. New York: Thames & Hudson, New York, 1992
Goossen, I. W., *Navajo Made Easier; A Course in Conversational Navajo*, Northland Press, Flagstaff, Ariz. 1979
Greenberg, J. H., *Language in the Americas*, Stanford University Press, Stanford, 1989
Langacker, R. W., *Fundamentals of Linguistic Analysis*, Harcourt Brace Jovanovich, New York, 1972
Pullum, G., *The Great Eskimo Vocabulary Hoax and Other Irreverent Essays on the Study of Language*, University of Chicago Press, Chicago, 1991
Sapir, E. & Swadesh, M., *Nootka Texts: Tales and Ethnological Narratives*, Linguistic Society of America, Philadelphia, 1939
Sapir, E., *The Collected Works of Edward Sapir*, Mouton de Gruyter, Berlin, 1987
Shopen, T., *Languages and their Status*, Winthrop Pub., Inc., Cambridge, Mass, 1979
Wolfart, H. and Carroll, C. & J. F., *Meet Cree: A Guide to the Cree Language*. 2nd ed., University of Alberta Press, Edmonton, 1981

2.7 Pidgins and Creoles
Bickerton, D., *Roots of Language*, Karoma, Ann Arbor, 1981
Crowley, T., *From Beach-la-mar to Bislama: The Emergence of a National Language in Vanuatu*, Clarendon Press, Oxford, 1990
Holm, J., *Pidgins and Creoles* (2 volumes), Cambridge University Press, 1989
Keesing, R. M., *Melanesian Pidgin and the Oceanic Substrate*, Stanford University Press, 1988
Mühlhäusler, P., *Pidgin and Creole Linguistics*, Blackwell, Oxford, 1986
Romaine, S., *Pidgin and Creole Languages*, Longman, London, 1988
Romaine, S. *Language, Education and Development: Urban and Rural Tok Pisin in Papua New Guinea*. Oxford University Press, 1992
Wurm, S. A. and Mühlhäusler, P. (eds.), *Handbook of Tok Pisin (New Guinea Pidgin)*, Pacific Linguistics, Canberra, 1985

3.0 Writing Systems
Antonsen, E.H., "The Runes: The earliest Germanic Writing System," in Senner, pp. 137-158, 1989
Bellamy, J.A., "The Arabic Alphabet," in Senner, pp. 91-102, 1989
Bonfante, G. and Bonfante, L., *The Etruscan Language*, New York, 1983
Bonfante, L., "Etruscan" in Hooker, pp. 321-378, 1990
Bricker, V., *A Grammar of Mayan Inscriptions*, New Orleans, 1986
Chadwick, J., "Linear B," in Hooker, pp. 137-195, 1990
Cook, B.F., "Greek Inscriptions," in Hooker, pp. 259-319, 1990
Coulmas, F., *The Writing Systems of the World*, Oxford, 1989
Cross, F.M., "The Invention and Development of the Alphabet," in Senner, pp.77-90, 1989
Daniels, P., and Bright, W., *The World's Writing Systems*, Oxford, 1996
Davies, W.V., "Egyptian Hieroglyphs," in Hooker, pp. 75-135, 1990
Diringer, D., *The Alphabet*, 3rd edition, New York, 1968
Driver, G.R., *Semitic Writing*, London, 1976
Fischer, H.G., "The Origin of the Egyptian Hieroglyphs," in Sennner, pp. 59-76, 1989
Gelb, I. J., *A Study of Writing*, Chicago, 1963
Green, M.W., "Early Cuneiform," in Senner, pp. 43-57. 1989
Healey, J.F., "The Early Alphabet," in Hooker, pp. 197-257, 1990
Hooker, J.T. (introduction), *Reading the Past*, Berkeley and Los Angeles, 1990
Jeffery, L. H., *The Local Scripts of Archaic Greece*, Oxford, 1990
Keightley, D.N., "The Origins of Writing in China: Scripts and Cultural Contexts," in Senner, pp. 171-202, 1989
Lehmann, R.P.M., "Ogham: The Ancient Script of the Celts," in Senner, pp. 159-170, 1989
Lounsbury, F.G., "The Ancient Writing of Middle America," in Senner, pp. 203-237, 1989
Page, R. I., *Runes*, Berkeley and Los Angeles, 1987
Reeves, N., *The Complete Tutankhamun*, London, 1990
Sampson, G., *Writing Systems*, Stanford, 1985
Schmandt-Besserat, D., "Two Precursors of Writing: Plain and Complex Tokens," in Sener, pp. 27-41, 1989
Senner, W. (editor), *The Origins of Writing*, Lincoln, Nebraska, 1989
Stroud, R.S., "The Art of Writing in Ancient Greece," in Senner, pp. 103-119, 1989
Ventris, M. and Chadwick, J., *Documents in Mycenaean Greek*, 2nd edition, Cambridge, 1973
Wallace, R., "The Origins and Development of the Latin Alphabet," in Senner, pp. 121-135, 1989
Walker, C.B.F., "Cuneiform," in Hooker, pp. 15-73, 1990

4.0 Epilogue
Ball M., (ed.), *The Celtic Languages*, Routledge, London, 1995
Fishman, J., *Reversing Language Shift*, Multilingual Matters, Clevedon UK, 1991

Index

Page reference in italics indicate illustrations/maps and/or their captions. Page references in bold indicate sections other than main text.

Acknowledgments

Key: *a* above; *b* below; *c* center; *l* left; *r* right

Image Bank 2-3, 6, 7 & 9; Karl Ammann/Ace 10; Image Select/Ann Ronan 12-13; Fortean Picture Library 14; L Le Plante/Panos 15; C M Dixon 17; Japan National Tourist Organisation 18; Pictor 19; Pictor 21*c*; Jay Freis/Image Bank 22; La Belle Aurore 23; from the collection of George Stern, courtesy of Michael Nicholson 25; AKG Photo 26; ET Archive 29; Image Bank 31; ET Archive 34; AA Picture Library 37 & 38; Mansell Collection 39 & 40; Pictor 42; C M Dixon 43; Peter Barker/Panos 44; Luis Castaneda/Image Bank 45; Jon Spaull/Axiom 50; J C Tordai/Panos 51; Mansell Collection 52; ET Archive 53 & 54; Andrew Driver/Ace 55; Pictor 57; ET Archive 58 , Andrew Conway/Ace 58-9*a*; John Readon/Rex Features 59*b*, from the collection of George Stern, courtesy of Michael Nicholson 60; Image Bank 61; Jean-Leo Dugas/Panos 62; AnneRippy/Image Bank 64 & 66; Alain Le Garsmeur/Panos 68; Nigel Hicks/Ace 69; Alain Le Garsmeur/Panos 70; Pictor 73; Adrian Boot/Retna 76; Jeremy Hartley/Panos 79; Sean Sprague/Panos 80; Trygve Bolstad/Panos 82; Betty Press/Panos 83; Powerstock 85; Nick Robinson/Panos 87; Jeremy Hartley/Panos 88; M Coyne/Image Bank 91; ET Archive 96; Ben Simmons/Ace 99; David Horwell 100; Ace 101; Pete Turner/Image Bank 103*a*; J C Callow/Panos 104; Geoff Smith 106; La Belle Aurore 111; Pictor 112; AKG Photo 114; Penny Tweedie/Panos 116; Roberto Matassa/Ace 11; Linda Freeman 118-119*r*; Pictor 121; John Miles/Panos 123; Retna 124; Steel Photography/Ace 125 *bl*; Graham Bibby/Ace 124*br*; P & M Walton/Ace 127; Ben Glass/Orion Pictures 128; Pictor 129; ET Archive 133; Peter Newark Pictures 137; Fotopic/Ace 140; Northwind Picture Archives 141; Solvang Conference & Visitors Center, USA 142; Ben Simmons/Ace 145; Tim Motion 146; ET Archive 147*a*; Pictor 147*b*; Rex Features 150; Geoff Smith 152; G A Rossi/Image Bank 153; Mansell Collection 156; David W Hamilton/Image Bank 158; Guido Rossi/Image Bank 159; Andrew Driver/Ace 161; Peter Newark Pictures 163; Oriental Institute, Chicago 164; Spectrum 166; Visual Arts Library 166; ET Archive 168, 169, 170 & 171*b* & *b*; C M Dixon 171*a*; Hulton-Getty 174; C M Dixon 177, 178, 179, 180 & 182; ET Archive 185; Lesley & Roy Adkins 186; ET Archive 187; Italian State Tourist Board 188; ET Archive 189; C M Dixon 190; ET Archive 191; Neil Cooper/Panos 195*a* & *b*; ET Archive 201; Japan National Tourist Organisation 204; Ann Ronan at Image Select 206; The Times/Rex Features 211; Richard Brook/Ace 212; Rafael Macia/Ace 214; Pictor 215.

All other photographs are the copyright of Quarto Inc.

Every effort has been made to acknowledge copyright holders. Quarto would like to apologise should any omissions have been made.

Quarto would like to credit the following for allowing us to reproduce or adapt copyright material:
p94 table adapted from Clark, R. "Austronesian Languages" in Bright, W., Ed, *Encyclopedia of Languages and Linguistics*, vol. 1, Oxford University Press, New York, 1992; p176 mono- bi- and triconsonantal figures reproduced from Hooker, J. T., *Reading the Past: Ancient Writing from Cuneiform to the Alphabet*, University of California, Berkeley, 1990. Copyright © 1990 Trustees of the British Museum; p181 (left) reproduced from *Recueil des inscriptions en lineaire A*, vol 5, pXXII, Ecole Française d'Athenes; p184 adapted from p244, J. Hooker, *Reading the Past*, University of California Press, 1990; p202 (top) adapted from a table in *The Origins of Writing*, edited by Wayne M. Senner, by permission of the University of Nebraska Press, copyright © 1989 by the University of Nebraska Press; p202 (bottom) adapted from Cambell, G., *Compendium of the World's Languages*, Routledge, 1991; p206 adapted from Coe, Michael D., *Breaking the Code*, Thames and Hudson, 1992; p208 adapted from Akira Nakanishi, *Writing Systems of the World*, Charles E. Tuttle Co., Tokyo, Japan, 1980.